Foreign Affairs
India at 70

Foreign Affairs November 2017

TABLE OF CONTENTS

Introduction

"After more than a half century of false starts and unrealized potential, India is now emerging as the swing state in the global balance of power," C. Raja Mohan, the director of Carnegie India, wrote not so long ago in the pages of Foreign Affairs. Ever since its founding in 1947, the world's largest democracy has, as Mohan suggested, prompted both lofty expectations and frequent disappointment about its economic potential and international role. But given turbulence around the world, challenges in India's own region, and growth and dynamism within India itself, the question of where the country goes from here has never mattered more than it does now, 70 years after its violent birth.

There are many ways India can swing: east or west, inward or outward. Understanding its course demands analysis of not just the forces of India's present but also the forces of its past. At Foreign Affairs, we have been charting India's successive transformations from the beginning: from British colony to sprawling multiethnic democracy, from nonaligned-movement leader to emerging nuclear power, from chronic underachiever to economic powerhouse.

In this collection, we feature the voices of both key participants and keen observers. The Earl of Halifax, the British viceroy from 1926–31, reflected within these pages on the end of British rule, while an early U.S. ambassador noted the young country's potential to shift the balance of power in the Cold War. Jawaharlal Nehru, the country's first prime minister, wrote in Foreign Affairs on the roots of nonalignment, and a decade later, his daughter, Indira Gandhi, followed up with an essay marveling at all that India had weathered in its first quarter century. More recently, Foreign Affairs has charted Narendra Modi's rise to power and considered what his grand economic plans and rousing populist call for a "New India" will mean.

The story of India's first 70 years is as fascinating as it is significant. The question of what happens next may be even more consequential — for understanding not just the course of what will soon be the world's most populous country but also its impact on Asia, on geopolitics, and on the global economy.

© Foreign Affairs

India: Two Hundred Years

The Earl of Halifax

PHOTO DIVISION, GOVERNMENT OF INDIA

A refugee special train at Ambala during the partition of India

WHAT is now happening in India has rightly held the attention of the civilized world. Here is a country containing a fifth of the inhabitants of the entire globe and occupying a highly strategic position, which — suddenly, as it must seem to a world preoccupied with grave questions of national and international politics—emerges from a position of political subordination to the status of a fully autonomous member of the family of nations. Quite apart from the powerful repercussions which such a development is bound to produce upon the equilibrium of human society, the dramatic quality of the events which have accompanied the last stages of India's transition from tutelage to self-government is such as to arrest the imagination of all spectators. That must be the justification for such a review as is attempted here.

The roots of the Indian problem lie deep in history, and recent events are the outcome of a long chain of contributory causes. For the decision of the British Government to relinquish its control over the Government of India is no arbitrary decision reached in haste, and most emphatically it is not the outcome of weakness or the abandonment of any of the ideals through which the British Commonwealth of Nations has grown, and for which it stands today. On the contrary, this decision of His Majesty's Government is the natural fruit of a century and a half of political, social and economic development in India, and, so far from being alien to the present spirit and purpose of the British Commonwealth, it may in fact prove to be the most striking realization of them which has so far been achieved. The world wars have but speeded up a process which has been under way for many decades.

II

Let us first see what it was that His Majesty's Government decided. Briefly it was that after a fixed date in the near future, India should be completely free to work out her own destiny under a constitution of her own choosing; and that by August 15, 1947, India, whether still united or partitioned, should enjoy the same status as other self-governing members of the British Commonwealth. To this end His Majesty's Government declared that if the predominantly Moslem areas so desired, India should be partitioned to form two new states, one predominantly Moslem, the other predominantly Hindu.

The areas in question are Bengal and a part of the neighboring territory of Assam in the northeast of India, and, in the northwest, the Punjab, the Province of Sind, the North-West Frontier Province and British Baluchistan. In regard to Sind, no troublesome questions arise because its population is overwhelmingly Moslem and all but a small minority of these wish to be included in the Moslem state, to be known as Pakistan. Bengal, the Punjab and the North-West Frontier Province are more difficult. In both Bengal and the Punjab, Moslems have only a narrow majority over Hindus and others, and to include these two vitally important provinces en bloc in Pakistan would be felt as an intolerable hardship by the many millions of Hindus in Bengal, and by Sikhs as well as Hindus in the Punjab. It was decided therefore to give the legislatures of these two provinces an opportunity of declaring, first, whether they wished them to be partitioned into predominantly Moslem and predominantly non-Moslem areas, and if, as has in fact happened, both the legislatures declared for partition, then the members representing constituencies in the predominantly Moslem and the predominantly non-Moslem areas, meeting separately, would declare whether they wished to belong to what is to be termed India or to Pakistan.

The case of the North-West Frontier Province is different from that of either Bengal or the Punjab, for there the great majority of the population is Moslem but nonetheless has hitherto supported a government allied to the Congress Party. And the Congress Party, of course, has always bitterly opposed the determination of the Moslem League and its leader, Mr. Jinnah, to partition India. The people of the Frontier Province were therefore given the opportunity, through a plebiscite, to declare their wishes for the future allegiance of their province.

Finally, as soon as the wishes of the peoples of these disputed areas had been made known, boundary commissions were set about the very delicate business of demarcating the actual dividing lines between the contiguous Moslem and non-Moslem areas in Bengal and the Punjab. In the latter case, a new and large complication is introduced by the presence of the Sikhs who are a separate community, neither Hindu nor Moslem. Although only about 4,000,000 all told, they were masters of all the Punjab, except its extreme south, and practically all the present North-West Frontier Province, until the conquest of the Punjab by the British a hundred years ago. Martial qualities, a proud tradition of past dominion, communal solidarity — all these combine to give the Sikhs an importance quite disproportionate to the fewness of their numbers. Yet no dividing line in the Punjab which the Moslems would ever accept could do other than leave a material proportion of the Sikh community inside Moslem Pakistan. And this is only one example of the kind of difficulty that is bound to arise in greater or less degree over the practical issues of delimitation and demarcation.

However, these conflicts of incompatible claims are well understood by the Indian peoples and their leaders, and no useful purpose will be served here by trying to suggest solutions in advance. It is something to the good that, now that the principle of partition has been accepted, both Governments in India will assume the status of self-governing members of the British Commonwealth, without prejudice to the right of their respective populations, once the boundaries have been finally settled and partition is complete, to decide for themselves whether they will retain their membership in the Commonwealth or leave it altogether.

The scheme for India's future is thus drawn on large lines, and, having regard to the place that India holds, and will hold, in the world, the world cannot be indifferent to the success or failure of it. Every Britisher who has served India — and vast numbers of Indians outside the Congress Party will share their feeling — must deplore the necessity of disrupting India's hard-won unity. As the Viceroy, Lord Mountbatten, said in his broadcast to India on Tuesday, June 3: "For more than a hundred years, four hundred millions of you have lived together, and this country has been administered as a single entity. This has resulted in unified communications, defense, postal services and currency, an absence of tariffs and customs barriers, and the basis for integrated political economy." That nation-building unity, temporarily at least, now disappears. We must understand why it has not been found possible to preserve it.

III

The reasons are older than even the establishment of British rule. Many foreign students who have no first-hand knowledge of India and its affairs have been puzzled by the Moslem League's bitter opposition, expressed through its leader and spokesman, Mr. Jinnah, to any scheme for a union of all India based on the cardinal democratic principle of majority rule. Their attitude has been represented as the attempt of a minority in India to dictate to the majority. Such judgment is not perhaps unnatural, but is certainly too harsh, and takes insufficient account of the realities of human life.

It is true that the Moslems form approximately only one-quarter of India's population, and that the Hindus outnumber them roughly by three to one. Nevertheless, the Moslems are conscious of deep traditional, historic and emotional differences between themselves and the majority community. They can never forget that they once ruled India as alien conquerors, and, although many Indian Moslems today are the descendants of Hindu converts to Islam, the great majority nevertheless now identify themselves with the Moslems who entered India in successive waves of invasion from the eighth century of our era onwards. And their thoughts constantly turn back to the great period of their rule, the Mogul Empire of Babur and his successors, the greatest of whom was Akbar, a contemporary of our English Queen Elizabeth. But from the last quarter of the seventeenth century onwards, as the Mogul Empire fell into decay, India became the battleground of rival potentates carving out kingdoms from its derelict dominion. Mahrattas in the center, Sikhs in the north, the Viceroy of Bengal in the east, the rulers of Hyderabad and Mysore in the south — all these were setting up successor states, and it looked as though India might sink into her old condition of uncertain equilibrium and intermittent domestic war. At this point the British, partly to establish order for the trade which had led them to India in the first instance, and partly in pursuit of their world-wide clash with the French, began their hundred-year conquest of India, which, beginning at Plassy in the east, ended at Gujerat in the northwest.

In place of chaos the British thus gave the Pax Britannica. During this hundred years of conquest, nearly three-quarters of the whole country came under direct British administration, while the remaining quarter was left under the rule of Hindu and Moslem Princes of innumerable gradations of strength and prestige, responsible for the domestic affairs of their states but having no foreign or military policies of their own. In a word, the British "froze" the situation as it was in the eighteenth century and though, as will be shown later, the seeds of subsequent constitutional development were being steadily sown, it remained largely frozen until the end of the second decade of this century.

The Government of India Act of 1919, better known as the Montagu-Chelmsford Reforms, with its declared goal of responsible self-government for India, was recognition of the extent to which the eyes of Indians —Hindus, Moslems and Sikhs alike — had caught the vision of wider political horizons. The more far-reaching reforms of the Government of India Act of 1935, with its autonomous Provinces of British India and provisions for a Federation of all India between British India and the Indian States, were a further long step forward, and but for the war might have been hoped to solve the problem of how to fit the Indian States into the larger mosaic of all India. For that is another, and a very difficult, element in the Indian conundrum of which much more is likely to be heard.

The obstacles on the one hand to anything in the way of enforced adhesion of the Indian States to Hindustan or Pakistan, or on the other to the enjoyment by the States of complete independence of either, are alike formidable.

On British India the effect of the approach to the time when power, hitherto exercised by an outside authority, was to be transferred to Indian hands, was immediately to raise the question, "Into whose hands?" And as this debate proceeded, marked at times by savage outbursts of popular feeling, many old ideas, conditions and aspirations which men had long since thought dead and buried began to raise their heads. Of such sort were the Moslem and Sikh traditions of dominion, and with their resurrection came the revival of the ambitions of certain of the greater States to play once more an independent part in the life of India.

Between the Moslem religion and way of life and that of the Hindus a deep gulf is set. Their notions of social, political and even economic affairs are deeply divergent. The Sikh religion, too, with its complete denial of caste, which is the pith and marrow of the Hindu way of life, sets barriers between them and the majority community. But between Sikhs and Moslems also there are long generations of conflict, for it was under the hammer blows of Moslem persecution that the Sikhs first became a militant and then a conquering community.

So from all these different angles — religious, communal, historic, social and political — we catch a partial glimpse of the centrifugal forces which, today at any rate, seem to be moving in India, and which, if wise counsels for the general good were not to prevail over smaller hopes and fears, might come near to reviving some of the conditions of the eighteenth century. Such in brief are the reasons why it has not been found possible to preserve the political unity of India after the passing of the Pax Britannica.

But against such background we can measure the merits of His Majesty's Government's principal proposals of June 3. For instead of an anarchic struggle between a multiplicity of warring claimants, as happened when the Mogul Empire fell into decay, and on other occasions in India's history, it is hoped to secure a controlled division of India, agreed between Moslems and non-Moslems, with the rulers of the Indian States invited to come to peaceful and friendly terms with one or other of the two Indias which are now emerging. Moreover, as we have seen, these two Indias are offered full autonomous membership of the British Commonwealth of Nations, which means that, if they choose to accept it — and their choice will be absolutely free and uncontrolled — they will at once in this atmosphere of complete freedom become inheritor beneficiaries of the incentive and practice of friendly coÖperation, which every member of the British Commonwealth today enjoys.

I have no doubt that these considerations are present to the minds of Indian leaders; and friends of India the world over, British and foreign alike, may well hope that both the new Indias will walk together along this path. For thus they would retain, in addition to many advantages which are far from negligible, the priceless asset of common citizenship, and salvage for the India of the future a creative principle out of which other formal attributes of unity may grow.

IV

It is strange how little place has been given by historians of British India to the cardinal truth that the political development of India during the past 150 years has been the product, not only of her connection with Great Britain, but of her membership of the British Empire and Commonwealth. In the case of the other self-governing members of the British Commonwealth, the molding influence of the inclusive association to which they all belong is generally recognized, and it is therefore reasonable to assume that India is not likely to be a solitary exception to this rule. Nor does this general assumption lack support from the facts of history. I suppose the greatest event in the history of the British Empire is the secession of the American Colonies, which left so deep a mark upon the history of the Mother Country and all her daughter nations. It generated a ferment of feeling and a searching of heart, of which the great Reform Bill of 1832 in British domestic politics, and the Durham Report some years later in imperial politics, were two outstanding consequences. Pitt's India Act of 1784 may be regarded as a repercussion on India of the great event. For in Pitt's own words the Act was meant "to give to the Crown the power of guiding the politics of India with as little means of corrupt influence as possible." In other words, the doings of the employees of the East India Company, whose forces had already conquered large and important territories, were in the last analysis to fall under the scrutiny of Parliament. Here was an invaluable safeguard. The Charter of the East India Company, under which it carried out all its operations, became due for renewal every 20 years, and the renewal provided the occasion for a review by Parliament of the whole conduct of the Company. Thus when the Charter came up for renewal in 1833, the first year of the reformed Parliament, it was laid down as a result of the discussion in Parliament that the great principle of equality of opportunity and equality before the law of all British subjects should be extended to India. A quarter of a century later, after the Indian Mutiny of 1857, the administration of India by the East India Company was taken over by the Crown, and Parliament thus became directly responsible for the Government of India through its agent, the Secretary of State for India.

With the transfer of authority came revision of the system of government, and in 1861 Parliament accepted the principle of representation of the people of India in the Indian Legislative Council. The Council of that day was small and its powers restricted, as was the degree of representation established; but a principle vital to future development had been introduced. For between 1833 and 1861 a beneficent revolution was occurring in British imperial policy. The colonies, later to bear the name of Dominions, and led by Canada, the oldest of them all, had achieved, or were on the high road to achieve, responsible self-government, which in the case of Canada had already become complete autonomy in her domestic affairs. By curious accident, Lord Elgin was Governor-General of Canada during the fateful closing years of the 1840's, which saw this transformation, and in 1861 he was Viceroy of India. Whatever may have been his direct connection with the framing of the India Councils Act of 1861, the new conception of imperial relationship which was growing up in the older colonies can hardly have failed to exert decisive influence upon the policy adopted in regard to India.

Looking back, we may judge it to have been inevitable that India should follow at her own distance and her own pace after the other members of the British Commonwealth. The process was cautious, but the general trend is unmistakable. The India Councils Act of 1892 asserted the principle of election for the Indian legislative body, and in 1908 the Morley-Minto Reforms greatly widened both representation and election, and the scope and powers of the Indian Legislature. In a true sense, 1908 was the direct precursor of 1919, the date of the Montagu-Chelmsford Reforms, just as these sign-posted the road to the great Act of 1935. To these two last reference has already been made, and it is inevitable that they should have somewhat overshadowed what was done in 1908. But the date 1908 is significant for its close correspondence in point of time with one of the most fruitful acts of all British imperial statesmanship, namely, the grant of responsible self-government to the then recently annexed Boer Republics of South Africa.

Other examples might be given to illustrate how intimate has been the interaction between developments in British Commonwealth relations and the system of government in India. But the broad picture is clear enough. As the conception of equal partnership in the British Commonwealth took root, India moved naturally and inevitably along the track already blazed by the constitutional pioneers which was to lead on to Dominion status. And during all these years, the strong centralizing rule of the British was investing India with the material apparatus and many of the formal attributes of a united nation. Law and order were impartially enforced. The strong arm of the Pax Britannica gave India security from external menace. From end to end the country was linked together by modern communications — railways, roads, telegraphs, shipping, and, latterly, wireless and aircraft. Great irrigation schemes were developed; famine no longer took cruel and all too frequent toll of the population; departments of public health, education, industry and commerce, and all the other activities of modern government came into operation; until to all outward appearance, India was a single and united nation.

The achievements of British and Indians working together on the material plane should not be underrated, for they were indeed remarkable. Speaking in the House of Commons on the Charter Act of 1833, Macaulay described the task of the British in India as "the stupendous process of the reconstruction of a decomposed society." He did not exaggerate, as many narratives of travellers, historians and officials can testify, and the India of today, despite many shortcomings in material equipment and in social and economic conditions, is a visible record of one of the most surprising administrative achievements in history.

But the unifying of India went much deeper than the outward evidences of material activity. And there could be no more impressive symbol of the deep unity achieved under British auspices than the Indian Army, in which Indians of all creeds and communities have been proud to fight side by side twice in a generation for a common cause. The system of education, particularly of higher education imparted through the medium of the English language, accomplished on the spiritual plane much of what communications, medicine, law and order, and the rest had accomplished on the material. The English language has been a great nation-building force in India. Not only has it unlocked for Indians the storehouse of the world's learning, a task which no Indian language could have performed, but it gave them for the first time a common language suitable both for politics and learned intercourse. In and through English the ideals of Indian nationalism have found expression. Without English no nationwide nationalist movement could have come to birth or flourished in India, for there would have been no universal medium of communication and no heaped-up stores of inspiration and experience on which to draw. For English is the language of freedom, the most potent of all the weapons in freedom's armory.

It is well that we should remember these things now, for in them we may detect mighty unifying forces below the surface, which may be powerful in the years to come. The political ideals which animate both Hindu and Moslem leaders are those which they have inherited as their birthright, like their fellows elsewhere in the British Commonwealth. The English language will never be completely displaced from the education of the Indian people, although Hindi, Urdu, Tamil, Ooriya, Bengali and other Indian languages will undoubtedly be more important media of instruction than they have been hitherto. For the English language and all that it means for the human spirit have become an imperishable part of India's heritage, and will impel unseen hands to reach out towards each other from both component parts of the India we have known. May it not perhaps be that the experience of free participation in the Commonwealth, with all that this implies, will prove itself a potent and unifying instrument?

There are some signs that the above may not be just pious aspirations. For some months past a Constituent Assembly representative of the different communities and interests of India, but at first boycotted by the Moslem League, has been meeting to consider the framework of the Constitution for the new self-governing India. Now that partition has been decided upon, the Moslem League, while having its own Constituent Assembly, will also be represented in the other, in order to hold a watching brief for Moslem interests outside Pakistan. A number of committees were set up by the Constituent Assembly, and one of the most important of these, the Constitution Committee, had as its task consideration of the fundamental structure of the Constitution. In the last days of June that Committee, having considered the respective merits of the American and British systems, decided in favor of the parlimentary system common to the United Kingdom and all the other self-governing Dominions. Moreover, it recommended that the official languages should be Hindi, Urdu or English. Hindi is an Aryan language spoken over a great part of India, mainly by Hindus, while Urdu, with its strong admixture of Arabic, is a lingua franca of the Indian Moslems. But in Hindu India there will be many who can speak neither Hindi nor Urdu, and English is bound to maintain a strong position alike in the law courts, in the legislatures, and in higher education. It is probable that when the Pakistan Constituent Assembly meets, it will come to similar decisions on these two vital points, for the Moslem objections to a system of government based on the fundamental democratic principle of majority government apply only to a government of all India, in which they would be in a permanent minority. Thus the nation-building forces of the English language and the British parliamentary democratic system will in all likelihood remain operative after the two Governments in India have set out upon their separate ways.

V

So as we cast up the credit and debit balance of the partition of India, we see that the debits, although they are visible and tangible enough, receive some offset from invisible but weighty credits. There are others which may properly be included. One of the greatest is the disappearance of the age-old suspicion of British motives on the part of Indians, in the face of a British-proclaimed policy that is so unmistakably clear and unconditional. In the difficult days which lie ahead this will be a great asset to Indians, because, with the actual process and details of partition, the most difficult and dangerous of all the stages of their political revolution has been reached. And both sides now know that in the British Government and people they have friends who will put their unrivalled political experience and their unstinted help at the service of the two Indias which are emerging. There will be no hidden purpose and no self-seeking behind such advice and help, and assuredly the Indian people will draw on it.

It is easier now than it was a few years ago to see that to expect Indians to reach full agreement among themselves on their political future before they had full power in their own hands to implement whatever they might decide was not the right approach. Now such power has been put into Indian hands, and, as nearly always happens, the acquisition of power has been followed by the growth of a sense of responsibility. As we read the dispatches from India today, we see deep searchings of heart, not only among Indian political leaders, but among the best of their followers, concerning the partition of their country. If the Moslems have insisted uncompromisingly on the creation of Pakistan, they nevertheless feel deeply the division of India between themselves and their Moslem compatriots. And this, too, is an item to be set on the credit side of the balance because, as nostalgic hopes of a united Punjab and a united Bengal continue to be held by Moslems (as they will be held) it will surely be seen that such union can be had only within the wider shelter of a united India. And so long as Hindustan and Pakistan remain members of the British Commonwealth of Nations, they can never be foreign to each other.

India stands today face to face with destiny. The choice that will make her future lies solely in Indian hands. Great Britain, with more than 200 years connection with India, is happy to have it so, for everything that is passing into history as I write is the logical and natural issue of the history of the last two centuries. That Great Britain has through those long years made mistakes no Britisher would deny. But where mistakes have been made they have either been honest mistakes of judgment or mistakes which the rising standards of a later generation have been quick to criticize and condemn.

And I would not hesitate to make two assertions: first, that on any impartial appraisement the British record in India is something of which the British people may rightly be proud; and second, that greater than anything which they have done or not done in India is the fact that they have by their contact with India introduced to that immense portion of Asia the principles of freedom and justice which are the foundation of the life shared by the English–speaking world.

Here is the taproot by which the new Governments in India will be fed. Here, too, is the source and inspiration of a policy that will leave to India the choice, free and unfettered, of her continued partnership in, or departure from, the British Commonwealth. Here too, perhaps, may be the key to open one more, and perhaps the greatest, chapter in the long story of our Commonwealth of Nations which began — where it might well have ended — at Boston 170 years ago.

THE EARL OF HALIFAX, Viceroy of India, 1926–31; Secretary of State for Foreign Affairs, 1938–40; British Ambassador in Washington, 1941–46; also formerly Secretary of State for War, Lord Privy Seal and Lord President of the Council

© Foreign Affairs

India as a World Power

An Indian Official

ABBIE ROWE

Jawaharlal Nehru and his sister with President Harry Truman during Nehru's visit to the U.S. in October 1949.

THOUGH the Indian Union is an infant state, India is no newcomer to history, no offshoot or colony newly risen to nationhood. She is a mother country, venerable in her own right; and her past, which is ancient as civilization, belongs to the essence of man's achievement on this planet. Nor has India lain broken and buried under the tides of history for so long that, in her reëmergence, she is a mere vestige of her former self. Measured against the millennia that went before, the two centuries of British rule formed only a brief, if critical, interlude. Now that is over, and India steps once more with unimpaired vigor into the main stream of human affairs.

Not only history, but India's geographical position, the idealism of her national movement, and the personality and teachings of Gandhi have combined to give her the distinctive place she holds in men's minds today. Standing midway between the east and west in more senses than one, she is, in terms of population, the largest single political unit in the world. Her initiative in calling the Delhi Conference on Indonesia in January 1949 brought together and successfully coördinated on an important question the views of a number of nations which had never met before as a separate group. And her leaders have behind them a lifetime of devoted public work with Gandhi, under whose guidance India turned a political campaign into a moral exercise on a national scale.

It is not easy to fit in Gandhi's teachings with any of the current social philosophies. As against the abstractions of the various "isms," he pleaded for attention to the elementary needs of humanity and enjoined a method of action and an attitude of mind and spirit as the necessary preconditions of clear sight and right judgment. He reiterated the most ancient ethical precepts, but he gave them meaning in terms of practical action and deduced from them social ideals which continue to be the inspiration of the great political party that he led to its goal.

The free India that came to birth on August 15, 1947, the India that acclaims Gandhi as the "Father of the Nation," has been largely preoccupied, so far, with problems arising from the conditions in which freedom was achieved.

Independence brought with it partition, and partition was the outcome of communalism. In India, in the last phase of British rule, communalism had developed into the demand for a "Moslem state," backed with the contention that Hindus and Moslems constituted separate nations. Gandhi during all his life had resisted this disruptive doctrine and striven for harmony between the communities. Partition itself was brought about by mutual consent. Even in the best of circumstances, the divisions and readjustments it involved would have caused some dislocation. As it happened, the long agitation that preceded it had inflamed communal fanaticism, particularly in the Punjab; and the intercommunal strife that broke out in that province thrust upon the new state a multiplicity of urgent and unforeseen problems. The prompt restoration of order was perhaps the least formidable of them all. In its wake came the immense task of organizing, within a few weeks, the movement of no less than 6,000,000 refugees, of improvising arrangements for their immediate relief, and devising plans for their permanent resettlement and rehabilitation. When was a "refugee problem" of this magnitude set before an untried government in the very first days of its existence and solved with equal expedition and success?

Besides surmounting this crisis, India has also had to undo the "partitions" effected a hundred years ago which had turned the land into a checkerboard of independent Princely States. More than 550 of them, varying from units of the size of the United Kingdom to hundreds of states each with an area less than ten square miles, were scattered over the peninsula. The internal frontiers that they raised – artificial in most cases — divided peoples who were otherwise homogeneous in every respect. There was never any social or economic justification for this arrangement, and nationalism had expressed itself as a popular movement within each state for the termination of autocratic rule and union with the rest of India. The political raison d'être for these hundreds of subservient enclaves disappeared with the disappearance of the imperial system in 1947, but the orderly liquidation of the powerful dynastic interests involved was a task as delicate as it was essential to the peaceful progress of India.

Constitutionally, the Viceroy had provided the link between the states inter se, as also between the states as a whole and the rest of India. When this nexus was broken, an indeterminate situation arose which might have caused endless trouble and disorder. The new Government, however, succeeded within a remarkably short time in obtaining the "accession," for defense, foreign affairs and communications, of all but a few of the states whose territories were enclosed by or contiguous with those of the Indian Dominion. By this means the Union Government resumed some of the powers formerly comprised in the concept of paramountcy, but the territorial fragmentation and the despotic personal rule remained as before. Since then, however, through patient negotiations and persuasion, these basic evils have also been practically eliminated. Except in a few cases, the states have all been either merged with the adjacent provinces or grouped together into larger units or sub-federations within the Indian Union. Simultaneously with this process of territorial reintegration, a fundamental change has been brought about peacefully in the internal structure of the states as a result of which representative and responsible governments have in all of them superseded the previous personal régimes.

II

In the two largest states, Kashmir and Hyderabad, the transition has been prolonged and complicated by the injection, from within as well as outside, of the communal issue. When the two new Dominions were created, the National Conference in Kashmir — a popular and predominantly Moslem, though politically non-communal movement, which had for many years striven for democracy in the state — took the view that a settlement of the question of Kashmir's relations with India and Pakistan should be deferred until such time as a popular and freely elected government in Kashmir was able to consider it. But the tribal incursions and the invasion by Pakistan nationals and the Pakistan Army in the autumn of 1947 precipitated a decision, and the National Conference as well as the ruler of the state separately applied to accede to India. Seeing especially the urgency of extending protection to the populace against the lawless depredations of the hostile forces, India accepted the accession, but stipulated that it should be confirmed by means of a plebiscite after the restoration of peace. As is well known, the dispute with Pakistan was subsequently referred, on India's initiative, to the Security Council of the United Nations.

Hyderabad, unlike Kashmir, is not a frontier state. It lies within the heart of India, surrounded completely by Indian Union territory. For social and economic, no less than for political and geographical reasons, an independent Hyderabad pursuing policies at variance with those of India would be as intolerable and dangerous an anomaly as an independent Kansas or Missouri in the United States. Hyderabad has therefore throughout its history been subordinate to the strongest power in India, the British, or the Mahrattas and the Moguls.

The attempt to reach a negotiated settlement with Hyderabad — as the Union Government had reached with the other states — was repeatedly foiled by a communal faction, the Ittehad-ul-Muslimeen, which had seized control of the state. To remain passive, in the hope that time would produce a solution, was to let the Ittehad, in a state where the population was predominantly non-Moslem, continue the rabidly communal campaign in which it was engaged, employing terrorist gangs and instigating hatred between the communities. India was not disturbed by the foolish threats that were being broadcast against her, but there was a real danger that communal disorders, spreading over Hyderabad, might break out all over India. Rather than permit, through its inaction, the occurrence of a tragedy much graver than the Punjab massacres of the previous year, the Union Government thereupon reluctantly decided to move its armed forces into the state.

The Union Government, like the national movement of which it is a product, has consistently opposed all manifestations of communalism and communal fanaticism. It has not lacked the will or the strength to deal sternly with both Hindu and Sikh communalists. It is determined that India shall not be a communal state, but a secular state, as it is, with a mixed population belonging to all religions. Its Moslem citizens, numbering approximately 40,000,000, enjoy equal rights with non-Moslems and occupy some of the highest and most vital positions in the state. Pakistan, too, has a mixed population, including a considerable proportion of non-Moslems; but Pakistan owes her origin to communalism, and the communal orientation has continued to color her policies. For communal reasons, there has been interference in Indian affairs — armed intervention in Kashmir (on the ground that the population is mostly Moslem), and diplomatic and political intervention in Hyderabad (because the dominant ruling minority there was Moslem).

In spite of these adverse factors, the bitterness aroused by the partition and its attendant disorders has gradually subsided. Frequent and friendly consultations have been held, and agreement has been reached on a wide variety of subjects. Hyderabad, under a régime that will become increasingly democratic, has ceased to be fit material for exploitation for communal purposes; and tension over Kashmir, the main outstanding subject in dispute, has greatly relaxed.

Thus although the new India got off to a somewhat shaky start, she has in less than two years magnificently recovered and stabilized herself. Political Cassandras foresaw chaos as the sequel to partition and the departure of the British. Intercommunal strife, on the one hand, and the ambitions of a multitude of sovereign princes, on the other, they feared, would rend India and keep the sub-continent in turmoil for years to come. These prognostications have been proven false. India is stronger and more united than ever. Partition, no doubt, meant a "loss," among other things, of territory and population. On the other hand, there has been a "gain" (other than national freedom) in that, through bloodless revolution, territories and populations that had for a century or more remained apart have reunited with India. Considering that they account for 48 percent of the total territory and 27 percent of the total population of the Dominion, this is no small achievement. There are no longer "two Indias" — the provinces and the states — but one India — the Indian Union, larger than either of the two, and more stable.

With the two interlocked conflicts out of the way — the conflict with the British and the conflict over partition — India is today giving herself a constitution which will reflect her new unity and freedom. Her main domestic problem is that of social and economic development, of obtaining the tools with which to carry out her projects of reconstruction. The solution of this problem, however, in all its ramifications, is inseparable from the present state of international relations, political and economic.

III

The broad facts about India's position are obvious enough. There are few parts of Asia where internal conditions are equally peaceful and stable. Her manpower and her latent resources give her an enviable advantage. Underdeveloped as she is, her organized industrial and military capacity still exceeds that of any nation in the east. She has no traditional enemies, nor has she acquired new ones; she has no vested interest of any sort in world affairs, except an interest in peace, a tradition of friendliness to all, and a readiness to coöperate with others for constructive ends.

Within this context, two specific objectives immediately define themselves as of concern to India: the abolition of racial discrimination and the liberation of subject peoples. They are intimately connected with her own recent experience and she cannot fail to pursue them. Her own liberation struggle was conceived, in one essential aspect, as a contribution to the freedom of all nations, and some progress has undoubtedly been made in this direction. But there are still a number of territories, mainly in southeast Asia and Africa, where the colonial status is being maintained, and the emancipation of which is being resisted by force. Racial discrimination, again, exists in more than one continent, notwithstanding the widely diffused sentiment against it, and its supporters are perhaps more outspoken and better organized than before.

In dealing with these problems, India is not actuated merely by emotion. If she has been vigorous in her opposition to the racial system in South Africa, and in her championship of Indonesian independence, it is not from any feeling of antagonism to the Dutch or the Europeans as such in South Africa. True, members of a community Indian by origin are among the victims in South Africa; and in Indonesia the victims are a people who have long cultural and historical associations with India. But more than sentiment is involved in these issues. Race discrimination and the colonial system, offending as they do the dignity of men and nations (and not only because they so offend), are essentially a part of the malaise of the world, and until they are removed there can be no health and strength in the world order.

Problems affecting dependent peoples, and involving discrimination and oppression, are specially acute in Asia and Africa. To resolve them, and promote the revival of these continents, and particularly of Asia, must therefore stand in the forefront of India's interests. Intrinsically, this is a just purpose and needs no ulterior motive to validate it, but it is bound up with the major conflicts in the world today and cannot be fulfilled in an isolated or self-contained manner. It calls basically for a new relationship with the west. For the understanding and consent of the west, given without arrière pensée, would ensure that the liberation movement advances without further violence and bloodshed, while the coöperation of the west could open the road to well-being for millions who are at present condemned to sub-civilized standards of living.

But the west is relevant to India and to the peoples of the east generally, not only because it must do its part in bringing about the peaceful transformation of an untenable relationship. It is relevant above all because, owing to the immense power at its disposal, the good that it can do is world-wide in its scope, as is the evil it can do. The initiative, on a global scale, lies in its hands. If it acts in unison and with goodwill it can guard the world against insecurity and divert incalculable resources from destructive to beneficent ends; and when it is divided, as now, the rift is a calamity in itself and may well be the prelude to the horrors of a world war. To whatever degree India may be drawn into such a war — and she will, let it be said, defend her soil and her freedom with every ounce of her strength — she is bound to incur, as she has incurred, her share of the suffering and starvation that will descend upon all nations. She has therefore a vital stake in peace. It is of paramount importance to her to avert a rupture between the colossi of the west, to mitigate the severity of the existing tensions, and to promote, as opportunity occurs, a reconciliation that can be only of benefit to the whole world.

There are conflicts and disputes in every continent today, affecting not only the local populations but the leading Powers of the west and, ultimately, the whole world. The alternative to a pacific adjustment would be so catastrophic that it is not wildly irresponsible to hold that the conflict or dispute itself may in the long run be of less consequence than the spirit in which it is approached and the methods by which it is resolved. This is not to imply that the substance of an international dispute or of its settlement is a matter of indifference to India. But, in forming her judgment, she cannot fail to distinguish between the elements of varying worth that enter into the complexity of each of these problems.

There are, first, the well-being and freedom of the people directly and immediately concerned, whose territory forms the locale of the dispute, and possibly a real disagreement over fundamental politico-moral principles (though here the area of conflict may well be narrower than one is always ready to admit). Secondly, there is, of course, in the case of many of these conflicts an element of preparation for future hostilities — an anticipatory manœuvring to gain, or retain, positions of strategic advantage. Thirdly, there is the political and propaganda aspect, amounting to an interpretation of what is involved in the dispute.

Naturally, this interpretation of what is at stake is couched in terms derived from the particular background, traditions and policies of one or the other of the dominant Powers; generalized to cover all disputes in all parts of the world, it tends to influence the evaluation even of problems (such as Asian problems) which have a specific character independent of the conflicts of the west. A common practice is to formulate the issue as one of preserving or extending some particular "way of life," or civilization, or one economic and social system as against another. When these concepts are presented in terms of the west, and the reference is to a western way of life, or what is called Christian civilization, or some social philosophy that is stated to be identical with them, their appeal can scarcely be compelling to the masses in India or, for that matter, elsewhere in Asia. Being herself so different from the west in many respects, Asia can receive with only mild interest any argument that appears to carry with it a totalitarian implication that the world should forego its variety and the vitality that comes of peaceful intercourse between its component parts and adopt instead a uniformity of beliefs and institutions originating in one particular region or country.

Besides, the peoples of the east who have just regained their freedom, or are on the verge of it, face unique problems of their own. They have not only to repair the damage and straighten out the dislocations caused by two world wars and arising out of the present unsettlement. They have to make up for centuries of lost time. While in subjection, their natural evolution was arrested: the changes that a free society would have effected for itself, and within itself, under the pressure of changing conditions were deferred or suppressed so long as a foreign Power was able forcibly to control the course of events. Today their problem is nothing less than the renovation of their ancient civilizations; and they will guide themselves, not by the doctrinaire prescriptions of one social philosophy or the other, but, in addition to their own inherited genius and the specific conditions prevailing in each country, by such experiences and experiments as they may consider relevant from all the rest of the world.

Where international disputes are concerned, India, therefore, can do no other than endeavor to view them without fear or prejudice or passion; to appraise them, without parti pris, in the light of the specific facts of each case; to disentangle and concentrate attention on the human and moral factors that may be involved, and strive for a settlement by conciliation and agreement. This she has sought to do, notably in the cases of Korea, Palestine and the problem of atomic control. Such a critical and dispassionate approach is not compatible with a ready-made preference for policies and programs evolved in one particular capital. It rules out India's association or identification with any international grouping as such, whereby she might be regarded as having entered into commitments relative to a future war. It rules out, in short, her alignment with any power bloc.

This position has, no doubt, its drawbacks, but to abandon it would be unwise, and certainly contrary to the interests of world peace. The whole aim of nationalization in the east has been to free the countries concerned from implicit adherence to the decisions of a foreign Power. It would be strange indeed if, on attaining independence, nationalism were to consent to enter into a relationship where in the nature of things the power of ultimate and binding decision must rest with the other party. India, at any rate, is too conscious of her responsibilities, and of the need to preserve and develop the innate strength and self-reliance of her people, to participate in any arrangement that might induce a sense of dependence or compromise her freedom of action.

Moreover, the forces driving to war can be checked only by the most persistent and patient effort to bring and hold all sides together — not by helping to build up the preponderance of one side, which in itself, and through its example upon others, can have no other result than that of widening the cleavage, pulling down the bridges and pushing the world a little nearer to the brink. This conviction is the mainspring of India's foreign policy. It impels her — not toward isolationism or any fictitious neutrality — but to extend the hand of friendship to all, provided only that the price of friendship is not conformity or subservience; to retain and develop all existing friendly contacts as well as to establish new ones. It was in this spirit that she considered the problems connected with her relationship with the United Kingdom and the other countries of the Commonwealth and reached the accord announced at London on April 28.

It is in this spirit, also, that she has adhered to the Charter of the United Nations and the organs established under it, which make possible the widest coöperation among peace-loving nations for constructive social ends and the maintenance of international security. India has participated fully in all phases of its work, and loyally accepted its jurisdiction, e.g. in the Kashmir dispute. Inevitably, the U.N. reflects not only the accord but the discords between nations, and the conflict between some of its dominant members is now acute enough to deprive the organization of one of the conditions of its effectiveness — continued agreement and understanding between the leaders of the wartime alliance against Fascism. To bring together the divergent points of view and seek to heal a breach which may ultimately spell disaster for mankind have been among the main aims of Indian policy in the United Nations.

IV

India's relations are bound to have a special degree of intimacy with the new group of nations coming into prominence in Asia, each as a separate entity and with an independent status in world affairs. During the era of western domination the links between them had been severed; they were cut off from each other more effectively perhaps than before the days of steam and electricity, and could not even meet together except under alien auspices. Their former contacts are being renewed gradually; and direct relations, it may be expected, will pave the way for frequent consultations and collaboration in matters of common interest and unity of action as and when needed.

For these countries have a tradition of peace and friendship among themselves. Predominantly agricultural and potentially wealthy, their resources are largely undeveloped or have been misapplied and directed to purposes other than their own well-being. They face in common a herculean task in increasing production and supplying their peoples with food, clothing, housing, education and health services. Practical wisdom dictates that they should concert measures of mutual aid in these matters. A world war — whatever it may do for others, and it will do no one any good — will mean for them the retardation for an indefinite period of their hopes of ameliorating the condition of their people. The conflicts, the animosities, the ambitions that threaten such a war are not of their making. Yet they cannot stand idly by, or imagine that they can insulate themselves against it; they must seek, with what power they have, to avert it, and by acting in unison secure for their joint policy an effectiveness that it would not otherwise achieve.

The distinction between the terms east and west, which we have freely used, is not merely geographical. It is more truly a distinction between peoples and governments preoccupied with the elementary needs of humanity, with food and freedom and peace — and peoples and governments preoccupied with the more complex aspirations arising out of the possession of vast power. It is the distinction, as one might say, between the spinning wheel and the atom bomb. This is what lies at the root of the protest against "power politics" that is so often to be heard in the east. A population roughly equal to that of the rest of the world is for the first time claiming its rightful influence in the councils of the world. It demands that power shall be the servant of human welfare, not its master. There are still obstacles to be overcome before its voice can be heard clearly or before it can translate itself into unity of action. But its appearance should cause no anxiety except to minds too long accustomed to think of Asia as "a tool or a plaything."

It is time for a wider recognition in the west that we have come to the end of an historical epoch. The eclipse of India in the eighteenth century was not an isolated phenomenon: it was part of the world movement by which the science and technology of Europe captured Asia and turned it, under different forms, into an appanage of the west. India's reëmergence is likewise related to the revival of the entire continent. It is not a racial movement: it is not animated by any hostile intent. It does not further the aggrandizement of any nation. Its purpose is wholly pacific and constructive--to broaden freedom and raise the standard of living. It is in consonance with all that is liberal, humane and disinterested in the western tradition. Its ultimate result must necessarily be to transform the politico-economic map of the world, and establish a new relationship between east and west. But the process is intertwined with what must surely be the supreme endeavor of our generation: to reduce and dissolve the disputes which, if widened or exacerbated, must plunge all the world into catastrophe. Whatever changes the future may bring, the Government and people of India will bend their energies to this twofold task.

AN INDIAN OFFICIAL, Anonymous

© Foreign Affairs

New India

Chester Bowles

The Sardar Sarovar Dam, the foundation of which was laid by Jawaharlal Nehru, who called multi-purpose projects "Temples of Modern India."

AFTER centuries of inertia, Asia today is wide awake and on the move. From Cairo to Manila, vast populations only recently emerged from colonialism are struggling to take shape as modern nations. Some Westerners find this new situation both bewildering and unpleasant. Some diplomats, indeed, confronted for the first time with the task of assessing the impact of their policies on Asia, find themselves yearning for the "good old days" when the European's word was law. But there are other Westerners — and I believe them to be a substantial majority in America — who look to this new Asia with hope and expectancy. They see developing there a democratic opportunity for hundreds of millions of their fellow human beings who have long been denied the right to choose their own governments and the means to achieve a better life.

The challenge to us is to reaffirm what is best in our long liberal tradition. By pursuing sympathetic, intelligent and patient policies the West will find it possible to work with most of the Asian nations on the basis of mutual respect and understanding in the building of a more stable world. By shirking the task of understanding Asia, and by refusing to recognize the realities of 1952, the West will surely alienate a vast continent and may eventually bring about its own downfall.

Even if we show the best of intentions we shall encounter many pitfalls. For years to come, fundamental differences in the cultural backgrounds of Asians and Americans and in their ways of life will make it difficult for each side to understand the other. Some Western visitors to India, for instance, still see only the Rudyard Kipling-Katherine Mayo land of tiger-hunting maharajas, sacred cows and cobras, against an endless backdrop of tradition-bound, poverty-stricken humanity. But for the visitor who looks below the surface there is a new and immensely exciting India — a five-year-old democracy of 360,000,000 people, working earnestly and with considerable success to solve their country's staggering problems. The outcome of this great Indian effort will profoundly affect the world in which we live. Indeed, the success or failure of the effort being made in India and other Asian countries to create an alternative to Communism in Asia may mark one of those historic turning points which determine the flow of events for many generations.

In China 500,000,000 people are working under a ruthless Communist dictatorship to increase Chinese food production, expand Chinese industry, strengthen the Chinese armed forces and indoctrinate Chinese youth with an aggressive Communist faith —all in the interest of an alien imperialism. A revolutionary challenge such as this cannot be met successfully with slogans, or with vituperation and threats. It can be met over the years only by the example of other Asians who are able to demonstrate in unmistakable terms that democracy not only guarantees the rights of the individuals, but also provides the most practical and quickest means to raise the living standards of the people.

Thus the future of Asia, and eventually the world balance of power, may rest on the competition between democratic India on the one hand and Communist China on the other. If democracy succeeds in India, regardless of what happens in China, millions of Asian doubters will develop new faith in themselves, in their ancient cultures, and in the ideals of the free world.

II

What, then, is the outlook for the future of democracy in India? What, to begin with, has the record been since India won her independence five years ago? An objective study of this record must convince any unprejudiced observer that the new Indian Republic is off to a remarkable start.

During the five-year period India has set up a democratic state which guarantees freedom of speech and freedom of religion to all citizens and freedom to vote to all men and women over 21 years of age. The Indian Constituton has drawn generously from the Constitutions of the United States and of other Western countries. The Indian judiciary generally follows Anglo-Saxon systems of jurisprudence.

To organize the Indian Republic was in itself a tremendous task. When the country became independent, five years ago this past August, there were nine partially self-governing provinces and four small centrally-administered provinces. In addition, there were 584 princely states. Of these only Kashmir, Hyderabad and Mysore were of significant size, while 202 had areas of less than ten square miles. Although theoretically responsible to British officials, many of the petty autocrats who previously ruled these states held the power of life and death over their subjects. In most of them there was little to differentiate the ruler's private bank account from the public reserves.

These feudal relics are now gone. Mysore, Hyderabad and Kashmir were established as separate states in their entirety. All of the former princely territories, covering an area of 588,000 square miles with a total population of more than 100,000,000 people, have been merged with each other, or with the former provinces, or otherwise integrated into workable administrative units. India now consists of 28 states which have much the same relationship to the central government as the 48 states of our American Union. The maharajas have been paid off with lifetime pensions, which although sizable by ordinary standards amount to a small fraction of their original princely incomes. Democratic institutions have been broadly established.

This extraordinary transition was accomplished largely by persuasion and with almost no violence. Kashmir, still torn between India and Pakistan, remains a sore spot. But it is a tribute to the wisdom of the princes and Congress leaders alike that there were not 50 Kashmirs.

Last winter India held her first nation-wide election. One hundred and six million citizens cast their votes. This is a higher percentage of those eligible to vote than is likely to go to the polls this year in our American elections. They came by bullock cart, by bus, by truck and on foot, and the women voters were as numerous as the men. There was free speech, and some of it very free indeed. Yet violence was rare, and there was no scandal.

Democratic assemblies based more or less on the British parliamentary system were elected in all of the states. A central government was chosen, made up of the House of the People, similar to the British House of Commons, elected by direct vote, and the Council of States, elected by indirect vote, mostly by the members of the state assemblies. Jawaharlal Nehru, as the leader of the majority party, was chosen Prime Minister. The President, whose powers are similar to those of the President of France, was elected by the combined vote of all members of the state and central assemblies.

India's success in unravelling a feudal-colonial complex involving 360,000,000 people, speaking a hundred different languages and with strong religious differences, and turning it into a united, effective democracy in five years' time will go down in history as a spectacular achievement. The bulk of the credit belongs to the Indian leaders and the Indian people. But most of them would be quick to grant a generous share to British public servants such as Lord Mountbatten, and to those many princes who peacefully turned over their power and authority to democratic governments.

The democratic organization of the new Indian Republic is only one chapter in the story. The record of parallel achievement in the economic field is all the more remarkable because it has been accomplished with only a moderate amount of foreign aid. Since 1947 the Indian Government has coped successfully with a refugee problem substantially greater than the one faced in Western Germany and involving five or six times more people than that which arose in the Near East. There has not been a penny of outside assistance. Today the great majority of the 8,000,000 refugees from areas which are now part of Pakistan are self-supporting. Only a relatively small minority are still receiving assistance from the Government and only 72,000 remain in camps —a figure which is being rapidly reduced.

The Indian rupee, valued at approximately 21 cents, is sound. During 1951 the Indian Government incurred new debts of $105,000,000; but in the same period it retired $180,000,000 of outstanding internal debt. Public works costing far more than this were paid for out of income. Future economic development will be guided by the new Five Year Plan, first presented in draft form a year ago. Because India's biggest problem is food, this plan properly places its primary emphasis on increased agricultural production.

India's huge and rapidly-growing population has often suffered from a shortage of food. Her history records many famines. In 1943, 3,000,000 people died of famine in a single province. The partition of colonial India between the Republic of India and Pakistan in 1947 involved the loss of extensive agricultural lands and made the food problem even more critical. Now, however, government officials are confident that by 1956 India can raise enough food to support the growing population, and at a higher dietary level. They point to the facts that the density of population is far less in India than in Italy and only a little more than half that in Great Britain, Germany and Japan; and that the annual population increase on a percentage basis is no greater than that in the United States, and substantially less than in Puerto Rico or Japan. Pilot studies have demonstrated that with India's year-round growing season, she can, if need be, double her food production once modern agricultural techniques and sufficient irrigation water are made available to the peasants.

And yet the hard, practical problems of the immediate future cannot be ignored. Some 50,000,000 tons of grain, in addition to other foods, are now required yearly to supply the average Indian daily diet of 1,800 calories. Last year India was able to produce only 45,000,000 tons because of the failure of the monsoon rains, and had to import 5,000,000 tons from abroad. More than half of this grain came from the United States, part of it paid for in cash, part by a loan. In the present year substantial imports again are necessary. This means that simply in order to maintain her present inadequate diet India must continue to spend some $600,000,000 in foreign exchange, which might otherwise be used to build up her steel industry, expand her transportation system and provide new factory jobs for Indian workers.

The Indian Five Year Plan boldly sets out to meet this challenge. The aim is to attain an annual production of 10,000,000 additional tons of food by 1956, and also a substantial increase in cotton. If these goals are reached, the average daily diet can be improved, food and cotton imports will no longer be necessary, and foreign exchange can flow at a much higher ratio into industrial expansion.

One of the first steps in increasing Indian food production is to provide the farmers with greater incentives, and in this connection the first effort being made is to give millions of them ownership of the land they till and to free them from the grip of the money lenders. For several years land reforms were held up by court disputes over what constituted adequate compensation for the landlords. In April 1952 the Indian Supreme Court handed down its decision and now the state governments are free to move rapidly ahead. Intense opposition from strongly entrenched and politically powerful landlords will, however, continue. If the Congress Party is to retain the confidence of the peasants, this opposition will have to be squarely met.

New lands are also being rapidly opened up for cultivation. Several million acres, long unused because of deep-growing weeds, malarial conditions or for other reasons, will soon be adding substantially to India's food supply. But the major increase in food production is expected to come through better use of land which is already under cultivation, and here the opportunities are very great.

Indian farmers have always made much poorer use of fertilizers than have the Chinese; their seeds often are of low quality; and hundreds of billions of gallons of water which could vastly increase food production on parched lands are being wasted for lack of adequate irrigation systems. In many villages farming methods remain much as they were before the British occupation. These problems are being tackled by the new Indian Government to the limit of its resources, supplemented by American Point Four assistance. All over the country, teams of agricultural extension workers are demonstrating what spectacular increases in food production are possible through modern methods of tillage, adequate fertilizers, improved seeds and better use of water.

The village-to-village program which is now unfolding is said to represent the biggest combined attack ever attempted anywhere on low agricultural production, disease and illiteracy. On October 1, 1952, the central Indian Government, in coöperation with the states, is scheduled to open up 55 community development areas, each containing on the average 200,000 people, or a total of 11,000,000. If sufficient financing is available, the program will be expanded to cover one-third of all the villages in India in the next four years.

One hundred village workers are assigned to each of these development areas. This means an average of one worker for each three villages or for each 1,800 people. These village workers, 3,000 of whom are just completing their training, will work with the villagers to increase agricultural production, improve sanitation standards, eliminate malaria and establish schools and adult literacy classes. To each development area, in addition, there will be assigned 22 specialists in engineering, education, public health and the various phases of agriculture to back up the village workers in their respective fields. More than 50 American extension workers are now actively engaged throughout India as consultants in the planning and development of this huge program. One hundred thousand tons of fertilizer purchased with Point Four funds will soon be available. American jeeps, D. D. T. for malaria control and steel for the production of improved tools by village blacksmiths are being put to work.

As I write, the exact amount of American aid for the present fiscal year remains undetermined. It is hoped that 55 more development areas, including an additional 11,000,000 people, can be opened up early in the coming winter, and that sufficient American supplies and technicians will be available to help carry this great program forward. But no one can accuse the Indian Government of sitting back and letting Uncle Sam carry the load. For every dollar of American aid going into this community development program, there are eight dollars in Indian rupees.

Another major part of the Indian agricultural effort is to increase irrigation. Present plans call for 8,000,000 acres of newly-irrigated land from major river valley developments by late 1956, plus another 8,000,000 acres from tube wells, improvements of present irrigation systems, additional shallow wells, storage ponds and other sources.

Three groups of big dams modelled on our T. V. A. or Boulder Dam systems are now being built at Damodar, Hiarkud and Bakhra-Nangal — the last-named alone to irrigate 3,300,000 acres annually. This is 70 percent more than is serviced by Grand Coulee, at present the largest irrigation system in the world. Point Four funds will provide bulldozers, pumps and other essential equipment for many of these irrigation projects. They also will help with the tube well program; our 1952 budget provides for 2,000 such wells to be dug, mostly in the great Gangetic basin of north India, each of them to irrigate an average of some 400 acres. They will pay for themselves in six or seven years. As in the case of the Community Development Program, this American contribution will be a small but essential part of the total investment.

Additional United States funds are going into an all-out campaign against malaria. The Ministry of Health and the Rockefeller Foundation estimate that there are 80,000,000 cases of malaria in India and more than 1,000,000 deaths each year. According to the experts, almost all of this human misery, to say nothing of the drag on India's productive capacity, can be wiped out in four years. The cost will be $23,000,000 for D.D.T., jeeps, trucks and spray machines and an equal amount in rupees for Indian labor and materials.

If sufficient American aid is made available by Congress, and if India continues her own present intensive effort to solve her great problems, there is every reason to hope that the great goal of the Five Year Plan — agricultural self-sufficiency by 1956—will be achieved. If it is, the new India will also have taken a long forward step in the world-wide struggle of democracy against Communist totalitarianism.

III

Even so, there are many urgent problems which will still remain unsolved, and one of the most important of them is the course of India's future industrial development. As Indian agriculture moves forward toward the Five Year Plan goal, fewer people will be required to raise the food needed to feed India's huge population. These workers will then be free for roadbuilding, construction, village industries, mining, and factory work in Indian cities. The transition will call for most careful planning. Foreign exchange totalling some $600,000,000 annually, now being spent for foreign food, must be largely diverted to industrial development. New capital, domestic and foreign, must be coaxed into constructive investment. New industrial managers must be trained. Here again there is every reason to be hopeful.

In the eighteenth century, at the time of the British occupation, India possessed a textile industry, technical skills and a level of artisanship that placed her in many ways well ahead of Western Europe. In the nineteenth century, under pressure from

British manufacturers, the industrial development of India was first curtailed and finally brought almost to a halt. One hundred years ago it was actually against the law for an Englishman to buy apparel made from Indian cloth. The basis for the modern Indian industrial plant was laid just before the First World War. Since then industrial development has moved forward gradually until today the statistics show that India is the eighth largest industrial country in the world. In view of her vast population, however, these particular statistics only emphasize how far she still has to go.

India is rich in natural resources. Her iron ore deposits are among the largest and purest in the world. She is one of the world's largest suppliers of manganese and mica. But her steel production is only a little more than 1,000,000 tons. Almost every major city in the country is short of industrial power. Her jute industry is her biggest dollar earner; but though it is the largest in the world, many of the plants need modernization.

Considerable progress is already being made in meeting these shortages. The many multi-purpose river valley projects now under construction should result in increasing hydroelectric capacity by two-thirds by 1957. Nearly one-fourth of the entire budget of the Indian central government is now being expended on these projects; and the total sum is expected to reach one billion dollars over the next five years, practically all of it to be coming from current revenue. Similar progress is in view in other fields. A plan is now under consideration by the World Bank which could increase India's steel production 70 percent by 1955, with the possibility of an additional 350,000 tons in that same period. The Indian railroads which were badly run down at the end of the war are being rehabilitated; and the program of modernization is being helped by a $33,000,000 loan from the International Bank. India's oil resources are at present very small, but there is some hope of future development. Meanwhile, one American oil company and one British group have completed contracts to build two large modern oil refineries in India, and a contract with another American company is under discussion.

Although the opportunity for future economic growth is great, once the present food deficits have been eliminated, the precise pattern of development is by no means clear. In theory, at least, most Indian leaders would prefer an economic system based on democratic Socialism. But in practice there are few who believe that Socialism could actually work in India except under the thumb of a dictatorial government, which would be no more welcome in India than in the United States. The preference of the average Indian leader for Socialism originates in the fact that the kind of capitalism which he considers as an alternative is not the incentive system which has been developed in the United States, but a European cartel monopoly concept based on high prices, wide profit margins and limited production. For this reason they believe themselves faced with a choice of evils, and this has resulted in a certain degree of confusion and contradiction in Indian industrial economic policy.

Fortunately, more and more Indian leaders are beginning to recognize that our American system of private enterprise is both far more efficient than Socialism and infinitely more socially conscious than the cartel capitalism which they have seen introduced from Europe. American businessmen who have visited in India in the last few months have seen tangible evidence of this new understanding. The three oil companies, which are now building refineries in India, for instance, were given 25-year guarantees against nationalization, and offered other inducements which would scarcely have been considered a year or two ago. Many observers believe that the Indian Government could afford to go further in offering practical inducements to new investors, domestic and foreign alike. Recently there has been considerable interest in the concepts introduced in Puerto Rico, where tax moratoriums on new investment and other inducements have resulted in rapid industrial development.

One possibility recently under discussion is the closer integration of the Japanese and Indian economies. Japan has a steel industry producing 6,000,000 tons annually, but at present is now forced to purchase much of her iron ore in the United States, which of course makes costs extremely high. India would gladly sell Japan substantial amounts of iron ore and some pig iron; indeed, as much as 5,500,000 tons of iron ore could be exported to Japan annually. What is needed is a rail link from an important source of iron ore in Orissa to the seacoast, plus the development of port facilities to handle the loading.

One thing, at least, is certain about India's future economic development. Whatever the system which emerges during the next few years, it will not be an imported carbon copy from America, Russia or any other foreign country. Another prediction which seems safe is that if political stability continues, India will develop a mixed economy, which, while borrowing generously from our American experience, will involve considerably more planning and tighter controls over the flow of capital. Most Indian government leaders are convinced that this is necessary in an underdeveloped country struggling to put its feet on firm economic ground. But side by side with this conviction is a growing belief that increased incentives to foreign as well as Indian investors must be a basic part of the plans for future development.

IV

India's new economic strength, however, is not to be based solely on new steel mills, new railroads and new power. Because transportation and housing are so inadequate, much of the industrial development must be decentralized and kept close to the villages. The need for small-scale industrial developments and cooperatives in rural areas will become increasingly apparent during the next two or three years as the effort to strengthen agriculture begins to pay dividends in the form of increasing food production.

Pilot studies in many parts of India have indicated that substantial increases in food production will be readily attainable within three or four years in those areas where more irrigation and commercial fertilizer can be provided, along with better seeds, better methods of planting and improved simple tools. Since most Indian villagers are not now getting enough to eat, some of this increased food production will be consumed by the cultivators and their families; but a major portion will be available to the cultivators in increased purchasing power, and in many areas this amount will be further increased through the new land reform programs which assure the cultivators a higher proportion of each crop. But this increase in food production will not be automatic. It can be assured only if the cultivators are given the incentives to produce the extra food made possible by modern techniques. If the incentives are lacking, the use of more modern techniques will merely reduce the number of hours spent by the cultivators in the fields.

This possibility has been clearly recognized. Studies are now under way in many villages, and as the community development program proceeds, knowledge of how to meet this challenge should rapidly increase. The answer lies largely in making more consumer goods available in the village bazaars at reasonable prices. There are tens of millions of Indians who have never owned a pair of shoes or a change of clothing. The market for new cooking equipment and simple comforts is almost unlimited.

Many students of the Indian economy believe that a sizable share of the increasing incomes of India's cultivators, and their energies during the off-seasons, can also be channelled into building roads, schools and hospitals. Those of us who are responsible for the Point Four program in India firmly believe that the labor and drive for this kind of local capital expansion must be provided by the villagers themselves. Every effort will also be made to build up local industry. Shoemakers and other village artisans and tradespeople will be urged to form cooperatives to handle their buying and selling. Small textile operations and cottage industries will be widely encouraged. To a large extent, the Indian Government is treading virgin soil, and answers to the problems that appear can be found only as the program proceeds. With this in view, plans for five of the 55 development areas which are opening this fall call for experimental work in local industries, cooperatives and the building of schools, hospitals and homes.

The principal responsibility for building the new India is clearly that of the Indian leaders and the Indian people, and this fact they fully accept. Indeed, it can be said that no people on earth have ever done more within limited resources than the Indian people have done since the birth of their new nation. The human material is here; the physical resources are here. The will to move ahead and to accept the challenge of Communism is also here. However, without a moderate amount of American aid each year for the next four years the objectives of the Five Year Plan are likely to prove unattainable.

We can be certain, I believe, that American resources spent in India will be used, not to perpetuate feudal institutions, but to build a modern democratic nation. This is vitally important, for if democracy is to survive in Asia, our efforts must start not at the top with the fortunate few but in the villages with the hungry millions. We must work in such a way that Asian people will come to look on democracy not just as a desirable but abstract goal, but as the most practical way to get things done.

American aid in Asia or anywhere else will be so much more money down the drain unless the local conditions are such that the program of aid has a reasonable chance for success. It is sheer waste to aid a nation which fails to establish a fair and equitable tax system, or an underdeveloped agricultural country which lacks the courage to establish land reform which gives the cultivators the right to till their own land. American money which strengthened only the upper income groups of revolutionary Asia would be not only wasted but would have a positively dangerous effect, for it would destroy the faith of the people of Asia in our American democracy.

Moreover, aid money spent simply for anti-Communist objectives has a hollow ring in Asia, for it points logically to the conclusion that if the noisy Communist minorities did not exist the interest of the United States in the welfare of Asian people would disappear. Nor, again, should we give aid in the mistaken belief that lasting friendship can be bought with dollars. Our primary objective must not be to develop gratitude in Asia toward America, but to create confidence in democracy as a vital force, and confidence among the people that under democratic government they have the ability to meet and solve the huge problems which confront them.

For this reason the methods which are used to increase production in Asian countries are almost as important as the production itself. Many argue glibly that the elimination of hunger in Asia will automatically bring about the defeat of Communism. This gravely oversimplifies the problem. Most revolutions are led not by hungry peasants but by frustrated middle-class intellectuals who have never known hunger in their lives. Living standards in India must certainly be improved, and with all possible speed. Unless this primary objective is achieved, the present democratic government will sooner or later be swept aside and the stage set for another devastating Communist victory. But India must do more than feed her people better. If democracy is to survive and grow, tens of millions of Indians must also be inspired with a dynamic new faith in the future and a sense of personal participation in building that future. In Jawaharlal Nehru, fortunately, India has a leader extraordinarily well equipped to provide the vital spark.

University students present both an opportunity and a problem. At present, there are 250,000 students in 800 Indian universities and colleges. Most of them receive a strictly liberal arts education (a hand-me-down from British days), and leave their universities with little practical training for the great battle of life which is in progress all around them. Except for the small minority who have received technical training in engineering, agriculture and public health, they find good jobs almost impossible to obtain. Thousands of recent graduates earn no more than eight or ten dollars a month. This produces frustration and many new converts to the Communist faith.

The Indian Government, which is keenly aware of this separation of the young intellectuals from the people and their problems, is now making every effort to close the gap and to develop a broad sense of democratic participation. Volunteer groups are being organized for road building and other construction work during vacation periods. Within the next few years some 60,000 young men and women, mostly college graduates, will be recruited as village workers to carry on the rapidly expanding work of the community development areas. As the program develops, the need for public health experts, welfare workers, doctors, engineers and other specialists should be almost unlimited.

In spite of every effort, however, the social problems of India seem more likely to grow than diminish in the coming years. The gigantic shakeup of Indian life, Indian attitudes and Indian traditions which is taking place is unloosening powerful forces. Most of them are good, but some are inherently explosive. The very success of the development program will in itself create new conflicts and new difficulties. They must be met with practical good sense, cool judgment and courage if India is to emerge a mature, stable democratic nation from the growing pains of her present strenuous effort.

V

What America does or fails to do in her relationship with India is clearly of the utmost importance to the outcome which I have been describing. It is also clear that whatever program we develop in the United States must receive the understanding and support of Republicans and Democrats alike. We cannot afford the luxury of a separate Asian policy for each major political party. We must develop a policy on which the great bulk of our people agree.

In adopting that policy and putting it to work we must understand that we cannot determine by our own efforts what will happen in Asia in general or in India in particular. In the new Asia the tides of hope, fear and conviction run deep and strong. We cannot control these tides. Asia will develop in her own way and the final dominant influences will be Asian, not American and Western. What we can do, however, is to understand the forces which are at work, and to seek patiently and sympathetically to strengthen those which are moving in democratic channels.

Soviet propagandists are now intensifying their campaign to establish Russia and China as the logical leaders of revolutionary progress in Asia, and it would be foolish indeed to minimize the effectiveness of their effort. In the Listener, a publication of the B.B.C., for May 24, 1951, Arnold Toynbee described the Soviet appeal to Asia in the following terms:

Yesterday I [Russia] was an old-fashioned peasant much as you are today. Like you today, I yesterday lived depressed, ignorant, hopeless, and tame. I was lying then as you are still, under the heel of a privileged native minority which was itself the creature of the Western masters of the world. But look at me now! See how I have pulled myself up by my bootstraps. And what I did for myself and by myself yesterday, you can do yourselves tomorrow if only you will take my advice and follow my example.

For those many Asians who are sophisticated enough to challenge the sincerity of the Russian interest in Asia's welfare, the propaganda spotlight is centered on China — which, it is claimed, "is now moving rapidly forward toward the dawn of a new day after centuries of exploitation by Western oppressors." In most of the Asian countries the Soviet Government works closely with local Communist party groups which are already well organized, particularly among the depressed classes and in the universities and colleges. The Communist purpose is first to discredit and then to undermine and destroy any government which seeks to develop an independent policy.

When Soviet strategy demands it, the local Communist Party will embark on open rebellion, as it did in many parts of India in 1948. But the Communist leaders are also familiar with Lenin's advice: "A tough, disciplined Communist minority needs no more than 10 percent of the popular vote to bring about the downfall of any democratic government. If there are five parties, you should work side by side with four to destroy the fifth. When there are four, ally yourself with three and destroy the fourth. When there are three, combine with two to destroy the third. And when there are only two, victory is in your hands."

India is a special target for the Communist effort because of her strategic position, her rich natural resources and the size of her poverty-stricken population. The Communist Party in India is well organized and amply financed, largely through the sale of Soviet literature. In the recent all-India elections, by far the largest in the history of the democratic world, it polled 6 percent of the total vote and established itself as the strongest opposition party in terms of elected representatives. Today, with Lenin's advice in mind, these Communist representatives for the time being are assuming a benign and patriotic look and are generously offering to work with "other democratic forces in pursuit of the ideals of the common man." Side by side with this the Communist cultural offensive continues, as does the attack on American "warmongers" and "imperialists." Every instance of racial prejudice in America, every Western failure to solve the problems and conflicts of colonialism, is exploited to the full.

The importance of this new and intensified Soviet effort in Asia should not be underestimated. Communist propaganda is particularly effective because in their hearts most Asians, non-Communists as well as Communists, still mistrust the West; and like many others before them, Asian nations are more conscious of the familiar dangers of the past than the yet-to-be experienced dangers of the future. There is, in consequence, a continuing bitter fear of the rapidly dying nineteenth century imperialism and a tendency to underestimate and to rationalize the danger of Soviet twentieth century imperialism — the real threat to their independence. But this is the situation with which we must deal, and we must approach it with imagination and realism.

The Soviet Union seems much more clearly aware than we have been so far that for Asia to become Communist would mean not only a drastic shift in physical power between the Soviet bloc and the Western democracies, but the broad deterioration of democratic morale in all parts of the world. Lenin made the blunt prophecy: "For World Communism, the road to Paris lies through Peking and Calcutta." His successors show the same belief that if they can overrun Asia they can build what Stalin has called "the road to victory in the West."

There is no reason why the challenge should not be met with confidence. If India's great democratic effort succeeds, if similar efforts suited to the needs of each country are pressed vigorously by the leaders of Japan, Indonesia, Pakistan, Thailand, Ceylon, Burma and the Philippines, and if these efforts are supported by patient, understanding policies on the part of the West, the next few years may see the emergence of a non-Communist Asia that will be both dynamic and democratic. That can swing the preponderance of world power in the direction of peace and freedom.

The road for American policy-makers working toward this goal will often be a rocky one. Many Americans who are deeply conscious of the crisis which confronts the free world are irritated by Asia's talk of "neutralism" and by the rebuffs which occasionally come our way from uncertain new governments which are still hopeful that Communism may turn out to be not as dangerous as we know it to be. But impatient criticism will only lead to equally impatient retorts. The situation calls, as I said at the beginning of this article, for a display of some of the best qualities in the American tradition: understanding and respect for the rights of others; humility in the face of strange ways and new problems; courage to remember that, in spite of the cynics, a little idealism mixed with the practical represents not weakness but strength; willingness to persevere in the face of difficulties. With these qualities, and with intelligence and imagination, we can, I feelsure, contribute to building an Asia that will have confidence in democracy and that will practise democracy.

© Foreign Affairs

For Principled Neutrality

A New Appraisal of Indian Foreign Policy

Acharya J. B. Kripalani

The 16th summit of the Non-aligned Movement (NAM), one of the founding fathers of which was Jawaharlal Nehru.

AS India before independence formed part of the British imperial possessions, the British Government decided her foreign policy. British interests were supposed to be also the interests of India. The foreign policy of England during the nineteenth century was directed to preserving her far-flung empire and safeguarding her world-wide economic interests. These objectives she tried to attain by a threefold strategy. One was to safeguard the routes to her imperial possessions. For this purpose she had to keep a strong navy equal to the combined navies of any two countries on the Continent. The center of the Empire was India. Therefore, the route to India was dotted with military bases in the Mediterranean — Gibraltar, Malta and Cyprus. England also dominated Egypt, the Suez Canal, the Arab countries and the Persian Gulf.

A threat to Britain's imperial possessions and her economic interests could come only from the industrially advanced countries of Europe. To avoid this contingency was the purpose of the second plank in British foreign policy: to keep the balance of power in Europe.

But Russia was both a European and Asiatic power, with expansionist designs in Asia. Therefore the third plank of British foreign policy was to contain Russia within her Asiatic borders.

After she won independence India had to evolve a foreign policy of her own, devoted to her own interests. However, it would be wrong to say that before then India had no foreign policy aims apart from those of Imperial Britain. The Indian National Congress, from the time the independence movement gained strength under Gandhi's leadership, developed its own foreign policy and this was generally accepted by the country. Naturally it had little to do with what is strictly called international diplomacy, carried on through envoys and other agents accredited for the purpose. India had none of these. Indian foreign policy before independence was confined to the enunciation of basic principles which would guide the country's diplomacy after independence. These principles, influenced as a matter of course by the principles that directed our whole struggle, were based on non-violence and truth. These are moral principles, but translated into political terms they mean disarmament and open diplomacy, principles enunciated by President Woodrow Wilson during World War I. India stood for the freedom of all nations and peoples and against all colonial or racial domination of one people over another; therefore she sympathized with all national struggles against imperialism. She stood for progressive disarmament and for world peace, supervised by some international organization wherein all nations participated equally.

After independence these principles were reiterated. At that time, the new expansionism of Communist Russia had not yet shown itself in its true colors. Soon, differences arose among the Allies who had fought the war against the Nazi and Fascist powers and Japan. Soviet Russia had been allowed to occupy the countries of Eastern Europe from which it had driven the Nazi armies with the help of local liberation forces. As these countries had resisted German occupation, the Russian occupation, like that of France by the Western Allies, was considered temporary. But soon it was apparent that Russia had no intention of withdrawing her armies and allowing these countries to manage their own affairs. On the contrary, through political coups supported by Russian armed forces, she imposed Communist régimes on them, subservient to her. The result was the cold war. The Western powers sought to strengthen themselves against expansionist Communist Russia by forming military alliances and pacts — NATO, SEATO and the Baghdad Pact. As a countermove, the Russians made so-called treaty arrangements with the satellite states — the Warsaw Pact. But the countries signatory to the Pact were not free agents, as was made plain when there was a general rising against the Russian-dominated Communist government in Hungary. A short-lived régime there, supported by the popular will, wanted to withdraw from the Warsaw Pact and remain neutral in the cold war. Soviet Russia would not allow this. One cannot imagine coercive action being taken by the dominant Western partners against any country that wanted to withdraw from one of the Western pacts!

In the present international circumstances, India, following her basic principles, has taken a position of non-alignment or neutrality as between the two power blocs, the Western and the Russian. But the Prime Minister of India has often said that Indian neutrality is not passive but dynamic. He means that India will freely express her opinion in international affairs and show her sympathy and solidarity with victims of aggression and injustice.

In spite of the fact that independent India was new to international diplomacy, her prestige in international affairs was somehow high, especially among Asio-African nations. This was due in part to the size of her territory, her geographical position and her vast population. It was also due to the unique character of the Indian struggle for independence, which put confidence and courage in colonial peoples everywhere by demonstrating that even an unarmed nation, if determined, could win its freedom. It was further felt that both before and after independence India's basic principles were just and humane. Though Western democracies mouthed the same principles, they were suspect, since they still held in an iron grip the remnants of their empires. The United States was not imperial in the West European sense, but it was thought to desire domination of other nations through its economic power. Its good faith was further suspect because of its alliances with imperialistic democracies and with non-Communist totalitarian and military régimes whose actions it could not control. The doctrine recently enunciated by President Eisenhower of "filling the vacuum" created by the dwindling influences of England and France in West Asia caused further distrust of American political motives. Both in Korea and Indochina the Western nations supported what Asians considered reactionary régimes. Naturally, therefore, Asio-African nations looked to free India for sympathy, support and guidance. Their representatives in the United Nations often consulted their Indian colleagues before making up their minds about policy decisions.

India's prestige in international affairs was enhanced when it was offered, and accepted, the chairmanship of international commissions appointed after the deadlock in Korea and Indochina. The big powers which had indirectly come to grips in these two regions knew that any further fighting might lead to a third world war. They found a way out by consenting to cease-fire agreements on the basis of the status quo and the appointment of international commissions to solve immediate problems. But they were not willing to play the game to bring about peace in these countries and their ultimate unification. The international commissions formed under Indian chairmanship therefore could not discharge their responsibilities effectively and in course of time they seem to have faded away.

Indian prestige was further enhanced when an Indian, a woman at that, was elected President of the U.N. General Assembly. It was not generally realized that owing to the jealousies and rivalries of the big powers this position of prestige, without power, could go only to prominent politicians in militarily weak countries.

Whatever may have been the failings of the Congress Party government in internal affairs, it could always with some justification show that it had added to the prestige and standing of India in the international world. But all this prestige did not advance any vital interests of India or diminish tension on her borders. Our relations with Pakistan are as strained as ever. The Kashmir issue remains internationally confused. In the case of the tiny Portuguese imperial possessions in India, no progress has been made; indeed the situation has deteriorated. On her northern frontier, India allowed the annihilation of the buffer kingdom of Tibet without a protest; we have recognized the legitimacy of the Chinese claim there. The question of the citizenship of Indian nationals domiciled for decades in Ceylon still hangs fire. There is no improvement in our relations with South Africa.

II

Why is this so? It is because the Indian Government thought that the whole business of diplomacy consisted in enunciating the principles of international policy. But international politics is not concerned merely with enunciation of abstract principles. It is very much concerned with international diplomacy, strategy and tactics. To use the old metaphor, it will not do to lose sight of the trees in contemplating the beauty of the forest, for it is the trees, after all, which yield useful fruit and timber. To take a historical example: President Wilson during World War I enunciated important moral and political principles to regulate international affairs, but after the war his weak diplomatic strategy failed and paved the way to World War II.

It is true that the international complications which faced India, and still face her today, especially on her borders, are not of her creation. They are historical legacies. But what is successful diplomacy? It is not that a country should enjoy international prestige, desirable as that may be, but that it should be able to safeguard its vital interests, without recourse to war. At least it should be able to reduce tensions. Successful diplomacy should counteract the adverse effects of historical circumstances. Another condition of successful diplomacy is to take appropriate action at the proper time. In politics, national or international, opportunities once missed are generally missed for good, or at least do not arise again in the same favorable form. The nation which fails to take advantage of a favorable opportunity has often to pay the full price of its mistakes, even as the merchant must for his miscalculated deals. The law of Karma is inexorable.

Let us take the example of the China-Tibet conflict. In resolution after resolution, the Indian National Congress before and after independence had denounced the domination of one nation over another. India never recognized unjust historical claims. If she had, her own struggle for independence would have had little justification. So it was, then, that immediately after independence when we invited to our country a conference of Asian countries, Tibet was included as a free nation. When the so-called Chinese liberation army marched into Tibet our government rightly protested. In surprise our Prime Minister asked: "From whom is Tibet to be liberated?" For this protest, Communist China dubbed us "the running dogs of imperialism." I am afraid we yielded to the usual Communist bullying tactics and allowed China a free hand in Tibet. Perhaps we were misinformed by our representative there about the nature of Chinese Communism. However that may be, we had no right to give our conscience a sop by taking refuge under the historic right of suzerainty claimed by Communist China. This suzerainty, as we know, or as students of history we ought to have known, was imposed upon Tibet by powerful imperial countries but was never accepted by the people or rulers of Tibet.

The question often asked is, what could India have done? We could not possibly go to war on this issue; but the alternative to war is not acquiescence in injustice. We denounced the aggression of Britain, France and Israel against Egypt, but this did not involve us in war. Today we side with the Algerian struggle for independence, but this has not meant the cutting of our normal and friendly relations with France. Acquiescence in aggression amounts to appeasement, which merely whets the appetite of the aggressor, as was seen at the time of Munich. England was not prepared for war with Hitler. But Chamberlain's mistake was to acquiesce in Hitler's aggression against Czechoslovakia by declaring it a distant country about which the English people knew little. In the case of China, we could have recognized the de facto Communist rule on Chinese soil and continued diplomatic and trade relations with the new government. We have such relations with France in spite of Algeria and with Russia in spite of Hungary. We have them with England even though she has not freed all her colonies. We have not ceased to be a member of the British Commonwealth, though some of its members are not friendly to us and indulge in racial discrimination against us. It is usual to recognize de facto governments, within their own borders, whatever their origin. However, when the means used to acquire power are of a doubtful character, the de facto and the de jure recognition should not be accorded immediately, especially the latter. One must wait and see if the new régime is accepted by the bulk of the people, without undue coercion. It was not even amiss to advocate the cause of Communist China's membership in the United Nations. It would not have been the first or only imperialist power represented in that august body. But we should never have put the seal of our approval on the rape of a virtually independent nation. India herself renounced her extraterritorial rights over Tibet, acquired under British imperial rule. We renounced these rights because we believed in the freedom of nations in spite of historical accidents to the contrary. India did not renounce these rights in favor of China but of Tibet. Even though we were assured that, unlike Soviet Russia, Communist China was democratic and progressive, we should have known that a régime that insists on unjust historical rights, derived from previous governments which it considered imperialist and reactionary, cannot be liberal or progressive. In their international affairs the Communist régimes in both Russia and China follow the expansionist and imperialist policies of the Tsars and of the Chinese emperors and Chiang Kai-shek.

In any case, by 1954, when the treaty between India and China was signed, the character of this régime was, or should have been, clear to the Indian Government. Yet by that treaty we confirmed the suzerainty of China. Since 1950, mine has been the solitary voice raised in the Indian Parliament against the recognition of the suzerainty of China over Tibet and in favor of Tibetan independence. Speaking in the House in 1958 on Panchsheel, I said that it "was born in sin in as much as by it we put the seal of our approval on the annihilation of a free nation." Subsequent tragic events have justified my criticism. Our recognition of Chinese suzerainty over Tibet is in clear contradiction to what our Prime Minister has often said: "Where freedom is menaced or justice threatened, or where aggression takes place, we cannot and shall not be neutral." This is dynamic neutrality. In the case of Tibet we have not been even neutral. We have dynamically sided with the aggressor.

Another example of the failure of our diplomacy is provided by the way we have handled the Kashmir problem. According to the "Instrument of Transfer of Power" from Britain to India and Pakistan, the rulers of the Indian States were free to accede either to Pakistan or India. The Kashmir ruler acceded to India. Legally, therefore, the integration of Kashmir with India was complete. Yet we made it a condition precedent to our accepting the offer of accession that power be handed over to the representatives of the people and that the Prince occupy the position of a constitutional ruler. This was done. Sheikh Abdullah, the leader of the popular party representing the people of Kashmir, was asked to form a democratic government. Thus not only was the condition laid down by the British Parliament about the accession of a princely state fulfilled, but India went further and helped in the establishment of a democratic régime in Kashmir. Yet we went out of our way to say that the accession of Kashmir would not be complete until a plebiscite had been taken. This was to create confusion about our legal and moral rights. Further, though we rightly described the action taken against the raiders from the North-West Frontier as a police action, we ordered a cease-fire without clearing the whole of Kashmir of outside raiders who were responsible for looting, murder, arson, rape and other atrocities on the people of Kashmir, both Muslims and Hindus. A police action does not come to an end by a cease-fire agreement with any foreign power, even at the instance of the United Nations. It is a matter of internal law and order, which cannot be ended unless the whole territory is cleared of the raiders from outside. However, if after the cease-fire we still stood by the promise of a plebiscite, we should have advised the Kashmir administration to arrange it in that part over which it had control, as soon as the situation was normal as regards law and order. But we did not do this.

Soon the Kashmir government under Sheikh Abdullah decided to convene a Constituent Assembly to frame a constitution for the region. This Assembly was obliged to review the question of accession even though it had already been decided legally. The Constituent Assembly's confirmation of the earlier decision should have laid at rest the question of a plebiscite. However, the Indian Prime Minister even then declared that the calling of the Assembly was without prejudice to the issue of a plebiscite.

No wonder that nations which are not necessarily prejudiced against India for reasons of their own misunderstand our position in Kashmir. Our representatives in the United Nations have laid most stress on India's legal rights there. The fact is that there are other more weighty, practical and humanitarian considerations for not disturbing the present position. If it is disturbed, there will again be a movement of population both ways and India and Pakistan will have a fresh refugee problem to face, even before the old one is satisfactorily solved. Further, the incorporation of Kashmir in Pakistan will be justified only on the assumption that religion is the basis of citizenship and nationality. The two-nation theory based on religion is reactionary and was never accepted by India. If it is accepted, every Muslim in India will be an alien in his country and every Hindu in Pakistan will be an alien there. Pakistan may welcome this, but a modern democratic nation like India can never accept such an undemocratic, reactionary and obscurantist solution. It will be the repudiation of our political principles, nullifying all our past. It will upset the whole of our mental thinking. India will have to make a new constitution. It will be in a sense totalitarian in as much as a large part of the community will not enjoy full citizenship rights. Further, India cannot and should not countenance a solution which will make Indian Muslims aliens in their home. This position can be better appreciated by the modern mind than insistence mainly on our legal rights.

III

There is always a danger in overemphasizing moral and ideological principles in international affairs. There are bound to be contradictions in the actual conduct of nations in dealing with each other. Our Prime Minister is never tired of repeating that "War solves no problems." Yet the expenditure on the Indian Army has been progressively increasing. As I once said in the Indian Parliament, supposing Pakistan was foolish enough to attack India, or if today China did so, would India fight? If she did, it would mean war. Would such a war be fought by India in the belief that war solves no problems? Armies are not maintained or military expenses incurred or wars undertaken on the assumption that war solves no problems. Rather the assumption is that, as long as the world has found no peaceful way of redressing international wrongs, war, in the last resort, is the only way of vindicating international justice and maintaining national dignity and independence. Today no nation maintaining an army which swallows a large part of its revenues, sometimes 50 percent and more, can with any logic or honesty hold that war solves no problems.

We also often say that the cold war is the result of fear. This is true. But we cannot talk too often of it, if we ourselves are afraid of Pakistan and of China. We cannot make light of the Russian fear of the United States, or vice versa. Even more, we cannot blame the Western European nations if they are afraid of Russia or if today the Asian nations fear expansionist China. Military power even for defense is born of fear. Only a determined nation, believing in non-violence, prepared for annihilation but unwilling to yield to injustice and tyranny, can really be fearless. This is what Gandhiji taught us, and he was right. It is no use reminding other nations of the faults from which we ourselves are not immune. Moral platitudes can be mouthed by politicians once in a while, but if they are repeated frequently, without appropriate action, their authors cannot escape the charge of hypocrisy.

For instance, the United States claims that if it ever goes to war against Communist powers it will be in defense of democracy and the free world. Do we believe these high and altruistic assertions when in pursuit of them the United States enters into alliances with imperialists and dictators? Would it not be better for the United States to say that it wants to safeguard its national freedom and is afraid of the expansionist designs of the Soviet Union? In that case, alliances with military dictators and imperialists to strengthen itself, however opportunistic, will not look so incongruous and hypocritical as they do today. If we are reluctant to believe in the pious utterances of others, we may be sure that such utterances by us, unsupported by appropriate action, will not be believed. Repeated platitudes will only confirm the belief, now so general, that the words of politicians have no meaning. They are blub, blub, blub. If words have no meaning, communication becomes difficult.

Take again the Panchsheel. Its principles if analyzed would amount to maintaining the status quo in international affairs, however inequitable. Neither the aggrieved nations nor the aggressor nations want or can maintain this status quo. For instance, there can be no peaceful coexistence between nations which have diametrically opposite apostolic missions to discharge and which want to do it through violence, war and crooked diplomacy. Nor can a conquered nation consent to peaceful coexistence with its imperial masters of whatever hue. Algeria can have no peaceful coexistence with France, nor for that matter can the Arab nations. Hungary cannot live in a state of peaceful coexistence with Russia or Tibet with China. The Portuguese dictator takes refuge under the Panchsheel doctrine of peaceful coexistence to deny the right of India in Goa or of the inhabitants thereof. Peaceful coexistence in such cases will be that of the lamb with lion, when the lamb is safe in its belly.

The same applies to other principles of Panchsheel. One cannot respect the sovereignty of imperial nations over their colonies, yet international law recognizes it as a fact. The independence of nations must be recognized and realized before there can be peaceful coexistence or mutual respect of each other's sovereignty. The Panchsheel principles are not moral imperatives that can be adhered to unilaterally. In international affairs, even moral principles have no unilateral application; much less can Panchsheel, which depends upon mutuality of rights and obligations. It is therefore no wonder that recently while on a visit to Nepal the Indian Prime Minister when questioned about Panchsheel was constrained to say, in effect, "Where is Panchsheel? It cannot be worked in the present international situation. It has become merely a slogan."

When all nations believe in war, in the ultimate, as the solvent of international problems, there is something to be said in favor of the doctrine of "brinkmanship," enunciated by the late Secretary of State, Mr. Dulles. As a matter of fact this is no new doctrine. It has been enunciated by politicians everywhere when they say, "Believe in God but keep your powder dry." On the basis of violence, no other kind of diplomacy is likely to succeed.

Unfortunately most nations have not powder enough to keep dry. It is also true that even the most powerful nation today cannot defend itself singlehandedly. It is therefore natural for nations to enter into military alliances for mutual protection. But there are countries which enter these alliances not for the purposes of defense but to safeguard their imperial interests or work their designs on their neighbors. For instance, Pakistan, as she has often said, has only one enemy — India. But for India, she would be neutral like most of the Asiatic countries which have recently achieved independence. France uses the military help she receives from the United States against Algeria. Portugal is in NATO to safeguard her imperial possessions. But in the confused international world of today this is inevitable, when both parties to the cold war want to strengthen themselves by any alliance, however doubtful.

It nevertheless is good that, in spite of any strength they might gain from military alliances, some nations have chosen to remain neutral. They do so for valid and weighty reasons. Not only do they have no expansionist designs, but they also feel that if they ally themselves with more powerful nations, and especially if they allow them military bases (ultimately it will come to that), they will impair their independence. Further, they believe that if more nations are linked in military alliances there is a greater danger of world conflagration, which, with the present nuclear weapons, may destroy humanity. If the number of neutral nations increases there will be a greater possibility of settling international problems through negotiations and conferences, below or at the summit. It will also mean more and more reliance on the good offices of the United Nations, thereby strengthening that organization. Even as it is, its services are utilized when the rival big powers feel that any further fighting in which they are directly or indirectly involved, if not speedily stopped, will produce complications leading to world war. This happened in Korea and Indochina and during the Suez and other West Asian troubles. In any case, regional military pacts weaken the standing and authority of the United Nations.

The underdeveloped Asio-African countries which have recently achieved freedom have so many political, economic and social problems of their own that they feel they must confine their attention to the solution of these rather than dabble in partisan international politics. They do not want to annoy any of the big powers. Furthermore, nations which have recently cast off the Western yoke are not quite sure that the colonialists have altogether abandoned the idea of regaining their old dominant position, given the opportunity. They therefore utilize the anti-imperialist assertions of Russia to keep in check fresh ambitions of the West. At the same time they are not enamored of the political and economic setup in Communist Russia or China. They therefore remain neutral. Further, they do not believe in the apostolic mission of reforming the world that both sides claim for themselves, one more fanatically and more aggressively than the other. No nation has been commissioned by God or His substitute, Historical Necessity, to reform the world.

These are good reasons for neutrality as between the two blocs, and they appeal to India. Therefore the policy of the Indian Government in this respect is generally accepted by the nation.

IV

But with all these advantages, there is no guarantee of noninterference, direct or indirect, by the power blocs if they feel that their real or fancied interests are affected. Under these circumstances the neutrality of uncommitted nations can be useful to themselves and to the world only if it is born of strength of conviction and not out of weakness or opportunist considerations. In the latter case they cannot stick to it under strain from one side or the other. Their moral influence can count only when they refuse to yield to the threats and bullying tactics of powerful nations. There must be no compromise on clear issues, involving questions of international justice and peace. It must be understood that no nation can keep intact its independence and whatever moral influence it has without taking risks. To suppose that right conduct, whether in the individual or the group, involves no risks is not true to the facts of life and historical experience. As we have said, the risks involved in appeasement in the long run are greater. Where physical resistance is not possible, one must not shrink from moral resistance to evil. That is the only way to save one's liberty and self-respect. Unfortunately, the world is so constituted that right conduct does not save one from material loss and suffering. In the struggle for independence, even though it was nonviolent, India had to take great risks at critical times; and she did not hesitate to take them. Neutral nations have to resist the temptation of inclining to one side or the other to gain temporary advantage. They must be impartial. They must avoid any action which may undermine the confidence of other nations in their neutrality and do everything that will strengthen it.

It is natural that India should want to be friendly towards her Communist neighbors. Neighbors are most likely to have conflicting interests and to find ready cause for a fight. In Europe, West and East, I have been told by every country that it was friendly to India. My reply usually was: "Why not? We are not neighbors." That India should be anxious for friendship with Communist Russia and China, in spite of difference in ideology, should not be difficult to understand; but this anxiety should not blind us to whatever they say or do, particularly where the freedom and interests of other nations are concerned. For instance, our condemnation of Russian action in Hungary in 1956 was so halting and belated that it lost its merit. We were more forthright in condemning British, French and Israeli action in Egypt, and also American and British action in West Asia, when troops were landed in Lebanon and Jordan. In the case of Tibet as I said earlier, our attitude from the beginning has been in contradiction with our avowed principles. It has had the appearance of weakness and opportunism, of purchasing Chinese friendship at the cost of Tibet.

On occasions, we have allowed our guests from Communist countries to denounce Western democracies, with whom we are on friendly terms, from our soil. We cannot stop nations from denouncing each other. But if they do so they must do it from their own country and not from ours. It is possible for nations so attacked to feel that we share the views of our guests. In any case, they naturally feel aggrieved.

In assessing historical events, we should not forget contemporary facts. Whatever the world has suffered and is suffering from overseas imperialism, we cannot ignore the fact that, for whatever reasons or on whatever pretext, a new variety of imperialism has made its appearance. It nibbles at its neighbors and swallows them. It waits for some time, brief or long according to circumstances, to pounce on other victims. It has not the merit of being democratic even at home. In a Western country the existence of democracy at home mitigates to some extent the rigors of its domination in colonial lands. In England, Labor as a party, and some of its leaders individually, advocated democratic reforms in India. Ultimately, the Labor Party not only supported the cause of Indian independence but negotiated on that basis. In Communist countries there can be no vocal public opinion against their aggression or tyranny. Not a single voice was raised or could be raised in Communist Russia or China against the aggression in Hungary or Tibet and the atrocities committed in these hapless and helpless lands. Within democratic France there is a section of socialists and the whole bloc of Communists who advocate Algerian independence. (In non-Communist countries, the Communists, though not very ardent patriots, are always the most passionate advocates of civil liberties and the freedom of the colonial peoples.) In the imperialist democracies, usually, when civil liberties are denied to colonial people or there is executive tyranny, some groups or individuals in parliament protest and rouse public opinion. This does not and cannot happen under dictatorships — Fascist, Communist or military. In the colonies of Western democracies, also, the legal system is generally modelled on the pattern of democracy at home, which affords some protection against executive highhandedness and tyranny. The legal system in totalitarian countries or their dependencies affords the individual no protection against political and executive highhandedness.

Toward the danger of this new imperialism the Indian attitude has not been as strong and unequivocal as it was toward the older imperialism from which India herself suffered. The old imperialism is thoroughly discredited and is on the decline. It no longer gets support from progressives and intellectuals even in imperialist countries. This does not mean that it does not weigh heavily on those who suffer from it. But the new Communist imperialism, now fast beginning to show its paws and claws, is more dangerous. It embraces in its vise both the home country and the dependencies. Moreover, it is imposed in the name of high principles and noble ends which may have an appeal for many intellectuals and idealists the world over.

As matters stand today, a neutral nation cannot afford to lean heavily on large loans from outside for the development of its internal economy, if it wants to maintain its independence of opinion and action. The anxiety for large loans has sometimes put India in an awkward position. Often when our representatives have gone to the West, especially to America, they have impressed upon their audiences the idea that if large loans are not advanced to India she will be overwhelmed by Communism; the great bastion of democracy in Asia will thus be destroyed. This appears to be a humiliating position for a great nation to take. If Communism is bad, India must resist it, loans or no loans. Unarmed India did not rely on foreign powers or foreign financial aid in order to win its independence. Today it cannot rely upon huge foreign loans to meet not only its economic needs but also an internal Communist danger. Furthermore, Western nations understandably do not appreciate our criticizing them, even on issues which do not adversely affect our vital interests, at the same time that we ask them for large loans. An independent nation which wants to maintain its right to free criticism and action will do best to rely upon its own resources for its economic development.

To sum up, then, the principles upon which the Indian foreign policy of non-alignment is based are correct. They are generally accepted by the country and are in keeping with the genius of our people. If more nations will accept the same attitude there will be a definite lessening of international tension. It is in details of diplomacy that our foreign policy has been weak and has sometimes gone wrong. Our mistakes have to some extent impaired our moral standing as a neutral nation and have often injured our interests in various ways. But, after all, India is new to diplomacy, and the world situation is extremely complicated.

ACHARYA J. B. KRIPALANI, Member of the Indian Parliament since 1952; leader of the Praja Socialist Party; President, Indian National Congress, 1946-47; Member, Constituent Assembly, 1946-51; author of "Gandhi, the Statesman" and other works

© Foreign Affairs

Changing India

Jawaharlal Nehru

AMBUJ SAXENA

Indian Institute of Technology (IIT), Kharagpur, the first IIT established in 1951.

August 1947 brought independence to India. In spite of the long-drawn-out struggle that preceded it, it came in peace and goodwill. Suddenly all bitterness of past conflict was forgotten and a new era of peace and friendship began. Our relations with Britain became friendly and we appeared to have no inherited problems and conflicts with any other country.

We had been conditioned for 30 years by Mahatma Gandhi and his gospel of peace which had left a powerful imprint not only on the minds of those actively interested in politics but also on the mass mind. Our success in attaining freedom through peaceful methods confirmed this way of thinking. Thus we entered the family of independent nations with a clean slate, without any inherited hatreds or enmities or territorial or other ambitions, determined to cultivate friendly and coöperative relations with all countries and to devote ourselves to the economic and social progress of India without getting entangled in national or international conflicts.

India had become free, but there were still some small parts of it under French and Portuguese control which were under colonial domination. Thus in our minds the freedom of India was not quite complete. We felt certain that France and Portugal would also follow the British example and that these enclaves of colonial territory would inevitably, and through peaceful methods, join independent India. We made the necessary approaches to the French and Portuguese Governments. The French enclaves became a part of the Union of India peacefully by agreement with France. Portugal proved much more intractable and gave a lot of trouble. There was serious trouble in 1955 involving the killing and wounding of many Indian and Goan passive resisters by Portuguese soldiers. There was also severe internal repression in Goa. Such incidents continued, and it was only after some show of military force, following further incidents in 1961, that this last remnant of colonial rule in India was ended. After that the independence of India was complete.

August 1947 brought long-cherished freedom to our country. But in the wake of it came the Partition of India and, immediately after, mass killing on both sides of the new frontier and vast migrations. We had hoped that the Partition of India, which was brought about by agreement, would lead to the creation of two states which would be friendly neighbors and would coöperate with each other. That was natural, as not only geography but a common history and culture and the same language and many other factors common to both would, we thought, inevitably lead to friendly coöperation.

But this was not to be. The events after the Partition left a trail of great bitterness. We were trying to get over the immediate results of the Partition when the State of Kashmir was suddenly invaded from Pakistan and a new conflict arose. To us, trained and conditioned as we had been by Mahatma Gandhi, this came as a shock, for we had hoped that there would be no military conflicts with any other nation. After 14 months, a cease-fire was agreed to and actual fighting stopped. Since then, although the Kashmir problem remained with us and gave a great deal of trouble, feelings in both countries gradually lost their bitterness and approached normality, in so far as the people were concerned.

We devoted ourselves to the major problem that confronted us-economic and social progress and the betterment of our people. Even before independence, we had given much thought to this matter and had come to the conclusion that we should proceed by the method of planning. Our resources were limited, and we wanted to utilize them to the best advantage to attain declared objectives. After independence, a Constituent Assembly was formed to draw up the new Constitution of India; this declared that India was to be a sovereign, democratic Republic which should secure for all its citizens: justice-social, economic and political; liberty of thought, expression, belief, faith and worship; equality of status and of opportunity. And among them all it was to promote fraternity, assuring the dignity of the individual and the unity of the nation.

On January 26, 1950, this new Republic came into existence and all our efforts were directed toward realizing the objectives laid down-political democracy and economic justice. We called the objective socialistic without adhering to any doctrinaire definition of the word. The system we evolved was consciously directed toward the welfare of the common man rather than to enrichment of the few; it is democratic because its processes are ultimately controlled by public discussion and by Parliament elected on the basis of universal adult franchise, and not by the secret purposes of a privileged minority.

While benefiting from foreign experiences-more especially, in the constitutional sense, from England and the United States-we did not wish to copy any foreign models. We believed that India had, by virtue of her long history and traditions, an individuality of her own and we should retain this without adhering to outworn ideas or traditions. We realized that the world was rapidly changing and we must keep pace with these changes without being swept away by them. We wanted to help, however modestly, in this developing pattern of international relations. We had no desire to interfere with other countries or impose our views on them. Thus, India started changes in her own life and institutions that are so decisive and far-reaching in their scope and intent that they may well be considered revolutionary, especially when viewed against the background of an ancient civilization and its ingrained conservatism. In foreign affairs, in a period when cataclysmic conflicts seem never too far below the horizon, she has invariably taken her stand with those who are striving for the maintenance of peace and for reconciliation and coöperation.

The twin policies which have guided us since independence are, broadly, democratic planning for development at home and, externally, a policy which has come to be named, rather inadequately, "non-alignment." Like the basic policies of most countries, these are not the product of any inspiration or arbitrary choice, but have their roots in our past history and way of thinking as well as in fundamental national exigencies. India's overriding and most urgent task is to raise the standard of living of her people, and in order to achieve this, to carry out structural and organizational reforms not only as speedily as possible but with maximum popular support and participation. In foreign affairs, we had no interest other than to cultivate friendly coöperation with all countries and to help to keep world peace, as the sine qua non of everything else.In our approach to these problems, our attitude and ideas had inevitably been shaped by our own recent struggle for freedom, as well as by the accumulated experience of centuries, and above all by Mahatma Gandhi's teachings.

It is no sign of complacency to recognize that these policies have met with an encouraging measure of success. India, with a population of 446,000,000 and an electorate of over 200,000,000, remains the largest functioning democracy in the world. Without deviating from democratic principles and procedures, she has launched upon extensive programs of modernization which are already bearing fruit. Far-reaching land reforms have taken place and our economy, still predominantly agricultural, is being steadily transformed by the spread of industrialization and the completion of vast new projects in the fields of power, transport and irrigation. Our Community Development schemes represent a rural reconstruction program which promises to transform the countryside and the vast population that live there. Recently, the Community Development movement has been extended to what is called Panchayati Raj; that is, there has been decentralization in favor of village-elected councils which have been given authority and resources to carry out schemes of development. Both industrial and agricultural production have increased substantially in volume as well as variety, and every effort is being made to ensure that the benefits of an expanding economy are shared equitably by all classes of the population. Education has spread remarkably at all stages and there are at present over 50,000,000 boys and girls in schools and colleges. Special attention has been paid to scientific and technical education. The health conditions of the people have also made substantial progress. In the 1940s the expectation of life in India was 32; now it is approaching 50. Our planning, designed to equip the country with the technical skills and the productive facilities of a modern society, is essentially welfare-oriented. Two Five Year Plans have been completed and the third is now in mid-course.

What is called "non-alignment" has also not fared badly. This, strictly speaking, represents only one aspect of our policy; we have other positive aims also, such as the promotion of freedom from colonial rule, racial equality, peace and international coöperation, but "non-alignment" has become a summary description of this policy of friendship toward all nations, uncompromised by adherence to any military pacts. This was not due to any indifference to issues that arose, but rather to a desire to judge them for ourselves, in full freedom and without any preconceived partisan bias. It implied, basically, a conviction that good and evil are mixed up in this world, that the nations cannot be divided into sheep and goats, to be condemned or approved accordingly, and that if we were to join one military group rather than the other it was liable to increase and not diminish the risk of a major clash between them. Essentially, "non-alignment" is freedom of action which is a part of independence. This attitude no doubt displeased some people to begin with, but it has been of service to the cause of world peace at some critical moments in recent history. A large number of countries, including most of the newly independent states of Asia and Africa, have adopted a similar outlook on international affairs. It is possible that India has influenced their thinking to some extent in this matter; but, however that may be, "non-alignment" is now an integral part of the international pattern and is widely conceded to be a comprehensible and legitimate policy, particularly for the emergent Afro-Asian states.

II

Consistent with our policy of promotion of peace and international coöperation, we welcomed the end of the civil war in our neighboring country China and the proclamation of the People's Republic of China in December 1949. We began developing friendly and coöperative relations with our northern neighbor.

The wanton and massive invasion of last autumn has, however, brought an incalculable, ominous and explosive new element into the situation. Peking's propagandists have tried to sow confusion in the public mind over this; but no amount of sophistry can conjure away the fact that the People's Republic of China is guilty of premeditated aggression. In 1954 India and China signed a general treaty on Tibet, in the preamble of which both parties pledged themselves to mutual nonaggression and respect for each other's territorial integrity. At that date, China knew precisely what the extent of India's territorial jurisdiction was; India, on the other hand, was not only not aware of the Chinese claims (they were not disclosed until five years later), but she had no reason even to suspect that there was any major question about the frontier.

All the fighting that has taken place, and the forcible seizure of territory by China, has been to the south and west-that is, on the Indian side-of the frontier as implicitly accepted by China herself in 1954. At no point have Indian troops ever gone beyond that line. The charge of aggression against the People's Republic of China thus holds, regardless of the controversy about the correct delineation of the border. This subject has been voluminously documented; what needs to be said here is that India's northern frontiers are not the result of any British imperialistic expansion, achieved in violation of China's rights or interests, but have their sanction in the facts of geography and history, and the generally accepted principles of international law.

It is difficult to forecast the further course of this dispute. Recently some non-aligned powers took the initiative in making certain proposals which, if accepted, could lead to talks between India and China on the merits of the question. We have accepted these proposals in their entirety. China has thus far not done so. We have suggested that we are prepared to refer these frontier disputes to the International Court of Justice at The Hague or to arbitration.

The initiative lies always with the aggressor, and the Chinese have been exceptionally devious and deceptive in their methods. What has happened so far serves to define, more clearly than before, certain considerations which must continue to govern our attitude and policy on this question.

First, it would be wrong and inexpedient, and also repugnant to every sentiment of national honor and self-respect, to acquiesce in aggression, as plainly established as it is in this case. We must, therefore, insist that the aggression be undone to our satisfaction before normal relations can be restored. Whether a peaceful settlement can eventually be reached, therefore, depends largely on China.

Secondly, despite our friendliness, China's behavior toward us has shown such utter disregard of the ordinary canons of international behavior that it has shaken severely our confidence in her good faith. We cannot, on the available evidence, look upon her as other than a country with profoundly inimical intentions toward our independence and institutions.

Thirdly, the Himalayan barrier has proved to be vulnerable. If it is breached, the way to the Indian plains and the ocean beyond would lie exposed; and the threat to India would then, likewise, be a threat to the other countries of South and Southeast Asia. India's determination to resist aggression and retain her territorial integrity is, therefore, a vital factor in the safeguarding of peace and stability throughout this whole area.

This is no doubt appreciated by all the friendly countries whom we have asked for military and other assistance in the present emergency; and the prompt response that the request evoked, particularly from the United States and Great Britain, has been warmly acknowledged by the Government of India and the leaders of Indian opinion. It is obvious, however, that the defense of India in any long-term view calls for a sustained effort by India herself-an effort, moreover, which cannot be conceived entirely or directly in narrow military terms. In the past, our preoccupation with the human problems of poverty and illiteracy was such that we were content to assign a relatively low priority to defense requirements in the conventional sense. We will now clearly have to give considerably more attention to strengthening our armed forces and to the production within the country, to the extent possible, of all weapons and equipment needed by them.

Measures to this end have already been taken in hand. But, over and above these, even for the specific purpose of defense, the prime requisite is a solid and broad-based economy and a population increasingly trained to make full use of the resources of modern science and technology. Our development plans and programs have had precisely these objectives; and with such modifications and minor changes in emphasis as may be necessary, it is, if anything, more essential than ever to press forward with them. We are aware that the additional burden on our resources, entailed by the larger defense expenditure, must in any event call for further sacrifices on our part. We are making these sacrifices and are determined to carry through the current Five Year Plan without any significant scaling down. We hope external aid in adequate measure will be available in support of this special effort.

I have mentioned earlier that Indo-Pakistan relations had been steadily improving in recent years. The Chinese attack on India has, however, caused a setback. Pakistan authorities tended to regard the crisis in Sino-Indian relations as an opportunity to press India to make all sorts of concessions to them.

A new series of talks has been started between the two countries, and we in India would be the first to rejoice if they helped to ease the tension. Without prejudging the outcome of these discussions, it may be said, however, that they have no direct bearing on the problems we face with regard to China. The boundary to be protected delimits the territories of the Indian state and their defense is the responsibility of the Indian Government. What India needs is not manpower but weapons and other military equipment, which in the short run she must get from other sources, and in the long run manufacture herself.

Pakistan, like other states, can help by refraining from giving aid and encouragement to China and thereby enabling her to multiply her pressures against us. Unfortunately, the attitude of Pakistan ever since the Chinese aggression on India has been the reverse of this, and this has undoubtedly added to our difficulties. We are eager to come to agreement with Pakistan in regard to Kashmir and other problems, but it must be remembered that the question of moving toward a possible change in Kashmir is so pregnant with explosive possibilities that any incautious step might have far-reaching effects involving the internal stability of the sub-continent, and thus weaken instead of strengthen our defenses. Also the settlement reached must be such that it makes for permanent improvement in Indo-Pakistan relations.

The conflict provoked by Chinese aggression raises wider issues than the simple demarcation of a remote border. It is difficult to understand why China chose to conceal her territorial claims for many years, pleading subsequently that "the time was not ripe" for revising her maps; or why she had to mount large-scale, concerted attacks from one end to the other of the two-thousand-mile-long frontier; or why she rejects any approach to settlement other than through bilateral negotiations in the context of military force; or why she has been conducting world-wide anti-Indian propaganda denouncing the whole range of India's policies and depicting India as a tool of reactionaries and imperialists.

The fact appears to be that China's anti-Indian policy flows from her general analysis of the international situation, and reflects the aims and assumptions underlying her foreign policy as a whole. This policy itself, while formally subscribing to such ideals as peace and coexistence-though in the special Chinese meaning of these terms-leaves no room for non-alignment. If the world is viewed as divided essentially between imperialists and Communists, between whom war not only is inevitable in the end, but between whom tension in some form must be kept alive and even intensified as opportunity occurs, then there is indeed no place in it for the non-aligned. The non-aligned nations must, in this context, seem to be occupying an unstable, anomalous position from which, if they could be dislodged, either by cajolery or coercion, the result would be to accentuate the polarization of world forces. It is logical to conclude that China's multiple campaign against India is an exercise in realpolitik on these lines. India is such an outstanding member of the non-aligned community that her defection, whether voluntary or enforced, cannot fail to bring grave and far-reaching consequences in its train.

III

If this analysis is well-founded, the challenge from China, as it has revealed itself, is not only to our foreign policy, but to our domestic policy as well. Both are rooted in our needs and interests, and spring from the same cultural outlook and the same scale of moral values. Tolerance, friendliness, the protection of the rights and dignity of the individual, peaceful settlement of disputes, the persistent effort to reach agreement through compromise and persuasion-these are the values we have been trying to uphold, imperfectly no doubt, in the conduct of our internal affairs. They represent a way of life, if I may so put it, a way of life that is anathema to the ruling ideologists in Peking, with their faith in power and violence as the instruments of benevolent change.

We are far from being averse to change, we have embarked upon far-reaching changes and we propose to persevere with our plans and programs; but we are convinced that the methods by which changes are brought about are at least as important as the changes themselves. Means are more important than ends-this was the basic policy on which Mr. Gandhi laid constant stress. We believe that any change should come about through our own volition, as a result of our own experience, and that it should not be foisted on us through any kind of force or pressure. In the pursuit of change, we should seek to carry the mass of the people with us and win their support. This way of dealing with our problems may not result in as swift or spectacular transformation as we might wish, but at least the progress achieved will have a solid basis in the nation's consent and avoid a degree of dislocation and disorganization that we can ill afford.

It is in this spirit that we have set our hands to the task of developing, in this ancient land, a system combining political democracy and economic justice.

Can this enterprise survive the new strains and tensions? The question goes to the heart of the issues involved in the present conflict, and the answer lies only in part, though perhaps in large part, with us in India. I am confident in my own mind that we cannot let ourselves be panicked into abandoning either the goal or the methods of our policy as I have stated it. The attack from across the Himalayas undoubtedly gave us a severe jolt; it aroused anger and disgust at what we felt to be a wanton betrayal of friendship. The immediate reaction was a spontaneous wave of national unity submerging all other disputes and dissensions. Even if some of them are revived, they are bound to be heavily colored by the implications of China's policy for our security as well as for other aspects of our life.

In India there are groups which may be called Right and others which may be called Left. But the antithesis between Right and Left is not so clear-cut as in some other parts of the world, or as widely permeating in its intellectual and political language. To the vast mass of our people, the reality is a deeply felt but undoctrinaire demand for better economic and social conditions, to which has now been added a troubled awareness of the Chinese threat and of the paramount need for safeguarding the nation's independence and integrity. This is the basic situation that our policies are designed to meet. Undoubtedly, grave new problems have arisen which we did not previously anticipate and which could conceivably disturb our internal equilibrium. The diversion of resources to military preparedness may slow down to some extent the improvement in living conditions, and we will have to adapt ourselves, psychologically also, to the presence of a powerful and hostile neighbor. These are highly unwelcome and distasteful necessities, and their emergence has prompted an earnest reappraisal of the course we have been following these last 15 years. That reappraisal, however, has convinced us that the basic policies we pursued in earlier years should not be changed, but should only be adjusted in order to meet the new dangers that face us.

The central fact is that the impact of China, whether it again takes an acute military form or makes itself felt more insidiously, is forcing the pace of growth in India. Both the Right and the Left have been affected, and the nation as a whole is growing up. It is learning that in the world today it is not enough to be devoted to peace, or to mind one's own affairs, but that it is also necessary to have adequate armed strength, to adjust our relations with friendly countries in the light of the changing actualities of the international situation and, above all, to preserve and consolidate national unity.

There is an interplay of domestic and external factors here which no one can ignore; our responses will inevitably be affected by the policies that others adopt toward us. While uncertainties are inherent in the situation, the political ferment that has been at work in India during the past few months has confirmed for us the essential and continuing validity of the principles on which we have hitherto taken our stand. The defense of our freedom and the social progress to which we aspire can best be assured in our view by the flexible democratic structure that we have evolved for ourselves. This is not only in conformity with our larger interests, but also with the larger interests of the world.

The Right in India has become more clamorous, basing itself on an extreme form of nationalism; the Left, though also nationalistic, is to some extent weakened. The Communist Party of India is in disarray, and the great majority of it has condemned Chinese aggression and declared itself in favor of the national stand. There is much heart-searching even in the Congress Party. But, on the whole, the picture that is emerging confirms the domestic and international policies that we have pursued, subject always to a general agreement about the necessity for increasing our armed strength for defense. If the frontier situation should deteriorate, we would naturally consider it desirable to take measures to tighten up the central authority. That is something that is likely to happen in a crisis under any system of government. But, even so, the basic democratic structure will, I think, continue.

It is pertinent to note that the Soviet Union and the Communist states of Europe allied to it have not considered it necessary to change their friendly attitude toward India in spite of open Chinese hostility toward us. Indeed, they have continued their aid to India in various ways. This implies a recognition on their part that India and other non-aligned countries have a vital role in the existing balance of forces.

I have endeavored to give, above, some explanation of the basic policy which China appears to be following in regard to India. It may be that this policy is partly affected by the growing rift between the Soviet Union and China. This may have led China to demonstrate, by her attack on India, that non-alignment has no reality and that the Soviet policy toward the non-aligned countries is wrong; the only right course is to work for a polarization of forces in the world. This might, according to Chinese thinking, justify their ideological difference with the Soviet Union.

Whatever temporary military success the Chinese may have gained by their aggression on India, I think it would be correct to say that they have failed thus far in their main endeavor. Not only have they converted a friendly country like India into one basically hostile to them and united and determined against them, but the policy of non-alignment has not broken down and stands confirmed. China has lost the goodwill of most of the non-aligned countries and even of many of her Communist allies. She stands isolated today.

Ever since the cease-fire and the Colombo proposals, the immediate excitement of day-to-day fighting on the border has naturally toned down. But it is generally recognized that the menace from China is a continuing one, and we must therefore prepare to meet it, whatever developments might take place in the near future.

The future is uncertain. But it may be said with some confidence that, while India continues to strengthen herself for defense, she is anxious that her economic development should not be impeded because of the increased expenditure on armaments. There is an increasing realization that this double burden must be borne by our people. There is also the hope that our friends abroad will help us by sharing this burden to some extent. But we realize that in any event the people of India will have to carry the main load.

IV

Whatever happens in India or elsewhere will be governed to some extent by international developments. Happily, there have been indications recently that a new phase may well be opening in international relations. Cuba suddenly revealed to us the thermonuclear brink on which we are all poised; it also brought reassuring evidence of restraint and moderation in high places, without which we cannot be sure of surviving the dangerous days yet to come. It may be that the cold war and the East-West antagonism of the 1950s will be gradually softened and transformed by the new pressures that have emerged within each bloc, as well as by the insistent demand of the "uncommitted" countries for a systematic and world-wide assault on hunger, disease and ignorance. But war, and nuclear war at that, still remains the spectre which must be exorcized before mankind can breathe freely again. That is why disarmament, particularly the abolition of nuclear weapons, beginning with the cessation of all further tests, is of such supreme importance. The technology of the arms race is acquiring a fearful momentum of its own, and is rapidly reaching a point where, if it is not checked and reversed in time, it may well pose insuperable problems of organized, social control. The responsibility for this naturally rests, in the first place, with the principal nuclear powers, and we must hope that they will be equal to it.

Meanwhile, Indo-American relations have seldom been as close and cordial as they are now. The deep sympathy and practical support received from the United States in meeting the Chinese aggression has created a wealth of good feeling and, apart from that, there is much in common between us on essentials. President Kennedy's vision of a world of free and independent nations, freely coöperating so as to bring about a world-wide system of interdependence, is entirely in accord with our own ideas. It is in this spirit that we have endeavored to collaborate in peaceful and constructive work with the new Afro-Asian states, and with Britain and other Commonwealth countries with whom we have a long historical association. It is in this spirit also that we are doing our best to further the purposes of the United Nations as, most recently, in the Congo.

The United Nations admittedly has numerous shortcomings. The government of a country representing a large part of the world's population is still not subject to the discipline and the responsibilities that membership in the world organization would impose. Often, moreover, the judgment and activities of the United Nations have been swayed or inhibited by the passions and prejudices of the cold war. None the less, the United Nations is the chief repository of our hopes for ever closer and more effective international coöperation for security as well as welfare. It is dedicated to peace, freedom and justice-noble ideals which embody the aspirations of all mankind-and it may yet lead us out of this fear and strife-ridden age into a more settled future when the full potentialities of science and technology could be applied to the well-being of all peoples.

© Foreign Affairs

Has India an Economic Future?

Charles E. Lindblom

Jawaharlal Nehru signing the Planning Commission's report on the first five-year plan in New Delhi, July 7, 1951.

Let us get down to cases rather than generalize grandly. In India, food-grain output is the pivot on which economic development swings. The most urgent demand of the population is for more to eat; the most acute problem of economic stability is keeping food-grain prices from rising too sharply as money demand outpaces the supply of food; and the core of development strategy has to be either an increasing provision of food-grains to satisfy new consumer demands in the urban and industrial sectors or deliberate retardation of industrial growth to head off the new demands. What is the record and prospect on food-grains?

In 15 years of planned development, India has increased food-grain production about 50 percent. Interrupted between 1961 and 1964, agricultural growth resumed with a 10 percent jump in production last year, the crop year 1964-65. The resulting gain in welfare has been partly drained away in population growth, so that the per capita gain in food-grain production is perhaps 15-20 percent instead of 50. Still, India has managed to put a poorly trained labor force, whose marginal productivity has often been estimated to be zero, to work with little capital on exhausted soil and somehow come up with a massive increase in product.

We know why the gain was not more. Exhausted soil. Poor seeds. Little mechanization. Crude tools. Primitive plows, and bullocks too weak to pull heavier ones. Untrained farmers. Little capital investment in the land. The low repute of manual labor. Caste rules that block innovation. Traditionalism. Ignorance. Insecurity. Corruption. Apathy. But how in the face of these obstacles was any progress made at all?

Perhaps between one-fourth and one-third of the growth in output in the last 15 years came from new acreage brought under cultivation. That is a substantial share, and it has implications for the future to which we need to return. But what of the rest of the increase? Given the power of the obstacles, one would question the possibility of greatly raising productivity. It should not have been possible. How was it done?

Output requires input, and in many parts of the world it is encouragement of the use of chemical fertilizer that has done the trick. But India has been using very little fertilizer, on an average about three pounds of nutrients an acre, compared with 300 in Japan, 180 in Taiwan and 100 in Korea. Because much, probably most, Indian fertilizer goes into its cash crops, the application per food-grain acre is even less than three. Moreover, the government of India has not clearly weighed in on the side of fertilizer promotion; it has restricted fertilizer production by private firms and then failed to push through its own modest plans for government production; it has restricted private sales of nitrogenous fertilizer and then boosted the price of fertilizer through co-op channels in order to protect high-cost government plants; and it has not either permitted or constructed a distribution system to get fertilizer to the farmers when they need it on credit terms that are possible for the majority of farmers. Although the government claims to be encouraging the use of chemical fertilizer, its various interventions have had other objectives as well and may have on balance restricted the rate of increase in its use. Fertilizer does not explain the big increase in production.

Irrigation? Between the beginning of the First Plan and the middle of the Third, India brought 20 million new acres under irrigation. But "under irrigation" does not mean what it does in the United States. It usually means providing water on an uncertain delivery schedule and in amounts insufficient for high yield. It is a valued method of drought relief, and what is often officially claimed for it is that it helps keep production from falling badly in drought, not that it greatly contributes to a secular upward trend in production. Disciplined delivery of water for sustained high yield is a concept of irrigation not yet accepted by the Ministry of Irrigation and Power. Nor, because the costliness of irrigation calls for austerity in project design, has drainage been incorporated into irrigation well enough to escape the charge, often made by foreign irrigation specialists, that major irrigation projects may have, through waterlogging and salinization, destroyed more productive acres than they have created. The government has invested heavily in irrigation; but it is a source of widespread complaint that major projects lag badly in construction, with the result that even the limited objective of drought relief is not effectively pursued. Clearly, irrigation projects do not explain the growth of output, and the big projects may have on balance retarded the growth of output.

Extension work? It has been largely incorporated into India's extraordinarily ambitious program of community development, in which tens of thousands of Village Level Workers, backstopped by specialists, have been scheduled to carry new ideas to villagers and new techniques to farmers. But the Village Level Worker has been, it seems everywhere agreed, over-scheduled. Even originally he was to be a general development officer; and he has been made into a messenger, tax collector and intelligence officer, ever taking up new tasks he prefers to agricultural demonstration, for which his training has turned out to be insufficient anyway. It is widely agreed that India does not have an effective agricultural extension service at this date.

Good prices? Compared with other countries, the ratio between output price and fertilizer price has been strikingly unfavorable to the purchase of fertilizer. More generally, food-grain prices have lagged behind industrial prices. The government's interest in incentive prices has taken second place to its more urgent concern for low food prices to hold down urban unrest. The result has been compulsory procurement at less than open-market prices as well as zonal and state restrictions on the movement of food-grains out of the most productive areas, both of which policies have driven prices down in the producing areas and undercut the monetary incentive to grow more food.

A similar account can be given of seed and insecticide programs. But we already have enough evidence to make three points of significance for India's future. First: it is not the new inputs of modern agriculture that have achieved the growth in food-grain output. Fertilizer, some new seeds and insecticides have contributed marginally; and irrigation water may have hurt as much as helped.

Second: developmental policies are not to be credited with the gain. As regards fertilizer, new seed and prices, they have probably retarded growth; on irrigation, they may have; and on extension, they have been ineffective. From other points of view, the policies have been good: irrigation for drought relief, low prices for urban consumers, Village Level Workers for general community development, fertilizer monopoly to help the co-ops. But they have not served the cause of growth and cannot possibly explain India's great gain in food-grain output.

No one knows just how the increase has been achieved. But it seems clear-and this is the third point-that there are powerful, pervasive, local and "spontaneous" forces for growth in Indian agriculture-even in this the most backward sector of the economy-without which the growth cannot be accounted for. There appears to be a greater expenditure of labor in agriculture than before and a shift toward better methods of cultivation, not because it has been so planned but because on their own initiatives Indian peasants have made the choice. They have done so for a variety of reasons: more mouths to feed, new aspirations spreading through the countryside by informal communication, new techniques communicated from neighbor to neighbor. Even if the governmental programs have accomplished more than we have just estimated, these spontaneous forces for growth are noteworthy in a society that gives so much evidence of resistance to change.

The implications of all this for the future of agriculture might be taken as hopeful. The near exhaustion of possibilities for bringing new land into cultivation is a threat to the future. But the record of the last 15 years assures us that the slow transformation of the countryside-of its attitudes, aspirations and dispositions to try new techniques-is well under way, so that the long-run trend is favorable. And as for India's acute need this year and next-that is, in the immediate and near future-for a more rapid annual increase in food-grain production than over the past 15 years, the evidence is that government policies for accelerating food-grain output are a weapon still largely held in reserve. They can now be thrown into the battle. It would appear that obvious policy changes could easily achieve a sharp acceleration of food-grain production-for example, to a minimum average over the years of 5 percent annual growth-a rate that would put an end to pessimistic speculation about the future of Indian agriculture.

II

That a future for Indian agriculture thus lies within grasp is typically missed in a preoccupation with the long-run necessity of more fundamental social transformation in rural India. It is everywhere said that Indian yields are no better than a fourth of what they could be with already known agricultural technology. It is then correctly inferred that a fourfold increase in yield would require a fundamental social transformation: new attitudes, aspirations, levels of education and training, specialized techniques, means of communication, market and career incentives, and the like. India, however, can afford to wait many years for a fourfold increase; and everyone, from Indian peasant to critical foreign observer, would rejoice in a steady 5 percent per year increase in production. For that level of gain, modest as it is, a social transformation need not be completed; it need only keep up its present steady pace. The indispensable new element that is required for the 5 percent annual gain is policy that will bring fertilizer, new seeds, water and insecticides to the farmer on price and credit terms advantageous to him-social transformation for the long run, inputs plus the financial incentives to use them for the urgencies of the near future.

Are Indian peasants ready and able to use the new inputs that better policies could bring them? We all wring our hands these days over the unreconstructed peasant who lacks the ambition to change his ways. There are millions of such peasants. There are also millions who have these past years been asking for credit denied them, who badger their more fortunate neighbors for seeds superior to those they can get through the state seed farms, who even without credit are buying all the overpriced fertilizer that is available to them, and who are eager for the new technical knowledge that the Village Level Worker cannot, because he lacks both time and training, give them. If both kinds of peasants have to be incorporated into a long-term program of bringing agricultural output up to levels achieved elsewhere in the world, only the latter, already in a high state of readiness, need to be counted on for a moderate 5 percent gain per year. Their readiness is indicated by their production last year. The extraordinary 10 percent jump in farm output realized in the year 1964-65 was not due wholly to better weather; it appears that the high prices of 1963-64 were, among other considerations, a powerful new incentive to produce. Good price policy could perpetuate such a force for those farmers who have proved their responsiveness to money incentives, even if other millions might remain untouched.

Can a set of new policies sufficient for accelerated growth be imagined? They would look something like this: on fertilizer, more imports; higher production targets than are emerging for the Fourth Plan; a big and immediate push on actual construction of fertilizer plants, public and private alike; a variety of distribution and credit channels to support fertilizer sales; and a lower price for fertilizer retailing. On new seeds, established foreign firms to enter the seed business, both to offer their own services and to shake up the state and central government seed farms. On water, an agreed new concept of irrigation with two main features: no design of irrigation without design of drainage; and no design of irrigation with exclusive attention to drought relief and without attention to the possibilities of disciplined delivery of adequate water for sustained high yield. On extension, the development, through both a training program and administrative reorganization, of a corps of Village Level Workers specialized not merely in agriculture but in agricultural demonstration and other field work. On prices, an end to zonal and state restrictions on movement of food-grains plus minimum support prices that do not serve as an excuse to requisition at less than market prices; that is, minimum prices that are not also maximum prices.

With the exception of the task of swinging the whole professional practice of irrigation engineering over to a new concept, no one can doubt that these policy changes lie within the technical competence of the government of India and of the states; they are not bizarre, unusual or especially difficult policies. If they were all successfully pursued, agricultural output could be expected to rise by a good deal more than 5 percent; hence, not all of them are essential for the modest 5 percent rate that would gratify everyone.

The prospects for India's agricultural future therefore rest-for some years to come-on the prospects for policy changes of this kind. Are they likely? It is a hard question to answer. That these policies are not already in force is no accident. Fertilizer importation and production have always suffered from the opinion, common in underdeveloped countries, that so precious an asset as foreign exchange should be saved for the industrial sector rather than given to agriculture. And the inefficacy of fertilizer distribution is rooted in a laudable Indian desire to build up a vast coöperative network, an ambition with understandably wide political support. Irrigation remains primarily concerned with drought relief because drought is a terrible problem; and humanitarianism joins with practical politics in sanctioning a system that spreads water widely even if thinly and irregularly. An intelligent concern with political stability in a periled democracy continues to make a kind of case for low rather than high farm prices. And so it goes; Indian policies fail to promote agricultural growth not out of oversight or foolishness but because there are good reasons for pursuing objectives other than agricultural growth.

Still, agricultural growth is looming larger as a policy objective. Political rhetoric is now all on the side of first priority for agriculture. It is coming to be believed that agriculture is the keystone of industrial growth and that foreign exchange is therefore worthwhile for farmers, that a failure to keep food-grain production well ahead of population growth promises the end of political stability, of Indian democracy and perhaps of the unity of the national state. These themes are repeatedly sounded in Indian public discussion.

More than that, specific policy changes are either under way or subject to intense debate. In the last two years, a debate on fertilizer policy has resulted in substantial increases in imports, an upward revision in earlier Fourth Plan production targets, a scheduling of new construction beyond earlier plans, and one great effort, significant even if it fell through, to enlist foreign enterprise in a coördinated program of plant construction. The price of fertilizer has already been somewhat reduced; and perhaps every state in the Indian Union is casting about, some with more energy than others, for credit and distribution facilities to supplement the inadequate coöperatives. It is reported that the Chief Minister of every single state has conceded the inadequacy of the coöperative distribution system and the need for a supplementary system. No doubt present policy on fertilizer is significantly better than it has ever been; whether it will be good enough is of course not yet certain.

On irrigation policy, the new concept of irrigation appears to be gathering adherents. A member of the Planning Commission declares, "We all are agreed on it!"-although what he must mean is that the new concept is carrying the day except among the professional engineers who build India's irrigation systems, and who not surprisingly remain a core of conservative resistance. The situation is reminiscent of American experience with unexpected deterioration of irrigated land because of inattention to drainage, of conflict between the agricultural interest and the engineering interest in irrigation, and of the conservatism of the professional engineers. Perhaps the battle progresses as well in India as in a comparable decade in recent American history.

The government of India is these days deep in a program of reorganization of the extension system. It was agreed in 1964 that the Village Level Workers should concentrate their efforts on agriculture; what remains to be done is to work out a manageable program of retraining those that can be made into effective agents of an extension system and to free them of tasks other than demonstration and field work. The relevant ministries seem clear about these necessities, and at least some top-level people in the ministries seem eager for ideas on how to transform a ponderous administrative system into what is necessary. Reform of the extension system is well advanced, although in a bureaucracy nothing is easier to sabotage than reform of the bureaucracy itself.

On price policy, it now begins to look as though the die has finally been cast for incentive prices for producers,. The government of India is now committed at least in principle to what may be as important a single policy shift as can be imagined for India. To be sure, continued anxiety about high consumer prices-it would be folly for the government not to be concerned-has compromised the new price-support policy by establishing maximum prices only slightly above the minimum, so that government still can and does sometimes requisition at below-market prices. But the new minima and new requisitioning prices are much higher than one would have believed possible only a short time ago; and, in addition, the government has pushed ahead to establish a semi-autonomous food corporation that can accumulate inventory and then enter the market as buyer or seller to support falling prices and stabilize rising prices without, it is hoped and planned, recourse in the future to legal maximum prices. The outlook for good price policy has never been better.

It is always possible that intended policies fail for lack of administrative energy or skill. On this score these new policies are not demanding. A big push on fertilizer can be had through administrative inaction; the government of India need only remove present restrictions on import, production and distribution of fertilizer. If it has the energy for active construction and promotion on its own, so much the better; but it is not essential. In price policy, a great gain would ensue from nothing more than the retirement of government from compulsory procurement, even though, again, positive action through the Food Corporation will in the long run be essential. In seed and insecticide programs, it would be enough to admit private firms to a larger role in production and distribution: whether in addition then the state and national seed farms can be revitalized would not be crucial. Improving the government extension service does indeed call for administrative energy and skill, and the whole program of reform may bog down for that very reason. But humble practical extension work of the kind India needs is done in the United States very largely by salesmen for farm supply houses; and the liberation of private firms in fertilizer, seed and insecticide offers the same possibility to India without administrative skill and energy. On irrigation policy there seems to be no prospect of substantial improvement without a thoroughgoing change of attitude on the part of the engineers in the civil service. But skill they have, and prodigious energy too, as proved by the scope of their present undertakings.

III

If India can make better headway with food-grains, it need not worry about the pace of industrial growth. It has been running for many years at about 9 percent annually, an acceptable rate as it stands but one that could be raised if a more rapid growth in food-grain output permitted a more expansionary monetary policy. The special problem in this field is exports; they need to rise sharply if foreign aid is ever to be terminated. Something like a jump from a current 3 percent per year (to hard-currency countries) to 5 percent would remove everyone's present concern.

The sluggishness of Indian exports is not attributable to weak demand in international markets or to lack of products to export. The traditional exports like jute products and tea have been suffering not from a falling world market but from a decline in India's share in it, attendant, it appears, on a slight but significant rise in the Indian selling price relative to its competitors' prices. In the very near future, India's excellent iron ore promises great new export earnings if it will only organize efficient mine-rail-seaport complexes and assure dependable delivery with quality control on the product. In the longer future, machine-made products, including machine tools, are a promising area for large expansion.

As in the case of agriculture, what stands between short-term potential and realization is not a hopeless paucity of resources or a backwardness in attitude and practice. Again, as in agriculture, there is backwardness in attitude and practice: inexperience in finding markets, in packaging, in quality control, together with a propensity to go for short-run gains in trade rather than to build up a lucrative long-term market. But if these are obstacles to the achievement of the maximum in exports, they are not obstacles that prevent the achievement of the gains required in the near future. These near-at-hand gains are denied India by a foreign-exchange and import-control policy that have the effect of making the acquisition of rationed import licenses inordinately profitable to importers, guaranteeing a highly profitable domestic market for goods that otherwise could be exported, and depreciating the price received by the exporter for exports. India's licensing system together with its overvalued exchange rate is a triple-threat attack on its own export possibilities.

Again, as in agriculture, these established policies are now under fire. A few years ago, India made a step forward through a system of special entitlements to imports based on export performance, and some more general way to increase the profitability of exports is now actively being sought. Old policy is defended because it possesses advantages, like protection of new Indian industries, which many Indians are fearful of altering even to achieve a desperately needed expansion of exports. The struggle is not a simple one between folly and wisdom but between two versions of wisdom, one version being heavily influenced by the prospect that aid will not forever continue to supply the imports that a weak export trade fails to do. Advocacy of a new import-export policy seems clearly to be growing; the probability that it will win in the near future (in contrast to the longer future in which it will surely win) is worth betting on, but lightly.

Population growth does not match India's growth in food-grain production and lags far behind the growth of industrial production. Population can continue to grow at its current rate of 2½ percent per year if gains in food-grain production run at 5 percent, fearful as is the prospect of indefinitely more mouths to feed. India's prospects on this score are better, however, than a simple race between output and uncontrolled population growth implies, for the new development of intra-uterine devices coincides with a fundamental change, marked even before Nehru's death, in the government's disposition to push birth control. India is currently in the throes of organizing, equipping and financing a big program of family planning following upon pilot programs in both urban and rural areas which have been successful in greatly reducing the birth rate. If it is too early to say whether the big operation will succeed, it is none the less clear that 1965 is a world away from 1962, when the government was both indisposed and without a feasible low-cost technique.

IV

Is it wishful thinking that assigns to changes in policy a reasonable chance for greatly accelerated economic growth? Is it naïve to believe that in a society as rigid as India's the will of government can sharply change the pace of social change? Again, it is necessary to distinguish between the prerequisite conditions for a modern India and those for a modernizing India. The mind boggles at the changes in thought, attitude and behavior of all participants in Indian development that would be required before India could bring itself into the modern world. In any case the requirements run far, far beyond any imaginable change in public policy. But man and social institutions are already changing in India fast enough to come close to meeting the requirements of a satisfactory rate of change-policy changes can push India across the line to success. It is not fanciful to imagine they will do so, even if it is not at all certain that they will.

That India shocks foreign visitors with poverty, filth, the inhumanity of caste, complacency, apathy, cynicism, corruption and mistrust says little about India's prospects. Such sharp reactions tell us what India is, not what it might be. If these distressing features of Indian society were absent, India would already be a developed nation; if they were already greatly moderated, India would already be among the nations far along the road to development; if they were only in process of moderating, India would be a staggeringly retarded nation slowly moving toward modernization. It is. These appalling aspects of Indian life are those that give any thoughtful man reason to interest himself in India's future, not reason to despair. They define India's problems; they do not prove the impossibility of solving them.

They are, of course, the reason that India requires foreign assistance, not, as is sometimes oddly proposed, reason for foreign lenders and donors to become despondent and pull out. Aid from the United States to India has been, relative to population and size of economy, about half as generous as aid to Pakistan, and greatly less than aid to Latin American countries, to say nothing of special cases like Viet Nam and Korea. It has never been large enough to cope with India's fundamental problems, and never will be. Since it is change in policy, not fundamental social transformation, that is within India's immediate grasp, American aid would make the most of India's prospects if it supported growth-oriented policies that promise annual gains in Indian income attainable next year, the year after, and the years that quickly follow after that. On fertilizer, seeds, irrigation, export policy, as well as on other policies like education and health, assistance from the United States, coming to the aid of good policies, could be critical for India and represent a high-payoff American investment.

Foreign lenders, especially the World Bank, have been criticizing Indian economic policy with increasing frankness in recent years. India responds in two ways: on the one hand, it is disposed to listen and consider; on the other hand, it takes umbrage, morosely speculating on whether to try to do without foreign assistance. The second reaction reveals a national pride with which Americans should feel sympathy; yet its practical consequences could be dangerous if it led India to starve itself.

Although the United States and other lenders would be mistaken if they tried to buy the policies they like in India by making aid contingent on India's accepting their advice, at the same time they will do well to make clear that the attractiveness of lending to India-the prospect that it will pay off either to India or to the lender-depends on Indian policy. India can be expected to understand that no prudent lender ignores the size of the payoff in calculating what it is willing to put into the growth process. Even on extreme assumptions about altruism in foreign lending, governments-especially democratic governments-cannot lend and give without tailoring what they do to fit their estimates of the contribution it will make to Indian growth.

The distinction between trying to buy, with aid, the policies we like and coming more generously to the assistance of policies that promise growth is a fine one; but it is a genuine one. Trying to buy desired policies opens up a range of possibilities for negotiation in which a foreign lender might, as a tactic for forcing India to knuckle under, offer less aid than the country's economic prospects warrant. Conversely, a foreign lender might, for a good enough bargain in the adjustment of Indian policies, offer more aid, or more aid of a particular kind, than is required in the light of prospects for growth. By contrast, supporting India less strongly when prospects for using aid effectively are poor, and more strongly when they are more promising, is a method of using foreign resources in a systematic way for encouraging Indian growth. This method challenges Indian sovereignty no more than does any significant mutual accommodation among powers.

India's capacity for reconsidering policy in the light of experience is not one of the conspicuous weaknesses of its development effort. American criticism of India often underestimates the rationality of Indian policy-making. We commonly allege that the Indian policy is doctrinaire-specifically, socialistically doctrinaire. But on the relative merits of private versus public ownership of industry, Indian policy, though strikingly different from ours, is exploratory, self-corrective to a degree and capable, as the record shows, of moving either toward or away from private ownership. The most conspicuous difference between domestic policy in the United States and in India is that U. S. policy is rigid in restricting public ownership to few fields, is less open, less exploratory, more governed by doctrine than is the Indian. Similarly, although Indian policy after independence began with a hardened position against foreign private investment, it has softened as the government of India gained confidence in dealing with large foreign firms. Although it is still timid and self-defeating, it shows more flexibility, more self-correction through feedback, than does United States policy, which has always been at least a little rigid. The point being made is not that Indian policies are correct and ours are not but that Indian policies are pragmatic to a degree unappreciated.

We have already noted that Indian policies are often hostile or indifferent to growth not because of oversight or folly but because other objectives stand in the way of growth. Of all these, the Indian desire for national political unity on a democratic basis is foremost. It is this praiseworthy ambition that has repeatedly produced compromise instead of a bold thrust on a new program, as illustrated in the deference shown states restricting food-grain movements out of their territories or in the distribution of inadequate irrigation to large areas.

Praiseworthy as is the ambition for democratic national unity, there can come a point at which its pursuit is at such a cost to growth that one believes both objectives cannot be simultaneously achieved. India's chances of finding itself at such a point have been diminished by a growing appreciation that more rapid growth will itself unify the society and strengthen the commitment to political democracy. There is as yet no major political leader, however, who acts as though he perceives the possibilities of combining the two objectives in a new coalition of political forces. Nehru himself seems to have thought in "either or" terms; Shastri has perhaps gone no further than to see, negatively, that too little growth can undermine national political unity and stability. A creative response to a chance to employ the aspiration for growth to achieve the aspiration for unity perhaps waits for another day, another leader. Indian political leadership is probably generally strong on compromising existing political forces but weak on the kind of political entrepreneurship through which interests are re-formed into new coalitions for new programs.

Of course, Indian political unity may crumble anyway-from conflict over language, regional disparities in interest, or from a military humiliation from China or Pakistan, even if the present border war does not promise to trigger the death of the Indian Union. To have maintained as orderly and democratic a government as India has maintained since independence, with an illiterate citizenry divided by caste and the isolation of the village, and to have achieved such orderly transfer of power to Shastri is, in the light of European efforts at democracy in the interwar period, a magnificent accomplishment. One is pained to think that even so fine an achievement is not enough to assure a unified, democratic future for India. It may turn out that India has no greater problem than its centrifugal tendencies, dangerous either because they pull the nation apart directly or because they undermine the prospects of growth to a point at which economic distress brings down the régime. But we have now ascended from the specifics of estimating food-grain production to the imponderables of guessing the future of a whole political system.

America and Russia in India

Chester Bowles

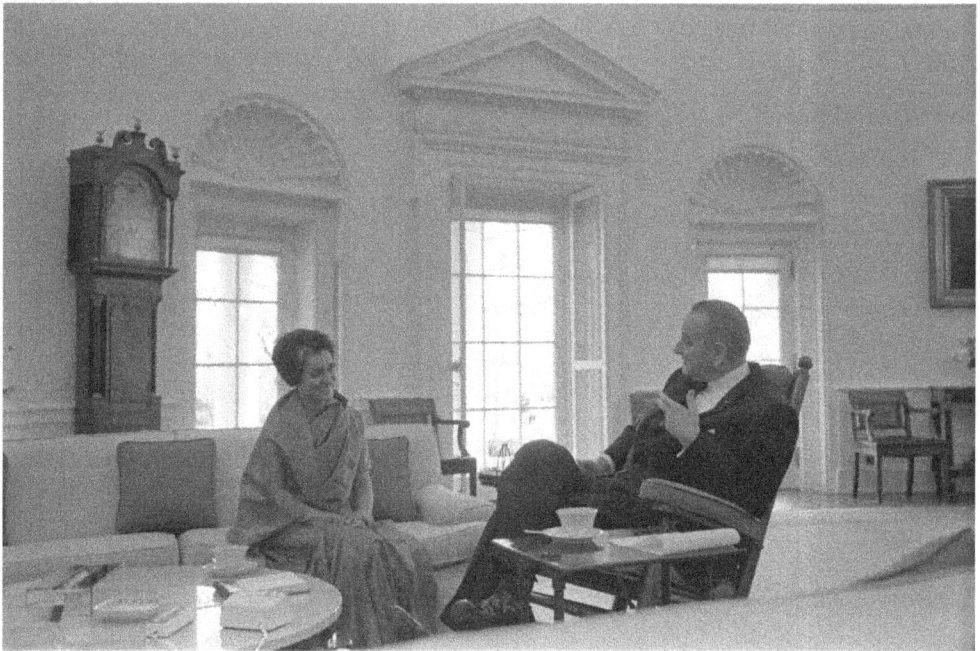

YOICHI OKAMOTO

Indian Prime Minister Indira Gandhi meets President Lyndon B. Johnson in the Oval Office, March 28, 1966.

As in many other parts of the world, the interests of the Soviet Union and the United States in India are widely assumed to be in "conflict." To what extent is this conflict genuine, and what are the implications for Asia in general and South Asia in particular?

America and Russia have each made major contributions to India's economic development. The United States has helped rebuild and modernize India's railroads, contributed 60 percent of the capital for India's power development, helped build and staff eight agricultural universities, provided nearly 40 million tons of foodgrains, printed millions of books for Indian schools, published four excellent magazines to help Indians better understand America, provided thousands of American technicians and made it possible for thousands of Indians to go to America for training and advanced education. The size of the U.S. Peace Corps in India has been double that in any other nation.

Although the Soviet economic investment in India is considerably less, it has been substantial. The U.S.S.R. has helped expand the production of steel and heavy electrical equipment and has provided close to one billion dollars to modernize India's army, navy and air force. Both the United States and the U.S.S.R. have, in addition, sent to India a steady stream of singers, musicians, and cultural exhibits, the number of Soviet programs being at least double our own. Both have large embassies in New Delhi.

Although Soviet and American activities and programs in India are somewhat similar, the political objectives and tactics have differed sharply. Let us first consider the U.S.S.R.

When Nazi Germany invaded the U.S.S.R. in June 1941, the promotion of Lenin's doctrine of worldwide revolution was muted and communist parties abroad were directed to focus all their energies on winning the war. This forced the Communist Party of India to coöperate with the British colonial government and largely to dissociate itself at a crucial moment from the struggle for independence. The reaction of the non-communist Indian leaders and the tens of millions who supported them was bitter. When official Soviet organs attacked Gandhi as a "reactionary Hindu" and depicted Nehru as the "Chiang Kaishek of India," the gap seemed unbridgeable.

After Stalin's death in March 1953, however, the Soviets began to ease their harsh line. In August of that year Malenkov spoke warmly of India's contribution to ending the Korean War and expressed the view that Indo-Soviet relations would "continue to develop and grow in strength." Contrary to the general impression, Nehru himself during this period had few illusions about the objectives of the Soviet Union and its leadership in India. A few days after Stalin's death, the Prime Minister described Stalin to me as "the coldest human being" he had ever met.

This shift in the Soviet mood coincided with John Foster Dulles' decision in 1954 to provide military equipment to Pakistan and convinced a reluctant Nehru that India should accept some assistance from Russia to "keep its options open." In 1955 the first Soviet loan agreement for Indian economic development was signed. On February 21, 1956, the Soviet Union agreed to finance and build India one of the most modern steel mills in Asia at a cost of $140,000,000.

Although the outside world had no clear indication of the growing differences between China and Russia until a few years later, the possibility of a split must have been apparent to Soviet leaders by the mid-1950s.[i]

When the break actually occurred in the late 1950s, Soviet assistance to India was sharply increased. Yet even when the Chinese-Indian conflict occurred in October-November 1962, Soviet leaders, still clinging no doubt to the hope that a tolerable relationship with China might be reëstablished, at first held back. Only when Khrushchev and his colleagues became persuaded that a rapprochement was no longer possible did India begin to receive its present high priority from Soviet policymakers.

While the U.S.S.R. certainly hoped for some additional dividends-India's support for Soviet foreign policy generally, the expansion of the "Socialist camp," etc.-the motivation of the U.S.S.R. in assisting India has since the mid-1950s been primarily based on the Soviet estimation of India's geopolitical importance as a partial balance to the political influence and potential military weight of China.

II

The United States Government, however, has never considered India to be of major political significance to the future of Asia. Our policies in India, like our policies elsewhere in Asia, have been the product of strangely diverse considerations, a fact which has not only confused most Americans but also many Asians. On the one hand, those who have been setting our policies have consistently failed to understand the political forces which are shaping Asia and to appreciate the limits of traditional military power in dealing with these forces. On the other hand, many of our actions have taken place within a framework of genuine idealism. Thus India has been seen as an impoverished nation struggling bravely but probably futilely to govern itself through democratic institutions, which for humanitarian reasons we have felt obligated to assist.

Our generally warm feelings for the Indian people and our concern for their welfare became evident in the 1930s and 1940s as the American people watched India's nonviolent struggle for independence under the leadership of Gandhi. During World War II, Roosevelt repeatedly pressed Churchill to agree to India's independence as soon as the war was over; indeed, two of Roosevelt's personal representatives in India supported Indian independence so openly that the British asked that they be removed.

When India became independent in 1947, the energies of the United States were largely focused on the economic and security problems of Western Europe. But in mid-1951, we provided India with two million tons of wheat, and in December of that year, during my first tour as Ambassador to India, I signed with Nehru the first developmental assistance agreement-an outright grant of $54,000,000 to assist Indian development. Since that time the United States has contributed $8 billion in loans and grants to bolster India's economy and to help feed its people.

Paradoxically, we have provided this massive assistance to a nation which most of our harassed top policy-makers in the State Department, White House, Pentagon and Congress have visited only briefly or in many cases have never seen, and of which consequently they have had only a limited knowledge and a hazy understanding. The

Bureau of Near East-South Asia Affairs, which has jurisdiction over our relations with India, stretches all the way from the India-Burma border to Libya. Understandably, the time of its key officials has largely been absorbed by the explosive Middle East. The average number of Representatives and Senators visiting India each year during my eight years there as Ambassador was nine-most of them for relatively short visits in and around the large cities.

Lacking firsthand knowledge of the complexities of Indian society and the hopes and fears of its people, it is not surprising that the Kiplingesque impression of India as an ancient land of cobras, maharajahs, monkeys, famines, polo players, overcrowded with cows and babies, still persists in the minds of many top officials in our government.

A relatively small number of able South Asia specialists in our universities have worked diligently to fill this information gap. But most of our "Asia specialists" are in fact Chinese, Japanese or Southeast Asia specialists; very few of them have had an opportunity really to know and understand India and to consider its relations to the rest of Asia.

The assumption that by giving India economic assistance we are at least assured of its friendship and hopefully of its support has generated reactions in New Delhi that have further confused our relations. The nationalistic leaders of India, as in most developing nations, are determined to demonstrate that they are now masters in their own house. When they assert their independence by refusing to see the world as our government sees it, leaders within the Administration and Congress have become by stages puzzled, frustrated, hurt and angered.

As a consequence, many overburdened officials in the State Department and White House have gradually lapsed into the comfortable rationalization that no matter how much assistance is given to India, its poverty is probably too deep and its population too vast to enable it to become a stable, viable nation. Only the fact that India is by far the largest underdeveloped nation, with the exception of China, and has somehow maintained in the world a democratic government for a quarter of a century, has enabled it to retain even its present precarious position on the back burners in the State Department and White House.

III

In 1963 the decisive factor in my decision to return to India as Ambassador was the conviction that in this role I might be able to contribute to the long overdue reorientation of our policies not only in India but in Asia. While skillfully marshalled arguments may establish doubts about the wisdom of an existing policy, it has been my experience that a policy itself is unlikely to be changed unless a major event shatters old relationships and forces a reëxamination of existing assumptions. The coincidence of four major events involving the Soviet Union, China, India and Japan, was, I thought, creating precisely such an opportunity.

These were the continuing split between the Soviet Union and China; the China-India conflict in 1962 which brought Nehru's efforts to create a live-and-let-live relationship with China to an abrupt end; the rise of Japan to become the world's third industrial power; and the beginnings of our blundering military involvement in Southeast Asia. The combination of these four "happenings," I felt, might force our government to reconsider its Asia policies as a whole and to give a higher priority to the one-seventh of mankind who live in India.

The promptness with which we responded to India's appeal for help following the Chinese attack in October 1962 seemed to reflect the new sense of priorities for which I had hoped. The emergency shipments of $70,000,000 worth of military equipment which we airlifted to India within a few days after Nehru's appeal reached Washington, was at the time assumed to be only the first step in the modernization of India's military forces. The Indian request for $500,000,000 of military assistance to be spent over a period of five years was less than half of what we had already given Pakistan. However, the old Dullesian arguments soon began to be raised again in the State Department and Pentagon, i.e. if we helped India even moderately to build up its defense capacity, we would upset our "loyal ally," Pakistan.[ii]

At first I was hesitant about India's request but for quite a different reason. Since World War II, most of our military assistance outside Europe, I felt, had been given not for legitimate purposes of defense but in effect as a bribe to persuade the recipient governments to support U.S. foreign policy. Once started, such assistance was hard to stop; sometimes we became political captives of the nations we were striving to defend.

I was convinced, however, that the situation in regard to India was radically different. Nehru clearly was not for sale and India's defense needs were very real. Its 2,500-mile long border with China had recently been breached by Chinese troops, and in addition there were 600 miles of border with Burma, which was in a state of general unrest. Although Pakistan's army, air force and navy had largely been equipped and trained by the United States, Pakistan had verbally supported the Chinese attack on India in 1962 and could not be depended upon to remain neutral if the Chinese should attack again. Under these circumstances our refusal to assist India while we continued heavily to support Pakistan seemed indefensible.

Moreover, in view of its recent clash with China, India was determined to modernize its defenses by one means or another. If we were not prepared to meet its legitimate security needs, I believed that India would turn, however reluctantly, to the Soviet Union. With Soviet concern over China growing, the response to Soviet advances would almost certainly be affirmative.

The possibility of this chain of events was rejected by almost everyone in the State Department, Pentagon and White House. India, it was assumed, had no place to go but to the United States. President Kennedy, however, seemed to agree with my view and asked me to explore the situation with Prime Minister Nehru and his associates immediately after my arrival in India in July. I should then return to Washington for further discussions with him.

In the summer and fall I had a series of long talks with Nehru, Defense Minister Yeshwantrao Chavan and other Indian officials not only about their own military security problems vis-à-vis China, but also about their willingness to take a greater measure of responsibility for the stability of Asia as a whole. In mid-November I left for the United States with a tentative understanding with the Indian Government in my briefcase. Quite unexpectedly, Nehru, who had been emotionally shattered by the recent Chinese attack, had volunteered to support a genuine effort by our government to negotiate a political settlement that could end the fighting in Southeast Asia. (This was before U.S. ground forces became directly involved in Vietnam.) He was also prepared to negotiate a ceiling on military expenditures with Pakistan. With this evidence of a new coöperative mood in New Delhi and with the President's backing, the way appeared to be open not only for a constructive relationship with India but even, with a bit of luck, a negotiated settlement in Southeast Asia.

However, these hopes were soon dashed. Kennedy's assassination six days after my arrival in Washington and Nehru's death six months later, in May 1964, when our government and an Indian negotiating team were on the verge of an agreement, resulted first in delay and finally in a decision by the Johnson Administration to postpone further consideration until the "situation had been clarified."

Three months later, the same Indian negotiating team visited Moscow and returned to New Delhi with all they had asked for, and more. Today India's 28 divisions, its 700-plane air force and its small but competent navy are largely supplied with Soviet equipment. It would be a mistake to exaggerate the political implications of the Soviet role as principal military supplier to the Indian defense force. But I believe that a major opportunity to use our own military assistance to promote greater political stability in Asia was missed.

IV

Because of the Soviet Union's greater awareness of India's potential role in Asia, Soviet operations in India are much more closely directed by the Foreign Office in Moscow than U.S. operations are directed by the State Department in Washington. As a result there has been a profound difference in tactics and in style between the Soviet and U.S. operations in India, which in spite of the continued indifference of Washington officialdom has helped keep our relationship with India on a reasonably even keel.

Most American embassies throughout the world are tied tightly to Washington by a combination of fixed policies, highly developed communications systems and frequent two-way visits. The embassy in New Dehli has been in a quite different category. There have been no clear national policies to guide its day-to-day operations. It is 10,000 miles from Washington and thus far, blessedly free of a modern telephone communication link. Most important of all, for the better part of 20 years it has been run by a series of independent-minded, politically expendable, noncareer Ambassadors who generally have had the support of the lower-level India specialists in the State Department.[iii]

Each of these Ambassadors travelled widely throughout India, and came to know on a personal basis most Indian leaders, and each spoke regularly to groups of college students, businessmen, educators and economists. Moreover, while not always in agreement with the policies of the Indian Government, each of them genuinely liked the Indian people. Their effectiveness was increased by the fact that they were supported by able staffs, most of whom shared their views.

Lacking clear policy direction from Washington, our remote and comparatively isolated embassy in New Dehli has within certain limits been able, independently and unofficially, to establish a less rigid set of goals. For instance, there has been a continuing effort to increase India's confidence in itself, to encourage India to broaden its perspectives on Asia and to understand U.S. difficulties in dealing with unfamiliar world problems. The New Delhi embassy has also consistently and with considerable success resisted pressures from Washington to use U.S. economic assistance as a lever to force India to see the world as we see it. In my eight years as Ambassador to India, I can remember no occasion when the State Department told me what to say or questioned any public statement I made.

The understanding and often close relations established with many Indian citizens and leaders by members of the American mission have been strengthened by nonofficial groups such as the American women's clubs in major cities which have taken an active role in social welfare projects and developed a genuine appreciation of Indian culture, religion and language. The several thousand impressive young Peace Corps Volunteers, who have served in India for an average stay of two years, and the 8,000 Indian students who attend American universities every year further strengthen these ties.

As a result, a great deal of common ground has been created in the last 20 years among influential Indians and Americans. Most Indians both in and outside the government remain critical of U.S. Government policies on such questions as Vietnam or East Pakistan, but with a few notable exceptions they have liked and respected Americans as individuals.

Since the Soviets devote a major share of their budget and manpower in India to an attempt to create distrust of America and Americans, the rapport to which I refer has been an important and perhaps decisive factor in keeping Indo-American relations relatively smooth. The Soviet effort to break these bonds and to turn the Indian people and government against the United States involves every device from forged letters to blistering attacks and accusations by Soviet-financed newspapers such as Blitz, Patriot, Link, and Radio Peace and Progress, which is specially beamed into India from Moscow. No doubt this effort has made an impression on some Indians. But because it is hard for most Indians to believe that the Americans they see and know are "imperialists" and "war mongers scheming to undermine India's independence," it has fallen far short of its objective.

The reasons for the persistence and intensity of the Soviet effort are unclear. Many believe that it reflects widely differing views of world affairs within the Soviet bureaucracy. In New Delhi, for instance, there are almost certainly deep differences between the younger and more modern-minded Soviet diplomats and those members of the KGB who still believe that Lenin's "revolution of the working classes" is in fact just around the corner. Similarly, some U.S. officials in the Pentagon and State Department still feel more at home with the rhetoric and tactics of the cold war.

Soviet activities in India have been further complicated by the fact that the original Communist Party of India has split into at least three sections. First, there is the Communist Party of India (CPI), which makes a determined effort to appear responsible and to coöperate with other "Socialist" parties. This group is largely financed by and directed from Moscow. It is small and compact, and therefore a less obvious target for criticism. But for that very reason it may have a greater potential influence than most people suspect.

The tactics of the CPI following Mrs. Gandhi's election in March 1971 have been shrewd. The first step was the announcement and later the introduction into Parliament of an appealing program to promote greater economic and social justice which generally reflects the liberal philosophy on which Mrs. Gandhi based her sweeping victory. If the new Congress Party adopts or supports all or part of such a program, the CPI can claim credit; if it fails to adopt the proposals, the CPI can charge that Mrs. Gandhi is still in the grip of the "reactionaries."

In addition, there is the Communist Party-Marxist (CPM) which came close to winning a majority in the recent West Bengal State Assembly elections. The CPM might be considered a Maoist party if it were not for the fact that it is momentarily in the Peking doghouse because of its persistent attempt to work within India's parliamentary process. Finally, there are the Naxalites, an extremist left-wing group which does not fit into any clear ideological pattern but which believes in ruthless violence and destruction as the necessary basis of revolutionary change.

Many observers in India are convinced that the differences among these three communist-marxist parties are more a matter of the timing of the "inevitable" revolutionary uprising than of actual ideology. However, I suspect that at least some of the differences run much deeper. This raises the question of whether Moscow really wants a communist India which, whatever its immediate advantages, would lead to further fragmentation of the communist "camp" and place an added burden on the juggling abilities of Soviet officials and ideologists.

V

What is the reaction of India to the lavish attentions it has been receiving from the world's two most powerful nations? Most Indians have become ever more disenchanted with the price that the Soviets have asked them to pay in terms of national dignity and sovereignty for their continued support and assistance. But because of their greatly increased fear of China, they now find themselves closer to Moscow than they really want to be.

India's decision in 1968 to abstain on the United Nations resolution vote in the Security Council condemning the Soviet Union for its invasion of Czechoslovakia illustrates its dilemma. If India had voted for the resolution, Mrs. Gandhi and her colleagues were convinced that there would be a dangerous slowdown in the flow of ammunition and spare parts from the Soviet Union for the Indian army, navy and air force. Consequently, India felt forced to abstain on an issue which had aroused strong feelings among most Indians.

The position of the U.S.S.R. in India has also been damaged by the high-handed manner in which Soviet representatives often negotiate economic and commercial agreements. Three or four years ago large headlines in Indian newspapers announced that the Soviets had agreed to buy 50,000 Indian-built railroad cars. However, when the bargaining began it became apparent that the euphoria was not justified. The Soviet price was far below the Indian cost price and as a result the deal fell through.

Nor is America wholly free of the charge of taking advantage of India's difficulties. During India's food crisis of 1965-66, President Johnson rather obviously attempted to use our wheat shipments to persuade India to take a more tolerant view of our military activities in Vietnam. Determined to demonstrate their sovereignty, the Indians predictably stepped up their criticisms of our bombing of North Vietnam. Angered, President Johnson responded by slowing down our wheat shipments at the very moment when they were most needed. This left scars.

Another factor in the relations among the three countries is India's increasing disenchantment with the heavy influx of "experts" from both nations. Not all of them-Russian or American-have been as capable as their Indian counterparts, and in some cases they have been insensitive to their surroundings and to Indian attitudes. Often India has accepted technical assistance from both the United States and the Soviet Union more to satisfy the donors than because of actual need.

VI

The remaining years of the twentieth century will be years of continuing unrest. In Africa, Latin America and Asia, corrupt governments, the pressure of college graduates without jobs, and the demands of the millions who work the land and operate the new industrial machinery to obtain a larger share of the wealth which they produce, will open wide the door for revolutionary change. Under these circumstances it is unrealistic to expect either the Soviet Union or China to forgo their professed revolutionary objectives. Nevertheless, the strength of Soviet and Chinese nationalism, with the two nations facing each other along a 5,000-mile border, coupled with the fact that the Russian Revolution is now more than 50 years old and is gradually losing its original fervor, suggests that they will follow quite different strategies.

The Soviet interest in India is only one facet, though a major one, in the Soviet effort to expand its influence throughout Asia. The increased Soviet naval force in the Mediterranean, the intense desire of the Soviets to reopen the Suez Canal and the presence of Soviet naval units in the Indian Ocean are reflections of this effort.

In June 1969, the General Secretary of the Soviet Communist Party, Leonid Brezhnev, noted in a speech at the World Communist Party Conference in Moscow, "We are of the opinion that the course of events is putting on the agenda the task of creating a system of collective security in Asia." This assertion has not officially been amplified, and consequently every government in Asia has been interpreting it in a different way. India's reaction to Brezhnev's statement was cautious: Mrs. Gandhi discreetly let it be known that India would prefer a nonalliance security agreement composed of Asian states, guaranteed by both Russia and America.

However, a key to Brezhnev's meaning appeared in advance of his speech in an article in Izvestia in May 1969, in which it was asserted that the same countries which have won their freedom from colonialism "will strengthen the peace by their own joint opposition to expansion and imperialism." The forces of "expansion" to which Brezhnev referred were clearly the Chinese, who were charged with harboring designs against a number of Asian countries. Peking promptly responded by accusing Brezhnev of "fishing in the dung heap of imperialism."

The U.S.S.R. is seeking to "contain" what it believes to be an expansionist-minded China-much as we have been trying to do-by associating whatever Asian nations can be persuaded to coöperate in a loose political organization under its leadership. When asked, "What is the basis of Soviet foreign policy in Asia?" a Soviet official recently replied with an eye to America's pullback from Asia, "We simply occupy the empty seats." But the U.S.S.R.-like China-is no more likely to succeed in forging such an association than we have been. The increasingly nationalistic Asians have no design to become the tail of the kite of any nation no matter how great its military power or how generous its offers of economic assistance.

Right now both the Soviet Union and India are concerned about the political thaw between the United States and China and the implications of China's support of the right-wing government in West Pakistan. The apparent easing of the Chinese attitude toward the United States is seen by many observers as the first step in a long-range Chinese program calculated to strengthen China's position in South Asia and eventually in Africa at the expense of the U.S.S.R., India and the United States.

A Soviet official with a touch of geopolitical paranoia might visualize the following sequence of events:

1. The Chinese, convinced that the United States is in fact prepared to withdraw from Southeast Asia and concerned about their own confrontation with the U.S.S.R., may seize upon the opportunity to establish a degree of rapport with the United States which might be useful to both nations in a number of ways.

2. If President Nixon will agree not only to pull all U.S. troops out of Southeast Asia but our air force and naval units as well (a move that would be warmly welcomed by most Americans, including leaders of Congress), China might seek to persuade the Hanoi government to release American prisoners and to take a more flexible position in the peace negotiations with the United States. This would serve the interests of both China and the United States and perhaps enable China to expand its trade with the United States and to ensure entrance into the United Nations, with the possibility that ultimately some degree of coöperation with the United States in regard to Pakistan and even the Soviet-Chinese conflict might become possible.

3. But a possible settlement of the conflict in Southeast Asia is only one aspect of a complex situation. China (ping-pong diplomacy to the contrary) believes that "the four seas are raging, the five continents are rocking," and its government may be expected to maintain its militarily cautious but politically aggressive revolutionary course.

A primary Chinese objective is the establishment of a solid Chinese presence in the Arabian Sea and the Bay of Bengal. This would enable China to outflank the U.S.S.R. (as well as the United States) and move thousands of miles closer to East Africa, a potentially rich and underpopulated area, in which for several years Peking has been taking an increasing interest. No one believes that the Chinese at the present time are prepared to run a serious risk of war in pursuit of this objective, but it is widely believed to be a major part of Chinese global strategy. According to Indian sources, 13,500 Chinese are now working in East Africa. There is also some fear that China may provide support to small guerrilla groups in Iran as they already have done in Oman. As a measure of its concern, India's leading China expert has recently been assigned to East Africa.

4. The present conflict in East Pakistan affords the Chinese an opportunity to move cautiously toward this goal. The fighting has placed an impossible burden on Pakistan's economy. With or without the Eastern wing, it will soon be in a state of near bankruptcy and in need of massive assistance. By supporting West Pakistan and by working with pro-Chinese Pakistani politicians, China will strive to establish a strong and eventually dominant presence there. With Sheik Mujibur Rahman removed from the scene, East Pakistan would also offer an opportunity for a new Maoist-oriented leadership. (India looks upon this latter possibility with particular alarm since it would almost certainly bring the Maoists in both East Pakistan and the CPM in West Bengal into a close association. This would create heavy pressures for an independent united Bengal, which would not only present another tempting target to the Chinese but would threaten the unity of India itself.)

This scenario may turn out to be no more than a bad dream, but there is no question that at the present moment many Soviet as well as Indian leaders are dreaming it-including some who are not normally subject to paranoia. The skeptics who dismiss it as farfetched are likely to be reminded that in the last 20 years several equally "impossible" developments have occurred in Asia: for instance, the sudden collapse of colonial rule, the dramatic emergence of Japan as the world's third-ranking industrial power, the disruption of the Sino-Soviet bloc and America's involvement in a major undeclared war in Southeast Asia in which nearly as many Americans have been killed as in World War I.

Far from being inevitably locked in a relentless confrontation, Russia and America have many problems, worries and objectives in common. By now each should have discovered that its own capacity to influence India and Asia is strictly limited. We have learned this lesson the hard way, and the generally cautious leaders of the U.S.S.R. are unlikely to repeat our folly.

With the passage of time (perhaps with an unexpected assist from some new "happening"), we may hope that the Soviets will abandon their present ineffective cold warring in India and put aside their nostalgic Leninist dream of a Soviet-dominated world, and that ultimately even the Chinese ideologists will come to see that their efforts to fish in troubled waters of South Asia and Africa are unproductive and dangerous.

As for the United States it is still not too late for us to bring our policies in Asia and particularly in India into line with the realities. Some steps we might take are as follows:

1. As an essential first step, the policy-making officials in the State Department and in the White House must broaden their perspective on India and its potential role in Asia. The following reorganization within the State Department would

do much to accomplish this: (a) A new Mediterranean Bureau would include North Africa, the Middle East areas and Afghanistan and Pakistan; (b) A new South and Southeast Asia Bureau would include, in addition to the Southeast Asian States, India, Ceylon and (if it manages to become an independent nation) Bangla Desh (East Pakistan); (c) A new East Asia and Pacific Bureau would include Japan, the Philippines, Taiwan, China and Korea.

2. The State Department should schedule regular in-depth visits to India and South Asia not only by its own key policy makers but by other government officials who are called upon directly or indirectly to deal with questions involving India.

3. All U.S. military aid to Pakistan should be stopped immediately. It can only lead to a comparable build-up in the Indian military, a reduced rate of development and the recurring possibility of war. Our lavish arming of Pakistan since 1954 will surely be considered by historians as one of our major follies. Until the political situation clarifies, economic assistance to Pakistan should be concentrated on the rehabilitation and relief of East Pakistan.

4. America, Russia and India should not only attempt to arrive at better understandings of one another, but also of China. Such understanding and the more responsible and constructive policies that may grow out of it are the long-term pre requisites for peace and more rapid economic development throughout Asia. A military conflict between the U.S.S.R. and China could be the ultimate disaster for mankind. We should therefore refrain from any temptation to play China and the Soviet Union against each other.

5. We should assure Mrs. Gandhi and her new government of whatever assistance, with no political strings, is necessary to support her effort to better the lot of the Indian people and to ensure the economic growth and stability of India. Unquestionably the newly elected government under Mrs. Gandhi's direction means business, but India's resources are strained to the breaking point.

Part of this assistance could be provided by a ten-year moratorium on the payments of principal and interest which India is now making on debts to the Western consortium nations including the United States and the World Bank. Next year these payments will total more than $600 million in hard currency.

By helping Mrs. Gandhi's new government to deal successfully with India's current internal problems we can help ensure the viability and political effectiveness of this cohesive democratic nation. With a population equal to that of Latin America and Africa combined, with a remarkable degree of political resiliency and depth of culture and with an effective administrative structure run by a generally competent civil service, an independent, confident India can play a major role in the stabilization of post-Vietnam Asia.

[i] In February 1957, shortly before the Soviet-Chinese break became evident, I had a lengthy discussion with Nikita Khrushchev in Moscow, most of which centered on India and China. When I remarked that both the Soviet Union and the United States might ultimately face a common problem in regard to China, he did not disagree.

[ii] For several years Pakistan had been manipulating American policies in Asia with a skill matched only by that of the Nationalist Chinese.

[iii] I refer to Ambassadors John Sherman Cooper, Ellsworth Bunker, John Kenneth Galbraith and myself.

India and the World

Indira Gandhi

Indira Gandhi and Jacqueline Kennedy in New Delhi, March 14, 1962.

This year India celebrates the twenty-fifth anniversary of her independence. These have been years of change and turmoil everywhere. Deep surging forces have torn asunder our past colonial feudal structures and have combined with the tides sweeping the world to give our post-independence evolution its unique qualities. But our own unvarying concerns have been two: to safeguard our independence and to overcome the blight of poverty.

Many crises and dangers from within and without have obstructed our path but we have taken them in our stride. Contrary to predictions, the country has not broken into warring states, We have not succumbed to civil anarchy.

There has been no widespread starvation; on the contrary, we have become self-sufficient in cereals. We have not jettisoned our free institutions, but instead gained greater political cohesion and economic strength. This does not justify complacency but it does give us confidence that the Indian people can rise to whatever challenge the future may hold. Under Mahatma Gandhi's inspiration, Prime Minister Jawaharlal

Nehru and the Congress movement formulated a set of principles which have served as our guidelines and which are still valid for us. These are democracy, socialism and secularism so far as our internal affairs are concerned, and nonalignment in our external relations. One or the other of these principles has been the subject of criticism within the country and abroad. But generally speaking, internally there is a more mature awareness of the forces and compulsions of our age, and these principles have come to form the essential elements of a national program accepted by virtually all sections of our people, even though there are differences of interpretation and regarding tactics. The massive majority with which the Congress Party was returned to power in the fifth general election in 1971 and in the state elections in 1972 is an indication of this.

What holds people together is not religion, not race, not language, not even a commitment to an economic system. It is shared experience and involvement in the conscious and continuous effort at resolving internal differences through political means. It is a sense of "Indianness" which unites our people despite ethnic, linguistic and religious diversity. Most conflicts and tensions in the world originate in the failure to take note of the importance of nationalism.

II

Two centuries and more of history marked by foreign intervention, domination and exploitation left India backward, apathetic and stagnant, The general scene was one of decay, reflected in the misery of the masses. For us, political independence became inseparable from economic freedom, which in turn could be meaningful to the extent that it served the interests not only of the few but of the many, of the nation as a whole. Hence our energies at home have been chiefly directed toward the reconstruction of our society.

Our national movement was committed not to a doctrine but to a purpose-the modernization of our society without loss of the Indian personality; the development and integration of industry and agriculture with modern science and technology; the uplift of the masses and the ending of archaic, hierarchical systems in which discrimination and exploitation had become entrenched.

In the economic field, it was clear from the beginning that we could not rely only on private enterprise and the play of market forces, that we would have to establish social control over the key sectors of the economy and adopt measures of economic planning appropriate to the stage of development reached. Our socialism is not a ready-made ideology but a flexible concept. Three successive Five-Year Plans have been implemented and we are halfway through the Fourth. None of them was beyond criticism in formulation or execution. And yet the overall progress of the last 25 years is by no means negligible. We have an impressive record of diversifying our industrial capacity and raising industrial output. The Indian peasant has quickly responded to the new strategy, with the state providing irrigation, improved seeds, better implements, fertilizers and pesticides. So marked has been the development of our industry and agriculture, our science and technology, our education and health, that some argue that India should not now be counted among the underdeveloped nations.

Although we have acquired certain features of an industrial state and although some classes and groups of our people are visibly prosperous, the vast majority still live in poverty and a substantial minority in crushing poverty. Moreover, the process of development has widened the disparities between different social classes and has created new imbalances between states and between districts within the same state.

Our very progress has drawn attention to the inadequacy of our achievement and to the magnitude of the tasks that still lie ahead. But it has increased our capacity to deal with them. We have realized that reliance on stereotyped processes of economic growth will not make an appreciable impact on the living conditions of the masses for decades to come. Hence, a basic review of our economic policies is now under way. We propose a more direct assault on poverty and its major manifestation, unemployment. Our next Five-Year Plan will emphasize investment and production programs which are closely related to a minimum level of consumption for all and are linked to the provision of employment opportunities on an extensive scale. This gigantic enterprise calls for institutional changes and innovations.

These radical policies do not conform to the code of capitalism and they may not adhere to orthodox doctrines of socialism but they are desired by the great majority of our people. The privileged do not hide their misgivings. Reform, as in every country where it has been an issue, is being hotly debated. Some of the more glaring inequities of the land system, e.g. absentee landlordism, were removed immediately after independence but the just redistribution of land and consolidation of holdings are yet to be satisfactorily completed. Industrialization and urbanization have given rise to new problems and have further accentuated disparities. However, our commitment to democracy is fundamental. Indian socialism is not a negation of democracy but its fulfillment, and democracy will be imperiled only in the measure by which we fail through lack of foresight or want of courage to respond to the aspirations of our people.

The resources for our economic development have come mostly from the sacrifices of our own people, but we have also received aid from abroad in the form of credits for the purchase of industrial equipment and food. Although aid was originally conceived of as external assistance for supplementing the self-help measures of developing countries, we have found that it is often used by some creditor governments as an instrument to enforce their short-term policy objectives and to secure political and economic concessions unrelated to our development. Aid is effective only if it is guided by considerations of development and when there is assurance of its continuity and not when it can be suspended or withdrawn abruptly,

While aid is generally tied to purchases from donor countries, repayment under many of the agreements has to be made in freely convertible foreign currencies, adding to our burdens. At present more than half of the external assistance to us goes for repayments of earlier debts. It is our policy to reduce reliance on aid progressively. We are determined to mobilize internal resources and technological capacities more intensively.

III

India's foreign policy is a projection of the values which we have cherished through the centuries as well as our current concerns. We are not tied to the traditional concepts of a foreign policy designed to safeguard overseas possessions, investments, the carving out of spheres of influence and the erection of cordons sanitaires. We are not interested in exporting ideologies.

Our first concern has been to prevent any erosion of our independence. Therefore we could not be camp followers of any power, however rich or strong. We had equal interest in the maintenance and safeguarding of international peace as an essential condition of India's economic, social and political development. In the bipolar world which existed in the immediate postwar era, Jawaharlal Nehru refused to join either bloc. He decided to remain nonaligned as a means of safeguarding our independence and contributing to the maintenance of world peace. Nonalignment implied neither noninvolvement nor neutrality. It was and is an assertion of our freedom of judgment and action. We have not hesitated to express our views on any major controversy or to support just causes.

In conformity with the objectives of our foreign policy, India sought friendship with every nation. We did not allow past conflicts to impede our new links with Britain within the framework of the Commonwealth. The problem of French possessions in India, unlike those held by the Portuguese, was solved in a civilized manner by peaceful negotiations. Thereafter, our relations with France grew in cordiality. We have similar relations with the Federal Republic of Germany and the German Democratic Republic and other European countries, both East and West. With the nonaligned countries in Asia, the Middle East, North Africa and Africa south of the Sahara, there exist special understanding and coöperation based on a common interest in safeguarding freedom and a common struggle against colonialism, neocolonialism and racialism. We have friendships with the countries of Latin America whose concern with problems of development is similar to ours. India has always held Japan in esteem as a dynamic Asian country, and our coöperation with Japan is steadily growing.

We have also tried to have normal relations with Pakistan,, Yet successive governments of Pakistan based the survival and unity of their country on the idea of confrontation with India. This has stood in the way of coöperation which would have been to our mutual benefit. India was partitioned in 1947 to solve what the British portrayed as irreconcilable Hindu-Moslem antagonism. Pakistan was based on the medieval notion that religion alone constituted nationhood.

Encouraged by the imperial power, the Moslem League claimed that Moslem majority areas were entitled to become an independent nation. Thus, Pakistan was born a geographical curiosity, its two halves separated by a thousand miles of Indian territory. India was left with a very large number of Moslems; they formed the largest of her many minorities. In keeping with her old tradition and the spirit of her nationalist movement, India adopted secularism-i.e. non-discrimination on grounds of religion-as a fundamental state principle. Equal rights and equal protection have been vouchsafed for the followers of all religions. The Moslem population of India has grown since partition from 35 million to 61 million. It is noteworthy that the 1971 census showed that there are 14 million Christians and 17 million others including Sikhs, Buddhists, Jains, Parsis and Jews.

Pakistan, on the other hand, clung to the political ideology which had led to partition. Those who came to power in Pakistan had sided with the colonial power in undivided India and had opposed the national struggle. These ruling elements, especially after the establishment of military dictatorship, set Pakistan on a course of pointless and seemingly endless conflict with India. Just as in the earlier days when the colonial power had used religious sentiments to blunt the nationalist drive in India, some powers sought to use Pakistan to offset India. Pakistan joined military alliances, which had been formed ostensibly to contain international communism, but which Pakistan used primarily in order to acquire weapons to be used against India. Moreover, it suited the West to play off Pakistan against India. China gave military assistance to Pakistan with the same purpose. Later, so did the Soviet Union in order not to lose leverage, but soon discovered its hazards. The consequence of this assistance was to strengthen the militarist oligarchy in Pakistan and inhibit the growth of democratic forces there. Hatred and suspicion of India were whipped up to maintain those in power and to divert the Pakistani people's attention from their demands. Since India remained outside military systems, our defense capacity, unlike that of Pakistan, had to be built up out of our own resources. We have bought defense equipment from a number of countries, however, particularly after the Chinese invasion in 1962 when we received very modest assistance from the United States and the United Kingdom.

Kashmir, as early as October 1947, was the first victim of aggression by Pakistan. This was at a time when there were no Indian forces at all in Kashmir-as acknowledged by the Foreign Minister of Pakistan at that time in the U.N. Security Council. A large part of that state has been under Pakistan's occupation for many years. India does not intend to recapture this territory by force; on several occasions we have given this assurance to Pakistan and have offered to conclude a "no war" pact Pakistan has rejected this offer repeatedly, trying to invoke third-party intervention in our affairs. Infiltrators and saboteurs have been sent into Kashmir and other territories, notably in the northeast. Early in 1965, our Kutch area was invaded, and later the same year the infiltration was escalated into an attack on Kashmir which led to fighting all along the western front.

The immediate background to the latest aggression against us in 1971 was the other battle which Pakistan had been waging for many months against its own citizens of East Pakistan (as it then was). India had no part in the internal developments of Pakistan-West or East. We would normally have welcomed the attainment of freedom by any victim of colonial oppression but usually it would have little direct impact on us. Bangladesh, however, was a part of our subcontinent. How could we ignore a conflict which took place on our very border and overflowed into our own territory? Ten million destitute refugees poured into densely populated areas which were also politically sensitive owing to the activities of Marxists and the Left extremists we call Naxalites. This posed unbearable strains on our economy and on our social and administrative institutions. The terrible stories of genocide and the comings and goings of Mukti Bahini, the resistance force of Bangladesh, created a volatile situation for us also. Could we remain indifferent to these developments?

As I told the leaders of the various countries which I visited in October 1971, the situation could not remain static. Several border clashes took place during these tense months, and there was one serious skirmish in November; but we treated these as local incidents. In the last week of November, President Yahya Khan publicly announced that war would begin in ten days and, sure enough, on the tenth day there was a massive air attack on seven of our cities and a ground attack all along our western border. Thus did Pakistan extend its war to India.

However, when 14 days later, on December 16, 1971, Pakistani troops surrendered on the eastern front, India unilaterally announced a ceasefire on the western front also. On March 25, 1972, we withdrew our troops from Bangladesh in consultation with the new government. The political map of the subcontinent has been redrawn and the notion of an inherent and insuperable antagonism between a secular India and a predominantly Moslem state has been discredited-not through any design on our part but because the idea itself was untenable and the military dictatorship of Pakistan, totally alienated from its own people, had followed a short-sighted and unrealistic policy. In his address to the nation on June 27, 1972, President Bhutto gave a perceptive account of the events when he said: "The war we have lost was not of our making. I had warned against it but my warning fell on deaf ears of a power-drunk junta. They recklessly plunged our people into the war and involved us in an intolerable surrender and lost us half our country. The junta did not know how to make peace nor did it know how to make war."

The shock of these events compelled Pakistan to exchange military dictatorship for civilian rule and opened the door to new possibilities for the peaceful resolution of the basic issues between the two countries. I took the initiative to invite President Bhutto for discussions. These have resulted in the Simla Agreement of July 2, 1972, by which Pakistan and India have proclaimed their determination to solve their conflicts bilaterally and without recourse to force, and to seek a durable peace and growing economic and cultural coöperation. The agreement which holds the promise of settlement of the Kashmir and boundary problems, has been welcomed by almost all sections of the Indian people. It is my hope that the implementation of this agreement in the spirit in which it was made will close the 25-year-old period of Pakistan's hatred of India, and that both countries will become good neighbors. I appreciate the courage and realistic approach which enabled President Bhutto to come to India. If Pakistan also shows the wisdom to come to terms with Bangladesh which, under Sheikh Mujibur Rahman, is building a secular, Socialist-oriented democracy, the subcontinent will at long last have overcome the main obstacle to its progress.

IV

I have dwelt at length on Pakistan and the problems of the subcontinent for their impact on us is immediate and deep. But we want better relations with China also. Even when we were fully absorbed in our own struggle for liberty, we supported China's parallel fight against imperialism and sent a medical team to Mao Tse-tung's Eighth Route Army. We have respect for their culture and cherish memories of past contacts. We were among the first in 1949 to welcome the establishment of the People's Republic.

Much to our disappointment, the last two decades have failed to fulfill our initial hope that India and China, both great Asian nations newly independent and faced with similar problems, would learn from and assist each other and so coöperate on the wider international scene. We began, as we thought, with mutual confidence and good will, but the events of the 1950s brought tension and misunderstanding, culminating in the entry of Chinese troops and their occupation of thousands of square miles of Indian territory in 1962.

It would be an oversimplification to regard this merely as the result of a border dispute. Simultaneous or subsequent developments-such as China's systematic support of Pakistan against India, her provocative criticism of India for alleged subservience to the United States and later the Soviet Union, and her persistent though futile efforts to promote internal subversion-leave us no option but to infer that the border dispute was the outcome of a more complex policy which was aimed at undermining India's stability and at obstructing her rapid and orderly progress. After the Cultural Revolution, conditions seem more tranquil, and there appears to be a new orientation of China's policies. We wonder whether this new mood will also be reflected in China's policy toward India. The earlier faint signs of a thaw have receded since China's unreserved support of General Yahya Khan's campaign against Bangladesh and India. We are not engaged in any competition with China, nor have we any hostile intentions. We hope that some day China will appreciate that coöperative and friendly relations between the 560 million people of India and the 700 million people of China are in our mutual interest.

Apart from the Soviet leaders, I think my father was the first Prime Minister to pay a state visit to China. Similarly, the exchange of visits with the leaders of the Soviet Union was memorable in that it was the first time since the October Revolution that a non-Communist personality of Nehru's stature and the head of a non-Communist government was welcomed officially by the Soviet government; it was the first time, also, that Soviet leaders traveled in a country outside the Socialist bloc. The talks held in Moscow and Delhi resulted in a significant measure of understanding that had more than bilateral implications. They demonstrated that it was possible for two countries such as India and the Soviet Union to maintain good relations and to work together in a friendly spirit in spite of very different social systems and without either having to modify its policies or sacrifice its philosophy and traditions.

The Soviet Union shares the Indian view on the maintenance of peace and the elimination of racialism and colonialism. On these issues it has supported the Afro-Asian stand in the United Nations and elsewhere. When matters vitally concerning our national security and integrity, such as Goa, Kashmir and more lately Bangladesh, became subjects of international controversy, the Soviet assessment of the merits of the case coincided largely with our own. In strictly bilateral terms also, there has been a steady increase in the range and volume of our coöperation-economic, commercial and cultural-to our mutual advantage. Economic relations with the Soviet Union are easier for us since we repay them through the export of our commodities. This mode of payment makes the Soviet credits self-liquidating.

The Treaty of Peace, Friendship and Coöperation concluded last year grew logically from this expanding relationship. It affirms the determination of both countries for greater coöperation in various fields and to consult one another, if need be, on suitable measures to safeguard their peace and security. There is nothing in the treaty to which any reasonable person or government could take exception. It contains no secret clauses, nor is it aimed against any county. Yet there have been some misapprehensions that the treaty dilutes India's nonalignment. It is strange that such criticism comes mostly from those who have vehemently denounced nonalignment all along. In the text of the treaty itself there is explicit recognition and endorsement of India's policy of nonalignment.

V

Our relations with the United States started off rather well. At that time, the American people and government showed considerable sympathy for the colonial peoples who were struggling for independence, and particularly for India. However, this phase was short-lived. With the rise of the United States to a dominant world position,

Washington's concern and respect for the national independence of India receded into the background. Everything was viewed solely in the context of checking communism and containing first the Soviet Union, subsequently China, and now once again the Soviet Union. There was a feverish building of military blocs and a continuous extension of a network of bases stretching across oceans and continents. The logical and practical consequence of this policy was to divide the world into two opposing camps and to expect each country to belong to one or the other-preferably the Western bloc.

A newly freed people, jealous of their independence, could not resign themselves to this position, nor could we isolate ourselves from what was happening around us. Successive U.S. administrations have ignored the fact that India must see her problems and her relationships in a different perspective. They have insisted on interpreting our nonalignment within the confines of a neutralism which they imagined to be slanted in favor of Russia. India was regarded with disapproval and resentment because of her independent policy. This could not but affect the bilateral relations between India and America. Despite fluctuations of mood, our relationship as a whole has been uneasy over a long period.

To our grave concern, U.S. policy as it developed impinged seriously on our vital interests. The admission of Pakistan into the U.S.-controlled system of alliances and the massive supply of arms to Pakistan were ostensibly part of the U.S. grand design against communism, but we cannot believe that the U.S. administration was unaware that these weapons could be and would be used only against India. We took considerable pains to point this out but our protests went unheeded.

Should not the people of the United States ask their government what they have gained from America's activities in Europe and in Asia? Has the United States succeeded in containing communism? On the contrary, has not the U.S. government been compelled to build bridges with the nonaligned and to woo the opposite bloc-the hated Communists? I have no doubt that if we had followed the advice of the Western bloc, conditions in India would have deteriorated and the extremists would have been strengthened.

In regard to Bangladesh and during the December war, the United States openly backed Pakistan at the cost of basic human values. This further strained our relations. I do not wish to analyze the U.S. role at that time or go into the misrepresentations which were circulated. But it is necessary to take note of the dispatch of the warship Enterprise to support a ruthless military dictatorship and to intimidate a democracy, and the extraordinary similarity of the attitudes adopted by the United States and China. Imagine our feelings. The original misunderstanding with the United States had arisen because of our contacts with China, the Soviet Union and Eastern Europe. We find it difficult to understand why, when the U.S. policy toward these countries changed, the resentment against us increased.

We do not believe in permanent estrangement. We admire the achievements of the American people. Indeed, a large number of Americans expressed sympathetic support for the cause of Bangladesh and India during the last year. We are grateful for the assistance from the United States in many areas of our development. We are ready to join in any serious effort to arrive at a deeper appreciation of each other's point of view and to improve relations. A great power must take into account the existence not only of countries with comparable power, but of the multitude of others who are no longer willing to be pawns on a global chessboard. Above all, the United States has yet to resolve the inner contradiction between the traditions of the founding fathers and of Lincoln and the external image it gives of a superpower pursuing the cold logic of power politics.

On fundamental questions such as disarmament, the abolition of nuclear weapons, the continuing struggle against colonialism and racialism, the widening gulf between the haves and have-nots, the war in Vietnam and the conflict in the Middle East, our stand has been consistent over the years and has been clearly stated in appropriate forums. In this article I have preferred to focus attention on the situation on our subcontinent because it is our special concern and has a significance beyond geographical frontiers. In considering the policies of some major powers, I have confined myself to bilateral relations which are intimately connected with their attitudes to the subcontinent as a whole.

VI

The international scene with which we had become familiar has considerably altered. Do the two recent summit meetings in Peking and Moscow indicate that communism and anticommunism will no longer be the ultimate criteria of political and moral values and that peaceful coexistence, which India has been advocating all these years, will be the governing consideration in international dealings? Whatever the motivation, the wisdom of these new approaches is beyond question, provided that the spirit of détente is also extended to other parts of the world. We cannot be sure if these flexible relationships necessarily point to a more stable world order. Coexistence by itself does not preclude policies, separately or in concert, which are detrimental to the freedom and interests of third countries. For example, coördinated action in the Security Council between China and the United States last year operated against an immediate restoration of peace in Bangladesh in keeping with the rights of its people. Agreements which promote the doctrine of balance of power or mark out spheres of influence are bound to increase tension and invite instability. No nation will be happy in a subservient role.

Europe has avoided war for more than two decades and is now attempting to build a framework of security and coöperation. But peace is indivisible and so long as there are conflicts and dissensions in Asia there will be no peace in the world. Asia has cradled many civilizations and contains a substantial section of the world's population. For more than two centuries, it has been drained of its resources and wealth which have contributed in no small measure to the industrial advance and affluence of the West. The countries of Asia are now politically free but the continuing interplay of international forces impedes our struggle against economic backwardness and the shadows of the past. We share many problems which can be solved through coöperation among ourselves rather than merely through assistance from the outside, which has tended to cause misunderstanding among us and which was motivated more by self-interest than by a genuine understanding of our needs.

Each country has its own heritage and distinct personality which it naturally wishes to develop in its own way. But we must also bear in mind our community of interests and take positive initiatives for working together among ourselves and with other countries in order to make a richer contribution toward the evolution of a world more liveable for all and of a socialorder more in consonance with the yearnings of modern man.

India After Indira

Paul H. Kreisberg

WARREN K. LEFFLER / LIBRARY OF CONGRESS

Indira Gandhi in Washington, D.C. in 1966.

Indira Gandhi's assassination on October 31, 1984, marked the passing of the generation that brought India to independence. Mrs. Gandhi was nourished, almost from birth, on the Congress Party's struggle against the British, and was particularly influenced by her party's close links with British socialism in the 1930s. She was deeply suspicious of the business class, even though it supported her with millions of rupees. She was convinced that only if the nation's industry, agriculture and services were closely guided by the state would equity and justice be assured. Wary of "imperialist" pressures on India — political, educational and economic — she never relinquished her belief that "foreign hands" sought to undermine not only Indian stability and independence but her personal political power as well. Although the United States seemed most often to be the target of her concern, the Soviets, British, Chinese, French and most of her South Asian neighbors were also frequently suspect.

Mrs. Gandhi shared the concern of her father's generation that India's unity and integrity were fragile and under continuing threat. The partition into two states, India and Pakistan, was the first great trauma for the independence politicians. Then, in the 1950s, came the integration of hundreds of small princedoms of the old British Raj and the struggle to prevent India from collapsing into a babel of independent linguistic and ethnic states. In the 1960s and 1970s, Mrs. Gandhi fought against political rivals at the national level, and sought to weaken and destroy politicians with strong regional bases who threatened to shift the political balance of power from New Delhi to the state levels; such a shift, she believed, would inevitably weaken the unity and authority of the central government.

Mrs. Gandhi was proud of India's technological progress but remained close to the traditions and customs of the countryside. Unlike her father, who openly disdained traditional religion, she regularly visited and worshipped at temples and shrines, and privately sought the counsel of astrologers. Her empathy was strong for the concerns of ordinary villagers, even though she herself never lived in rural India. Only once did she lose her grip on the pulse of her country, when a mass compulsory sterilization campaign got out of hand in 1975-76, arousing popular fears and anger, and resulting in her overwhelming defeat at the polls in 1977.

The confusion, division and incompetence of Mrs. Gandhi's political opponents (despite their strength in some regions), her determination to ensure that one of her sons would succeed her, her drive for vindication, and her sheer political grit and shrewdness, all led Indira Gandhi back to power in 1980. But her last four years were difficult, marked by growing internal political unrest, increasing public cynicism about politics and politicians, and the dangerous religious violence which ultimately took her life.

II

Rajiv Gandhi, who succeeded his mother as prime minister only hours after her death, was three years old when India became independent in 1947. For most of his life, politics and foreign policy seem to have held no interest for him at all. His view of the broader world is hard to trace, but his interests and priorities seem quite different from those of his predecessors. He expressed great suspicion of outside interference in India during his 1984 election campaign, but this seemed more tactical than (as with his mother) a residue of a lifetime of political conspiracy and anti-imperialist liturgy. He appears committed, in a personal sense, to the modern world and to reform and change in a way his mother was not. Religion, superstition and the life of the peasant have no place in his experience or interest.

He may wear a shawl and dress in plain white Indian pajamas in public, but in private he is a man of jeans and polo shirts. His career was aviation; his closest friends, young businessmen; his most persistent theme in speaking to national or grass-roots audiences is the importance of technology and modernization. Appalled at the garbled, disjointed records of the Congress Party, he put them on computers. He influenced his mother's decision to begin to liberalize the internal economy three years ago and to open up Indian economic development increasingly to the use of electronic communications and computer technology.

In his first two rather reluctant years as an apprentice politician after the death of his younger brother Sanjay — whom Mrs. Gandhi had originally seen as her political heir and for whom politics was life itself — Rajiv shied away from the older generation of Congress Party political figures and from the caste and religious politics that Mrs. Gandhi understood so well. He left visitors with a general impression of diffidence and lack of self-confidence. But, thrown suddenly onto center stage by the death of his mother, he instinctively rose to dignity, tranquility, firmness and a willingness to exercise power. These are the characteristics Indians want above all from their leaders; indeed, they are the characteristics that Indians associate with the gods. The underlying strength of the republic and its democratic constitutional system once again enabled India to make a smooth, essentially peaceful transition to a new national leader. The character of that new leader reinforced the support of the Indian people for the system.

In his first months as prime minister, Rajiv Gandhi made not a single false step. Indian voters rewarded this performance with an overwhelming vote of confidence in the national elections in December 1984, and with almost the same enthusiasm in the more complex state-wide elections in March. Like fairy dust, charisma has graced Rajiv's head, where no one had guessed it would settle.

In selecting Congress Party candidates for the December elections, Rajiv boldly tried to sweep away great numbers of venal, sycophantic and traditional politicians, pulling back only when it was clear that a frontal assault would tear his party apart. But his enormous victory at the national polls — he won 80 percent of the seats contested, giving the Congress Party its first clear popular majority since Indian independence — gave him great bargaining power to strike more effectively at these targets, and he did so before the subsequent state elections by refusing party endorsements to 40 percent of the Congress members seeking reelection to state legislatures. He has thus begun to generate new life in the Congress Party at lower levels, a vital step for future vigor in Indian politics.

To be sure, his post-election national cabinet is not brilliant; it is not markedly different in character from his mother's last cabinet. But he chose a number of new junior ministers of state, and pointedly told all his ministers that they would be judged promptly and finally by their performances. For the first time, there were junior ministers in their thirties, and even if the assortment of caste, religious and regional politicians which India's diversity and social complexity demands is still there, the older ministers can see all too clearly that new and younger substitutes are ready and in training to fill their shoes should they falter.

Rajiv feels most comfortable with his own generation and with individuals whose backgrounds are similar to his own. His closest advisers and the key managers of his election campaign were his classmates at the elite Nehru Dun boarding school for boys or friends from his years as a pilot for Indian Airlines. But he has also promoted more traditional politicians in his general age bracket, such as V.P. Singh, an attractive and shrewd Congress Party member of parliament in his mid-forties. Singh, Rajiv's finance minister, held several cabinet positions in Mrs. Gandhi's post-1980 cabinets and organized the Congress victory at the recent elections in the vital north Indian state of Uttar Pradesh, which has 119 million people and 84 parliamentary seats. He has the grass-roots links which Rajiv Gandhi still lacks, despite the prime minister's demonstrated appeal to the Indian voters, and yet is fully committed to honest, efficient and modern government. Singh is a man to watch for the future.

Simplifying the operations of government, speeding up the decision-making process and eliminating dead wood are Rajiv's central governing priorities. He has tried to shake up the 16 million bureaucrats of the country, condemning sloth and laziness, and demanding hard work. The objectives are impeccable, but Rajiv will find — and probably already knows — that their realization will be enormously difficult.

III

The major issues facing the new government are overwhelmingly internal, as would be the case for any Indian government. But India's relations with its neighbors — particularly Pakistan, Sri Lanka and Bangladesh — cut deeply across Indian domestic political sensitivities about national unity, and affect a wide range of political, military and economic options for New Delhi. Despite efforts to lead the nonaligned movement and excursions into global politics (more frequent in the 1950s and 1960s than later), events in South Asia have always been at the heart of India's foreign policy. These are the issues that affect most powerfully the political forces within India itself.

The collapse of law and order in the Punjab in 1984 clearly illustrates the point. Virtually all of India's attention and energy was focused for most of the year on the tensions between Sikhs and Hindus in the northwest Indian state. The Punjab, bordering on Pakistan and lying only 60 miles from New Delhi itself, is India's richest state, the breadbasket of the country and a center of modern industry and military facilities. Indian national security and the safety of the capital depend on the stability and security of the Punjab. No Indian government could tolerate a breakaway movement there.

It is true that despite occasional bursts of rhetoric, even during the worst of the violence between radical Sikhs and government authority in 1984, few Indian Sikhs sought an independent state. But another assassination or further acts of terrorism could arouse a new wave of violence by Hindus against Sikhs of the Punjab and elsewhere, with dangerous consequences for Indian stability, religious peace, and confidence in the army and civil service, where Sikhs hold many senior positions.

Indian strategic planners have always feared that Pakistan might take advantage of domestic Indian religious or social strife to weaken Indian unity and encourage dissidence. Some Indians strongly believed this was happening in 1984, but evidence for official Pakistani support of Sikh dissidents is fragile. In his December election speeches Rajiv Gandhi repeatedly struck the theme that India would exert every power at its disposal to ensure stability in the Punjab, vaguely but ominously warning against any outside involvement.

Pakistan's leaders consistently and indignantly denied any involvement with the Sikhs; since Mrs. Gandhi's death they have expressed strong and repeated interest in improving relations with New Delhi and with its new prime minister. Rajiv Gandhi responded warmly, but nearly 40 years of bad blood must be overcome, and hardly a month goes by in which there is not some expression of suspicion and fear by India or Pakistan about activities directed by one at the other: troop movements, alleged border incursions, negotiations for new arms, inflammatory radio or press broadsides. These suspicions can gradually be eased by efforts on both sides, but will swiftly revive if there is new internal unrest in either Indian or Pakistani border areas.

Thus, regardless of Pakistani professions of friendship and denials of interest in destabilizing India, Indian leaders cannot rest easy until political stability is fully restored in the Punjab. Reconciliation with the Sikhs and an easing of tensions in the Punjab are the most urgent internal tasks facing Rajiv Gandhi and, at the same time, key elements for peace in the subcontinent. The new prime minister is not without assets in facing this challenge. It was Mrs. Gandhi, not Rajiv, whom most Sikhs held responsible for the Indian army's seizure last summer of the Golden Temple, the sacred center of the Sikh religion. It was she, not he, who imprisoned or banned from political activity most of the leaders of the Sikh community. Emotions have cooled since then and Rajiv handled well the rioting in New Delhi after Mrs. Gandhi's assassination. Hindus and Sikhs alike were stunned by the looting and vengeance killings that followed the assassination, and Rajiv's calls for calm, unity and justice were welcomed by opinion leaders on all sides. Most of the issues under dispute are not that intractable, leaving aside the extreme claims of a handful of Sikhs committed to separation or radical reforms to distinguish a Sikh Punjab from the rest of India.

Rajiv, therefore, can start with a relatively clean slate, and moderates among the Sikhs are likely to be eager to try to work with him in the coming year. His release of key Sikh leaders in March 1985 was an important first step. Next would be a judicial inquiry into the rioting in New Delhi and the killings of Sikhs on Indian railways in the same period, but the prime minister has hesitated on such a step, possibly for fear of uncovering culpability among both police and Congress Party officials.

The Punjab, of course, is not the only domestic Indian area affected by relations with Pakistan. The shifting of millions of people during partition, as well as three Indo-Pakistani wars and the fact that India has the fourth largest Muslim population in the world, have produced intense sensitivity to any Pakistani developments. India's Muslims have shown themselves over the years to be genuinely Indian in their national loyalties, but they are also attentive to their Islamic neighbors. Many are deeply religious. Hindu-Muslim tensions have never been totally eliminated, and no year passes in which serious violence with religious overtones does not occur somewhere in the country. In 1984, hundreds died in such incidents in Bombay and Hyderabad. Indian government sensitivity to Pakistani actions — external or internal — that Indians believe might feed such violence is high and, while rarely the subject of direct diplomatic exchanges, remains just under the surface for politicians and officials of both countries.

IV

India's current problems with Sri Lanka stem from similar cultural, racial, economic and religious causes of long standing. The largest Sri Lankan minority, Tamils who emigrated from southern India to Ceylon as tea and rubber plantation workers in the nineteenth century, is Hindu; Sri Lanka's ruling Sinhalese are primarily Buddhists, with significant Christian and Muslim minorities. Hostility to the Tamils is strong among both the Sinhalese poor and middle class.

In Indian tradition, Sri Lanka was a land of demons and of the ogre king, Ravanna, who kidnapped and raped the bride of India's greatest hero, Rama. Even today, Ravanna is burned symbolically as the personification of evil by millions of Indians in India's most important annual religious festival. At the same time, he is portrayed as a national hero in Sri Lanka, and Sri Lankan folk tales abound with memories of the defeat of past Tamil invaders.

Indian-Sri Lankan diplomatic negotiations over the Tamil minority problem go back to the 1950s, but relations were generally amicable and cooperative until Tamil-Sinhalese tensions erupted into brutal violence two years ago. Moderate voices — Tamil and Sinhalese — were muted, and half a dozen Tamil "liberation" groups proliferated in Sri Lanka, dedicated to independence or total autonomy for Sri Lankan Tamils. The violence and political activity of these Sri Lankan Tamil groups aroused strong sympathy among the 50 million inhabitants of the Indian state of Tamil Nadu, including, inevitably, many of the state's political leaders. New Delhi would probably like to halt the training of Sri Lankan Tamil guerrillas in "secret" camps in southern India, but it has felt compelled to deny even the existence of these camps, despite widespread and detailed reporting on their activities in the Indian press.

Initially, Rajiv Gandhi had little room for diplomatic or political maneuver. Now that the state elections have been concluded, he may be willing to risk restraints on the Tamil "freedom fighters"; in any event, he has firmly rejected Sri Lankan Tamil appeals for Indian troops to come to the aid of their brothers in the south. India has repeatedly offered its good offices in resolving tensions and avoiding any escalation between India and Sri Lanka. Mediation efforts came close to success in the first half of 1984, but ultimately foundered on resistance by some influential Sinhalese nationalists to major concessions for local Tamil autonomy and participation in a proposed national conference of reconciliation.

Prospects for easing tensions or averting a new outbreak of violence in Sri Lanka are not promising, and would be worsened should Sri Lankan Tamils formally declare independence for their northeastern region of the island. Should that occur, a conflict similar to the decade-long tragedy of Cyprus could be replayed in the midst of the Indian Ocean. Internal Indian political tension would be heightened, and Rajiv Gandhi's current rejection of intervention would be gravely tested.

Bangladesh is the third major intersection of India's domestic and foreign policy concerns. Indian interests focus on the millions of illegal Bangladesh migrants who have streamed into the northeast state of Assam over the last decade and more. This has aroused growing resentment over land, jobs and political power, as many of the migrants sought to vote in Indian elections and Assamese fought back to prevent being overwhelmed at the polls. Large-scale violence between Assamese and Bengalis — mostly from Bangladesh but some from India's own state of West Bengal — began to erupt four years ago. Assam is India's primary source for onshore oil, and violence halted production at one point. India has begun building hundreds of miles of high fences to keep out Bangladesh border-crossers, a move bitterly criticized by the Bangladesh government in terms reminiscent of similar U.S.-Mexican exchanges. Political life in Assam has been disrupted to the point where, as in the Punjab, neither the 1984 national elections nor the local elections of 1985 could be held.

The aura of good will between India and Bangladesh, dating from India's role of "godmother" to Bangladesh independence from Pakistan in 1971, has long since faded. Not only the border migration question looms as an irritant; there are also intense disagreements over the allocation of river waters flowing through India's northeastern states into Bangladesh, conflicting claims to potential offshore oil in the Bay of Bengal, and smuggling of rice and jute between the two countries. Indian weariness over persistent internal Bangladesh political instability is growing. The problems intensely affect political and economic debate in the poorest and most volatile of India's states, West Bengal, Assam and Bihar.

The policies Rajiv Gandhi has adopted on these regional foreign policy problems do not yet differ significantly from those of his mother. This is not surprising, since his mother's foreign policy advisers still remain in place. More important, India's policies toward its neighbors are so closely related to difficult domestic issues that options for sudden or fundamental changes are almost nonexistent. But nuances in style on Rajiv's part may yet appear — perhaps a greater willingness to avoid confrontation, to deal with problems quietly and with at least the appearance of understanding, and greater seriousness about strengthening the fabric of the nascent South Asian Regional Cooperation grouping established four years ago by all the states in the area.

Formed without a secretariat, primarily as a forum for discussing issues rather than implementing programs, SARC has accomplished little so far. But if Rajiv is serious about a new Indian opening to his neighbors, the SARC summit planned for the fall will offer him the opportunity.

The key to better relations in the region is greater trust of India by the smaller countries, a trust Mrs. Gandhi did not engender. Like the "Widow at Windsor," of whom Kipling warned one should "walk wide," Mrs. Gandhi's forceful and, at times, abrasive assertion of a preeminent position on the subcontinent antagonized and alarmed bordering states. Rajiv may venture a smoother, softer stance. Even if much of the substance of Indian policy does not change, a shift in style would be welcomed by all the countries of the region.

V

Relations with the major powers have been heavily influenced by their respective policies toward India's regional interests. Indians have seen the Soviets as friends, the United States and China, more often than not, as adversaries, and Japan, France and Britain primarily only as trading partners.

Since independence, India's prime ministers have nourished relations with the Soviet Union. The U.S.S.R. has supported India on the Kashmir issue and in every other Indian conflict with other states. Since the mid-1960s, the Soviets have been India's primary source of military equipment and have alternated with the United States as India's primary trading partner. India has purchased military equipment — helicopters, ships, tanks, artillery and aircraft — from the French, British and others, but most imported Indian military hardware comes from the Soviet Union. Thus, for a sample four-year period (1978-82), of the $3.6 billion in India's foreign military purchases, $2.8 billion (77 percent) came from the U.S.S.R.

In a rare concession, the Soviets agreed many years ago to allow the Indians to manufacture analogues of almost all the equipment they purchase. This has enabled India to become both self-sufficient in basic arms and a potential exporter. India now places this condition on any military equipment it negotiates to buy; both France and Britain have reluctantly agreed.

In the last three years, India has taken some steps to diversify its sources of modern weaponry. Soviet prices, however, remain lower than those of any other suppliers, and can be paid in rupee-denominated exported goods rather than in scarce foreign exchange. This was enormously helpful when India was able to export to the U.S.S.R. low-quality goods for which international buyers were scarce. But now India wants fewer nonmilitary modern high-technology products from Moscow, and as its own exports become more sophisticated, the appeal of the Soviet market is declining. Indians have begun to worry about large ruble trade balances which are useful only for arms purchases.

After long estrangement on the matter, India and the United States have begun discussions about military sales in recent years. Each round has failed because of various Indian conditions: New Delhi has sought guarantees that supply will not be interrupted by U.S. political decisions; assured delivery of large quantities of spare parts; promises of technology transfer and indigenous production in India; relaxation of U.S. export controls; and other arrangements that the United States found objectionable. A recent sale of sophisticated American electronic equipment for tanks may be a harbinger of things to come. It is very unlikely, however, that the United States or any other Western country will supplant the Soviets as India's primary source of modern supply in the military field.

India has been sensitive to charges that this arms relationship produces political dependence on the Soviet Union. The Indians do permit Soviet ships to refit and refuel at Indian ports, but they note that the same benefits go to British and French ships. The Soviets sought to use Indian airfields for Indian Ocean reconnaissance flights in the early 1970s, but this was denied. And Indians insist that the Russians have no special access to Indian defense or production facilities once initial training and production technology transfer has been accomplished. There are no regular Soviet training or advisory teams with Indian military forces, other than when new equipment is phased in, and Indian officers are fiercely independent of any foreign military strategic or tactical advice.

Moreover, with only occasional exceptions, India's positions on most foreign policy issues, as measured by rhetoric and voting in the United Nations, have not differed significantly from those of Indonesia, China, or even Pakistan. (It is the occasional exceptions, including votes on Afghanistan, Kampuchea and the Korean Air Lines incident, which most irritate Washington.)

The Indians are particularly sensitive to Soviet activities in India's domestic life because of the sizable communist parties in the country. Indians are well aware of continuing Soviet disinformation tactics designed to implicate the United States in supporting Sikh nationalists, opposing India's leaders, and even being involved in Mrs. Gandhi's assassination, as well as encouraging Sri Lanka and generally interfering in India's internal affairs. Few senior Indian officials have believed such stories over the years, but they have had a cumulative political impact on many ordinary Indian newspaper readers.

India has felt free, or at least inclined, to criticize American foreign policy more than Soviet. Partly this continues a persistent and often sincerely voiced refrain from

Indian intellectuals, since Nehru's days, that Indians expect more from a democratic than a totalitarian power. During the 1950s and 1960s, moreover, the Soviets were the main international proponents of anticolonialism, an issue to which Indians were instinctively drawn — and on which they often found themselves at odds with the United States, as they admit, whether fairly or not.

Most important, however, is the Indian perception that American policy has favored India's adversaries — with the sole exception of the Sino-Indian conflict in 1962. Indian suspicion of China and of Pakistan — and of U.S. links to both countries, and those between the two — and unease over American naval might in the Indian Ocean have led Indians, for the last two decades in particular, to look to the Soviets for tacit balancing support against the United States and those states with which the United States seemed to have favored relationships.

The Indians are themselves uneasy about Soviet actions in Afghanistan since 1979. While Indian rhetoric has been constrained in public, Indians have privately made clear to Moscow their strong distaste for the presence of Soviet troops on the fringe of the subcontinent. Mrs. Gandhi bluntly and publicly told her Soviet hosts during a visit to Moscow in 1982 that Soviet troops had to leave Afghanistan. But the issue is complicated for New Delhi policymakers; they are uneasy that the primary guerrilla resistance to the Soviets in Afghanistan comes from fundamentalist Muslim groups, and they are even more uneasy that Pakistan is justifying a buildup in its military forces by emphasizing the Soviet threat on its border.

India is faced with a strategic dilemma: it does not want Soviet forces in the region, nor does it want the United States to send forces or military aid to Pakistan to resist Soviet pressures. While it is unable to reach an agreement with Pakistan that would enable both countries to present a joint front to all outside powers, India is unlikely to play a major role in persuading the Soviets to withdraw from Afghanistan.

VI

Relations between India and China have eased over the last five years. Rajiv Gandhi was a young man of 15 when the two Asian powers went to war in 1962, and it would not be surprising if he were willing to look toward the settlement of minor territorial disputes on the Sino-Indian border that Mrs. Gandhi still had difficulty contemplating. At issue, after all, are nothing more than impenetrable gorges, unclimbable peaks and four-mile-high Himalayan tundra where nothing grows and breathing is painful. India's national honor as the party defeated in the war has left it reluctant to relinquish territory without compensation. Negotiations are likely to continue to be protracted, but are not critical for either state.

India and China differ strongly on other issues, including Vietnam and Kampuchea. Indira Gandhi harbored strong feelings about Vietnam, dating back to Hanoi's struggle for independence from France and to her father's — and her own — admiration for Ho Chi Minh. Since the early 1960s, India has also seen a strategic interest in encouraging an Indochinese "buffer" between China and eastern India, barely 500 miles away across Thailand and Burma. The Indians held no brief for Vietnam's occupation of Kampuchea, but when balanced against Pol Pot's rule, and strong Chinese backing for the Khmer Rouge, India has been content to back the Heng Samrin regime in Kampuchea until Pol Pot can be eliminated and Chinese influence in the area reduced.

Indonesia is the only country of the Association of Southeast Asian Nations to have sought out good relations with India, primarily because Indonesia shared India's concern that China might be an active expansionist threat in the Indian Ocean region. The attitudes of other ASEAN countries toward India range from indifference to active dislike. But if Indian economic initiatives show promise of bringing trade and technical benefits to the countries of the region, and if Indo-U.S. relations improve, ASEAN self-interest is likely to lead these states to take another look at India and its new prime minister. Rajiv Gandhi's decisions on how to deal with ASEAN sensitivities over Vietnam and Kampuchea will depend primarily on how much room he decides he has in dealing with the Soviets. It would be surprising, however, if he wished to commit himself deeply on behalf of the Vietnamese; the "buffer" argument has long seemed somewhat limp, and Vietnam would seem to hold little appeal for someone dedicated to modernizing India. Rajiv's interest in mutual trade and technology cooperation within the region could be a new element. Japan, as usual ahead of most others, has been wooing India precisely in this way for the past three years. This may thus be an ideal time for moderate Asians — ASEAN and the Republic of Korea — to express an interest in improving ties with India.

Often heard in private conversation, but rarely in public speeches, is Indian resentment that the United States (and other Western countries) seem far more interested in China than in India. Many Indians compare the constant stream of businessmen visiting China with the still modest flow to India, and are skeptical that Western expectations for the China trade will materialize. At the same time — and this is only rarely articulated — they seem worried, with good reason, that China may penetrate international markets and preempt opportunities for Indian exports. Rajiv Gandhi may well use the goad of Chinese competition to drive his own business and bureaucratic communities to greater efforts.

VII

There is no evidence that Rajiv Gandhi holds any of Mrs. Gandhi's old personal suspicions of the United States, although he seems to have had few close relationships with Americans. He was sharply critical of alleged U.S. support for, or at least indifference to, the activities of Sikh nationalists in the United States last year. But he has also made plain to a variety of visitors that he would welcome friendlier and more active bilateral ties, particularly in science, technology and trade.

His government's handling of the aftermath of the disaster in Bhopal, in December 1984, in which over 2,000 persons died from poisoning after an accident in a Union Carbide plant, has been marked by concern to avoid damage either to Indo-American relations or to the prospects for future American investment in India. He has scheduled two visits to the United States in 1985—one in June and another to attend the U.N. General Assembly in October — and although he has also accepted invitations to visit China and the Soviet Union (thus demonstrating that India's nonaligned policies remain unchanged), the possibility of a new opening in U.S.-Indian relations seems enticing.

To be sure, the last four decades have seen other "openings" for improved relations, particularly under Ambassadors Chester Bowles, during the Truman Administration, and John Kenneth Galbraith, in the Kennedy Administration. Both proved short-lived because of tensions over American policies toward the region as a whole.

It was, of course, American links with Pakistan that were the central points of controversy both times. The U.S. bilateral security agreement with Islamabad and Pakistan's membership in pro-Western security treaties (the now defunct Southeast Asia and Central Treaty Organizations) in the 1950s, U.S. arms sales to Pakistan in the last 20 years and, above all, the Indian conviction that the United States has backed Pakistan in each of its conflicts with India remain constant themes in Indian political discourse. U.S. rationales, focused on the global balance and on Soviet threats to the Middle East, have held no persuasion for India. Indian resentment of the United States on these issues is deeply felt and broadly based, and is almost certain to infuse some of Rajiv Gandhi's thinking, as well as that of his advisers. It can be diminished in prominence; it can even be submerged if other aspects of Indo-U.S. relations develop. But the suspicion and its potential to emerge suddenly to impair bilateral ties remain under the surface and should not be ignored.

If large, currently planned increases in U.S. assistance to the Afghan guerrilla opposition materialize, Soviet air incursions and bombings inside the Pakistan border may become more intense. Mikhail Gorbachev took little time after assuming leadership in Moscow before warning Pakistan of the risks that support for the Afghan Mujahedeen might bring. The Indians are rightly concerned about the broad threat to subcontinental and, above all, Indian security that these developments pose. They are likely to oppose strongly Pakistani requests for stepped-up military assistance if Soviet pressure along the Afghan border mounts. And more direct U.S. efforts on behalf of Pakistan could easily lead to a replay of past deteriorations in Indo-U.S. relations.

At the very least, U.S. planning for Afghanistan, and for Pakistan, could well take much closer account of what the cumulative consequences of U.S. policy may be for India than has been the case thus far. Such cautions have been offered in the past but rarely have been heeded. Rajiv Gandhi's trip to Washington in June offers an ideal opportunity for the United States to listen to Indian concerns as well as to try to persuade the Indian prime minister of U.S. views. The key problem is whether the remainder of this decade will see a significant rapprochement between India and Pakistan. It would be an act of great strategic courage for Rajiv to seek such a real, long-lasting understanding with Islamabad, and for Islamabad to reciprocate. But, even if an effort to relax tensions is on his and Pakistani President Zia ul-Haq's mutual agendas for the next year or so, innumerable domestic and external hazards lie in wait to trigger tensions. The United States can do little to help change this state of affairs. But careful consideration of how U.S. policies — on arms, on help for the Afghan guerrillas, on nuclear proliferation and on aid — toward India and Pakistan may affect the other country is essential if the United States is to avoid being one of these hazards.

Any period of worsening Indo-Pakistani relations is also a bad period for Indo-U.S. relations. The real challenge for Rajiv — and for American leaders — will be to try to avoid such periods or to try to manage them when they occur.

Although the United States has wisely assured India it supports Indian efforts to seek a peaceful resolution in Sri Lanka, tensions between India and Sri Lanka are a lurking problem for the United States. The United States, sensibly, has made clear to both countries that it does not want to become involved. It has ignored recent Sri Lankan hints that the U.S. navy is welcome to call at the superb harbor of Trincomalee, which lies close to the area of heaviest Tamil population concentration on the island. A curious array of outside parties are already engaged in the Sri Lankan imbroglio, with China, Israel and Jordan quietly helping Sri Lanka, and the Palestine Liberation Organization and Libya assisting the Tamils. India, as usual, is suspicious of any outside moves in the area, and were Rajiv Gandhi not making a strong effort to keep the situation under control, it could easily boil over into generalized verbal attacks on "foreign intervention" that invariably would implicate the United States — even if only through Soviet disinformation efforts.

By building a broader framework for Indo-U.S. relations, both sides may have a stronger interest in minimizing the kind of damage to political confidence, and thereby to economic relationships as well, that has often occurred in the past. This is the strategy which the State Department, with support from the White House, is now following. The Indian government seems fully in support as well. It is a good policy but it cannot replace a strategy designed to avoid heightened military and political confrontation in the region.

VIII

For all the prime minister's zeal for modernization, development challenges for the Indian economy remain immense. Population growth continues to far outstrip the creation of new employment opportunities and services. The economy has been growing at four to five percent a year, but urban and rural poverty levels remain almost as high as they were 30 years ago, despite the rise of tens of millions of Indians into the ranks of the middle class. The economy is still heavily over-regulated, and bureaucratic control remains stultifying. Industry is inefficient and increases in productivity are almost non-existent. Power, transportation and communication are all in short supply, as are external and internal capital resources. New technologies will help, but they are costly for a country already facing mounting debt repayment challenges later this decade.

In contrast to all these elements is an enthusiastic, ingenious and entrepreneurial labor force with large numbers of high school and college graduates, including many engineers, doctors and accountants. The internal market is vast and, like the Chinese market, anxious for diverse, high quality, reasonably priced goods. If India's political and economic leaders can steadily hack away at the obstacles to growth — and that will require all the enthusiasm and commitment Rajiv Gandhi can summon — India's economic rate of growth might rise to six or seven percent over the next decade, probably not more. Ideally, New Delhi would like to attract development aid, but will probably have to make do with enhanced opportunities for trade and investment from abroad. Japanese, American and European businessmen who, with Indian counterparts, become part of this development process could reap great benefits if they are willing to take the risk and if the Indian government provides the incentives for them to do so.

Until very recently, the Indian attitude toward American investment and trade has been that the initiative was up to the United States — unlike, for instance, China's recent efforts to seek out, encourage and woo foreign investors, technology transfers and trade. Individuals and officials of India and the United States often grate on one another, in ways which Americans and Chinese seem to be able to avoid. The image of Indians has languished in the United States, though polls since 1983 show India beginning to move up in the general esteem of most Americans. The successful film Gandhi and positive reactions to A Passage to India and the television series The Jewel in the Crown seem to have helped foster an increasing interest in India among Americans.

The Year of India, scheduled to start in June 1985 and to be opened by Rajiv Gandhi and Mrs. Reagan, may build on this base and strengthen both real interest and sympathetic curiosity. American banks and major corporations have started looking more actively into India as a site for overseas expansion. They have been encouraged by the relatively buoyant Indian economy since 1982, India's strong credit rating, new investment in telecommunications and, probably, Japanese success in trade and investment ventures (five major Japanese car-makers plan to assemble and manufacture automobiles and trucks; other Japanese companies intend to produce electronic components). U.S.-Indian trade has been growing, and small but potentially significant contracts have been concluded for high technology transfers including computers, silicon wafers and telecommunications equipment between business firms. In November 1984, India and the United States concluded a memorandum of understanding on technology transfers, which may help further broaden cooperation and strengthen the hand of American businessmen in matching or beating European and Japanese competitors for the Indian market.

U.S. investment in India has grown steadily but slowly in recent years, mainly through technology licensing contracts. Total U.S. investment in India by the end of 1983 was $463 million, and was probably about $475 million at the beginning of 1985. As in China, the primary attraction for foreign investors has been the huge, relatively untapped domestic market and low wage rates. The overregulated character of the Indian economy, on the other hand, and uncertainty about the stability of the Indian labor force and political tranquility in the country, have argued for caution.

The liberal and rational economic policies of the last few years, on which the new Gandhi government seems determined to build, could ease the concerns of American companies and result in a significant upturn in Indo-U.S. economic ties.

IX

India has shown itself to be remarkably stable, despite the constant iteration of threats to national unity and integrity. Such warnings are echoes of past fears, not current realities.

A long list of challenges to this statement could be drawn from the preceding pages — economic, social, political, religious, sectional. But India's stability lies in its very size and complexity, and in the fact — and it is truly a fact — that, regardless of their diversity and of the tensions that exist as a result, Indians from the southern tip of Kanyakumari to the Himalayas do think of themselves as "Indians" with a common nationhood, and they are proud of it.

Instability in the Punjab is serious but, demonstrably, it does not generate weakness everywhere. If India's efforts to develop an electronics industry were to falter, this would be serious for some major Indian development objectives but would go almost unnoticed by most of India's 765 million people. The failure of the monsoon is always serious for millions of Indians, but monsoons rarely fail three years in a row and agriculture has become strong enough to produce significant surpluses in the good years.

Regardless of how bad the government in New Delhi may be or who rules there, the inertial weight of 3,000 years of history and custom, two centuries of British rule and 40 years of independent government, of well-established patterns of local village and district administrations, and of the myriad interwoven threads of Indian society, has proven a tremendous force for stability. If India is hard to move and to change, it is equally resistant to transient threats. A former member of the Indian Communist

Party summed it up: "I left the Party forty years ago, since Revolution in India seemed impossible. And nothing has happened to change my mind since."

India remains the anchor and bulwark of South Asia against outside invaders or aggressors. India has the strongest motives for joining with Pakistan in resisting full-fledged Soviet aggression, just as it would resist with vigor a Chinese, U.S. or any other "threat" to the region. There can be no doubt that on this issue Rajiv Gandhi, Indira Gandhi and any prospective Indian leader would stand as one.

The core of an effective American strategy in this region should be good relations with India. This does not entail an Indian veto on U.S. relations with Pakistan or other countries in the area, or require that those relations track at all times with those of New Delhi. Indo-U.S. relations are not likely to run smoothly and calmly at all times. But, in the long run, American interests will not be served by good relations with other countries of the subcontinent if its relations with India are poor. There will be hard issues on which American presidents and Indian prime ministers may have to agree to disagree, but close consultation and genuine concern for the interests of India may help to build bridges over these difficult issues.

This is likely to require the United States to take a less dogmatic view of Indian relations with the U.S.S.R. than has sometimes been the case in the past. But if Washington can show tolerance on this issue, and if Rajiv Gandhi is ready to look seriously and sympathetically at the broad American interests in Asia, the new Indian government could be the best thing that has happened for the United States, and for other friends of the United States in the region, in decades.

Paul H. Kreisberg served several tours of duty in India since 1952 as a Foreign Service offcer and was Deputy Director of Policy Planning in the State Department in the late 1970s. He is now Director of Studies at the Council on Foreign Relations.

© Foreign Affairs

Against Nuclear Apartheid

Jaswant Singh

The first nuclear blast site in India's western desert state of Rajasthan is seen in this picture released May 17 by the Indian government in New Delhi.

THE CASE FOR INDIA'S TESTS

While the end of the Cold War transformed the political landscape of Europe, it did little to ameliorate India's security concerns. The rise of China and continued strains with Pakistan made the 1980s and 1990s a greatly troubling period for India. At the global level, the nuclear weapons states showed no signs of moving decisively toward a world free of atomic danger. Instead, the nuclear nonproliferation treaty (NPT) was extended indefinitely and unconditionally in 1995, perpetuating the existence of nuclear weapons in the hands of five countries busily modernizing their nuclear arsenals. In 1996, after they had conducted over 2,000 tests, a Comprehensive Test Ban Treaty (CTBT) was opened for signature, following two and a half years of negotiations in which India participated actively. This treaty, alas, was neither comprehensive nor related to disarmament but rather devoted to ratifying the nuclear status quo. India's options had narrowed critically.

India had to ensure that its nuclear option, developed and safeguarded over decades, was not eroded by self-imposed restraint. Such a loss would place the country at risk. Faced with a difficult decision, New Delhi realized that its lone touchstone remained national security. The nuclear tests it conducted on May 11 and 13 were by then not only inevitable but a continuation of policies from almost the earliest years of independence. India's nuclear policy remains firmly committed to a basic tenet: that the country's national security in a world of nuclear proliferation lies either in global disarmament or in exercise of the principle of equal and legitimate security for all.

THE TESTS OF MAY

In 1947, when a free India took its rightful place in the world, both the nuclear age and the Cold War had already dawned. Instead of aligning with either bloc, India rejected the Cold War paradigm and chose the more difficult path of nonalignment. From the very beginning, India's foreign policy was based on its desire to attain an alternative global balance of power that, crucially, was structured around universal, nondiscriminatory disarmament.

Nuclear technology had already transformed global security. Nuclear weapons, theorists reasoned, are not actually weapons of war but, in effect, military deterrents and tools of possible diplomatic coercion. The basis of Indian nuclear policy, therefore, remains that a world free of nuclear weapons would enhance not only India's security but the security of all nations. In the absence of universal disarmament, India could scarcely accept a regime that arbitrarily divided nuclear haves from have-nots. India has always insisted that all nations' security interests are equal and legitimate. From the start, therefore, its principles instilled a distaste for the self-identified and closed club of the five permanent members of the U.N. Security Council.

During the 1950s, nuclear weapons were routinely tested above ground, making the mushroom cloud the age's symbol. Even then, when the world had witnessed only a few dozen tests, India took the lead in calling for an end to all nuclear weapons testing, but the calls of India's first prime minister, Jawaharlal Nehru, went unheeded.

In the 1960s, India's security concerns deepened. In 1962, China attacked India on its Himalayan border. The nuclear age entered India's neighborhood when China became a nuclear power in October 1964. From then on, no responsible Indian leader could rule out the option of following suit.

With no international guarantees of Indian security forthcoming, nuclear abstinence by India alone seemed increasingly worrisome. With the 1962 war with China very much on his mind, Indian Prime Minister Lal Bahadur Shastri began tentatively investigating a subterranean nuclear explosion project. A series of Indian nonproliferation initiatives had scant impact. In 1965, to make matters worse, the second war between India and Pakistan broke out. Shastri died in 1966 and was succeeded by Indira Gandhi, who continued the fruitless search for international guarantees. In 1968, India reaffirmed its commitment to disarmament but decided not to sign the NPT. In 1974, it conducted its first nuclear test, Pokharan I.

The first 50 years of Indian independence reveal that the country's moralistic nuclear policy and restraint paid no measurable dividends, except resentment that India was being discriminated against. Disarmament seemed increasingly unrealistic politics. If the permanent five's possession of nuclear weapons increases security, why would India's possession of nuclear weapons be dangerous? If the permanent five continue to employ nuclear weapons as an international currency of force and power, why should India voluntarily devalue its own state power and national security? Why admonish India after the fact for not falling in line behind a new international agenda of discriminatory nonproliferation pursued largely due to the internal agendas or political debates of the nuclear club? If deterrence works in the West — as it so obviously appears to, since Western nations insist on continuing to possess nuclear weapons — by what reasoning will it not work in India? Nuclear weapons powers continue to have, but preach to the have-nots to have even less. India counters by suggesting either universal, nondiscriminatory disarmament or equal security for the entire world.

India is alone in the world in having debated the available nuclear options for almost the last 35 years. No other country has deliberated so carefully and, at times, torturously over the dichotomy between its sovereign security needs and global disarmament instincts, between a moralistic approach and a realistic one, and between a covert nuclear policy and an overt one. May 11, 1998, changed all that. India successfully carried out three underground nuclear tests, followed on May 13 by two more underground, sub-kiloton tests. These five tests, ranging from the sub-kiloton and fission variety to a thermonuclear device, amply demonstrated India's scientific, technical, and organizational abilities, which until then had only been vaguely suspected. A fortnight later, on May 28 and 30, neighboring Pakistan predictably carried out its own tests in the bleak fastness of the Chagai Hills in Baluchistan, near the Afghan border. Suddenly the strategic equipoise of the post-Cold War world was rattled. The entire nonproliferation regime and the future of disarmament were at the forefront of international agendas.

THE FAILURE OF THE OLD REGIME

Since independence, India has consistently advocated global nuclear disarmament, convinced that a world without nuclear weapons will enhance both global and Indian security. India was the first to call for a ban on nuclear testing in 1954, for a nondiscriminatory treaty on nonproliferation in 1965, for a treaty on nonuse of nuclear weapons in 1978, for a nuclear freeze in 1982, and for a phased program for complete elimination of nuclear weapons in 1988. Unfortunately, most of these initiatives were rejected by the nuclear weapons states, who still consider these weapons essential for their own security. What emerged, in consequence, has been a discriminatory and flawed nonproliferation regime that damages India's security. For years India conveyed its apprehensions to other countries, but this did not improve its security environment. This disharmony and disjunction between global thought and trends in Indian thought about nuclear weapons is, unfortunately, the objective reality of the world. Nuclear weapons remain a key indicator of state power. Since this currency is operational in large parts of the globe, India was left with no choice but to update and validate the capability that had been demonstrated 24 years ago in the nuclear test of 1974.

India's May 1998 tests violated no international treaty obligations. The CTBT, to which India does not subscribe, permits parties to withdraw if they believe their supreme national interests to be jeopardized. Moreover, the forcing of an unconditional and indefinite extension of the NPT on the international community made 1995 a watershed in the evolution of the South Asian situation. India was left with no option but to go in for overt nuclear weaponization. The Sino-Pakistani nuclear weapons collaboration — a flagrant violation of the NPT — made it obvious that the NPT regime had collapsed in India's neighborhood. Since it is now argued that the NPT is unamendable, the legitimization of nuclear weapons implicit in the unconditional and indefinite extension of the NPT is also irreversible. India could have lived with a nuclear option but without overt weaponization in a world where nuclear weapons had not been formally legitimized. That course was no longer viable in the post-1995 world of legitimized nuclear weapons. Unfortunately, the full implications of the 1995 NPT extension were debated neither in India nor abroad. This fatal setback to nuclear disarmament and to progress toward delegitimization of nuclear weapons was thoughtlessly hailed by most peace movements abroad as a great victory.

Nor was the CTBT helpful. In negotiations on the CTBT in 1996, India for the first time stated that the nuclear issue is a national security concern for India and advanced that as one reason why India was unable to accede to the CTBT. Presumably this persuaded the nuclear hegemons to introduce a clause at the last minute pressing India, along with 43 other nations, to sign the treaty to bring it into force. This coercive clause violates the Vienna Convention on Treaties, which stipulates that a nation not willing to be party to a treaty cannot have obligations arising out of that treaty imposed on it. Even more galling, this clause was introduced at the insistence of China — the provider of nuclear technology to Pakistan. When the international community approved the coercive CTBT, India's security environment deteriorated significantly.

India's plight worsened as the decade wore on. In 1997 more evidence surfaced on the proliferation between China and Pakistan and about U.S. permissiveness on this issue. During Chinese President Jiang Zemin's recent visit to Washington, the United States insisted on a separate agreement with China on Chinese proliferation to Iran and Pakistan, which the Chinese signed instead of professing their innocence. Both the U.S. unease and the Chinese signature attest to Chinese proliferation as a threat to India's security. After all these assurances, China continued to pass missile technology and components to Pakistan. Despite this, the Clinton administration was still willing to certify that China was not proliferating or — even worse for India — that the United States was either unable or unwilling to restrain China. As the range of options for India narrowed, so, too, did the difficulties of taking corrective action.

A FINE BALANCE

Today India is a nuclear weapons state. This adds to its sense of responsibility as a nation committed to the principles of the U.N. Charter and to promoting regional peace and stability. During the past 50 years, India made its nuclear decisions guided only by its national interest, always supported by a national consensus. The May 1998 tests resulted from earlier decisions and were possible only because those decisions had been taken correctly.

The earliest Indian forays into the question of nuclear disarmament were admittedly more moralistic than realistic. The current disharmony, therefore, between India and the rest of the globe is that India has moved from being totally moralistic to being a little more realistic, while the rest of the nuclear world has arrived at all its nuclear conclusions entirely realistically. With a surplus of nuclear weapons and the technology for fourth-generation weapons, the other nuclear powers are now beginning to move toward a moralistic position. Here is the cradle of lack of understanding about the Indian stand.

The first and perhaps principal obstacle in understanding India's position lies in the failure to recognize the country's security needs; of the need in this nuclearized world for a balance between the rights and obligations of all nations; of restraint in acquisition of nuclear weaponry; of ending today's unequal division between nuclear haves and have-nots. No other country in the world has demonstrated the restraint that India has for the nearly quarter-century after the first Pokharan test in 1974.

Now, as the century turns, India faces critical choices. India had witnessed decades of international unconcern and incomprehension as its security environment, both globally and in Asia, deteriorated. The end of the Cold War created the appearance of American unipolarity but also led to the rise of additional power centers. The fulcrum of the international balance of power shifted from Europe to Asia. Asian nations began their process of economic resurgence. The Asia-Pacific as a trade and security bloc became a geopolitical reality. But the rise of China led to new security strains that were not addressed by the existing nonproliferation regime. The 1995 indefinite extension of the NPT — essentially a Cold War arms control treaty with a heretofore fixed duration of 25 years — legitimized in perpetuity the existing nuclear arsenals and, in effect, an unequal nuclear regime. Even as the nations of the world acceded to the treaty, the five acknowledged nuclear weapons powers — Britain, China, France, Russia, and the United States — stood apart; the three undeclared nuclear weapons states — India, Israel, and Pakistan — were also unable to subscribe. Neither the world nor the nuclear powers succeeded in halting the transfer of nuclear weapons technology from declared nuclear weapons powers to their preferred clients. The NPT notwithstanding, proliferation in India's back yard spread.

Since nuclear powers that assist or condone proliferation are subject to no penalty, the entire nonproliferation regime became flawed. Nuclear technologies became, at worst, commodities of international commerce and, at best, lubricants of diplomatic fidelity. Chinese and Pakistani proliferation was no secret. Not only did the Central Intelligence Agency refer to it but, indeed, from the early 1990s on the required U.S. presidential certification of nonproliferation could not even be provided. India is the only country in the world sandwiched between two nuclear weapons powers.

Today most nations are also the beneficiaries of a nuclear security paradigm. From Vancouver to Vladivostok stretches a club: a security framework in which four nuclear weapons powers, as partners in peace, provide extended deterrent protection. The Americas are under the U.S. nuclear deterrent as members of the Organization of American States. South Korea, Japan, and Australasia are also under the U.S. umbrella. China is, of course, a major nuclear power. Only Africa and southern Asia remain outside this new international nuclear paradigm where nuclear weapons and their role in international conduct are paradoxically legitimized. These differentiated standards of national security — a sort of international nuclear apartheid — are not simply a challenge to India but demonstrate the inequality of the entire nonproliferation regime.

In the aftermath of the Cold War, an Asian balance of power is emerging with new alignments and new vacuums. India, in exercise of its supreme national interests, has acted in a timely fashion to correct an imbalance and fill a potentially dangerous vacuum. It endeavors to contribute to a stable balance of power in Asia, which it holds will further the advance of democracy. A more powerful India will help balance and connect the oil-rich Gulf region and the rapidly industrializing countries of Southeast Asia.

To India's north is the Commonwealth of Independent States, a reservoir that has yet to be fully developed. The Soviet Union's successor, Russia, has considerably less international prestige. Inevitably, the previously existing alliance between India and the former U.S.S.R. has eroded.

On India's western flank lies the Gulf region, a critical source of the world's energy. India has ancient links to the area, as it does to the former Soviet lands. It also has extensive energy import requirements. The Gulf employs Indian labor and talent. However, this region and its neighbors have been targets of missile and nuclear proliferation. Long-range missiles entered this area in the mid-1980s. Since 1987, nuclear proliferation in the Gulf, with extraregional assistance, has continued unchecked.

Faced as India was with a legitimization of nuclear weapons by the haves, a global nuclear security paradigm from which it was excluded, trends toward disequilibrium in the Asian balance of power, and a neighborhood in which two nuclear weapons countries act in concert, India had to protect its future by exercising its nuclear option. By so doing, India has brought into the open the nuclear reality that had remained clandestine for at least the past 11 years. India could not accept a flawed nonproliferation regime as the international norm when all realities conclusively demanded the contrary.

India's policies toward its neighbors and others have not changed. The country remains fully committed to the promotion of peace, stability, and resolution of all outstanding issues through bilateral dialogue and negotiations. The tests of May 11 and 13 were not directed against any country. They were intended to reassure the people of India about their own security. Confidence-building is a continuous process to which India remains committed.

India's motive remains security, not, as some have speciously charged, domestic politics. Had the tests been motivated simply by electoral exigencies, there would have been no need to test the range of technologies and yields demonstrated in May. In the marketplace of Indian public life, a simple low-yield device would have sufficed. Since that marketplace did not govern the decision to experiment, the tests encompassed the range of technologies necessary to make a credible nuclear deterrent.

JOIN THE CLUB

India is now a nuclear weapons state, as is Pakistan. That reality can neither be denied nor wished away. This category of "nuclear weapons state" is not, in actuality, a conferment. Nor is it a status for others to grant. It is, rather, an objective reality. India's strengthened nuclear capability adds to its sense of responsibility — the obligation of power. India, mindful of its international duties, is committed to not using these weapons to commit aggression or to mount threats against any country. These are weapons of self-defense, to ensure that India, too, is not subjected to nuclear coercion.

India has reiterated its desire to enter into a no-first-use agreement with any country, either negotiated bilaterally or in a collective forum. India shall not engage in an arms race, nor, of course, shall it subscribe to or reinvent the sterile doctrines of the Cold War. India remains committed to the basic tenet of its foreign policy — a conviction that global elimination of nuclear weapons will enhance its security as well as that of the rest of the world. It will continue to urge countries, particularly other nuclear weapons states, to adopt measures that would contribute meaningfully to such an objective. This is the defining difference. It is also the cornerstone of India's nuclear doctrine.

That is why India will continue to support initiatives, taken individually or collectively, by the Non-Aligned Movement, which has continued to attach the highest priority to nuclear disarmament. This was reaffirmed most recently at the NAM ministerial meeting held soon after India had conducted its recent series of underground tests. The NAM ministers reiterated their call at the Conference on Disarmament to establish, as the highest priority, an ad hoc committee to start negotiations in 1998 on a phased program for the complete elimination of nuclear weapons within a specified time, including a nuclear weapons convention. The collective voice of 113 NAM countries echoes an approach to global nuclear disarmament to which India has remained committed.

One NAM initiative, to which great importance is attached, resulted in the International Court of Justice's unanimous July 1996 declaration that there is an international obligation to pursue in good faith and bring to a conclusion negotiations leading to comprehensive nuclear disarmament under strict and effective international control. India was one of the countries that appealed to the ICJ on this issue. No other nuclear weapons state has supported this judgment; in fact, they all have decried it. India has been and will continue to be in the forefront of the calls for opening negotiations for a nuclear weapons convention. This challenge should be confronted with the same vigor that has dealt with the scourges of biological and chemical weapons. In keeping with its commitment to comprehensive, universal, and nondiscriminatory approaches to disarmament, India is an original party to the conventions against both. In recent years, in keeping with these new challenges, India has actively promoted regional cooperation — in the South Asian Association for Regional Cooperation, in the Indian Ocean Rim Association for Regional Cooperation, and as a member of the Association of Southeast Asian Nations Regional Forum. This engagement will continue. The policies of economic liberalization introduced in recent years have increased India's regional and global linkages, and India shall deepen and strengthen these ties.

India's nuclear policy has been marked by restraint and openness. It has not violated any international agreements, either in 1974 or 1998. This restraint is a unique example. Restraint, however, has to arise from strength. It cannot be based upon indecision or hesitancy. Restraint is valid only when it removes doubts, which is precisely what India's tests did. The action involved was balanced — the minimum necessary to maintain an irreducible component of the country's national security calculus.

Even before 1990, when Congress passed the Pressler amendment cutting off economic and military aid to Pakistan to protest its development of a nuclear program, the genie of nuclear proliferation on the Indian subcontinent was out of the bottle. The much-quoted 1987 interview in which Abdul Qadeer Khan, the chief Pakistani nuclear scientist, verified the existence of Islamabad's bomb simply confirmed what New Delhi had long suspected. The United States, then still engaged in Afghanistan, continued to deny that Pakistan had crossed the nuclear threshold. The explosions at the Chagai Hills on May 28 and 30 testify to the rightness of India's suspicions.

After the tests, India stated that it will henceforth observe a voluntary moratorium and refrain from conducting underground nuclear test explosions. It has also indicated a willingness to move toward a de jure formalization of this declaration. The basic obligation of the CTBT is thus met: to undertake no more nuclear tests. Since India already subscribes to the substance of the test ban treaty, all that remains is its actual signature.

India has also expressed readiness to participate in negotiations in the Conference on Disarmament in Geneva on a fissile material cut-off treaty. The basic objective of this pact is to prohibit future production of fissile materials for use in nuclear weapons. India's approach in these negotiations will be to ensure that this treaty is universal, nondiscriminatory, and backed by an effective verification mechanism. That same constructive approach will underlie India's dialogue with countries that need to be persuaded of India's serious intent. The challenge to Indian statecraft remains to reconcile India's security imperatives with valid international concerns regarding nuclear weapons.

Let the world move toward finding more realistic solutions and evolving a universal security paradigm for the entire globe. Since nuclear weapons are not really usable, the dilemma lies, paradoxically, in their continuing deterrent value. This paradox further deepens the concern of statesmen. How are they to employ state power in the service of national security and simultaneously address international concerns? How can they help the world create an order that ensures a peaceful present and an orderly future? How are they to reconcile the fact that nuclear weapons have a deterrent value with the objective global reality that some countries have this value and others do not? How can a lasting balance be founded? While humanity is indivisible, national security interests, as expressions of sovereignty, are not. What India did in May was to assert that it is impossible to have two standards for national security — one based on nuclear deterrence and the other outside of it.

The end of the Cold War did not result in the end of history. The great thaw that began in the late 1980s only melted down the ancient animosities of Europe. We have not entered a unipolar order. India still lives in a rough neighborhood. It would be a great error to assume that simply advocating the new mantras of globalization and the market makes national security subservient to global trade. The 21st century will not be the century of trade. The world still has to address the unfinished agenda of the centuries.

Jaswant Singh is Senior Adviser on Defense and Foreign Affairs to Indian Prime Minister Atal Bihari Vajpayee and a Member of Parliament for the Bharatiya Janata Party.

© Foreign Affairs

India and the Balance of Power

C. Raja Mohan

Japan's Prime Minister Junichiro Koizumi and Indian Prime Minister Manmohan Singh sign an agreement in New Delhi, aiming to cope with the growing clout of China, April 29, 2005.

WILL THE WEST ENGAGE?

After disappointing itself for decades, India is now on the verge of becoming a great power. The world started to take notice of India's rise when New Delhi signed a nuclear pact with President George W. Bush in July 2005, but that breakthrough is only one dimension of the dramatic transformation of Indian foreign policy that has taken place since the end of the Cold War. After more than a half century of false starts and unrealized potential, India is now emerging as the swing state in the global balance of power. In the coming years, it will have an opportunity to shape outcomes on the most critical issues of the twenty-first century: the construction of Asian stability, the political modernization of the greater Middle East, and the management of globalization.

Although India's economic growth has been widely discussed, its new foreign policy has been less noted. Unlike their U.S. counterparts, Indian leaders do not announce new foreign policy doctrines. Nonetheless, in recent years, they have worked relentlessly to elevate India's regional and international standing and to increase its power. New Delhi has made concerted efforts to reshape its immediate neighborhood, find a modus vivendi with China and Pakistan (its two regional rivals), and reclaim its standing in the "near abroad": parts of Africa, the Persian Gulf, Central and Southeast Asia, and the Indian Ocean region. At the same time, it has expanded relations with the existing great powers — especially the United States.

India is arriving on the world stage as the first large, economically powerful, culturally vibrant, multiethnic, multireligious democracy outside of the geographic West. As it rises, India has the potential to become a leading member of the "political West" and to play a key role in the great political struggles of the next decades. Whether it will, and how soon, depends above all on the readiness of the Western powers to engage India on its own terms.

THREE STRATEGIC CIRCLES

India's grand strategy divides the world into three concentric circles. In the first, which encompasses the immediate neighborhood, India has sought primacy and a veto over the actions of outside powers. In the second, which encompasses the so-called extended neighborhood stretching across Asia and the Indian Ocean littoral, India has sought to balance the influence of other powers and prevent them from undercutting its interests. In the third, which includes the entire global stage, India has tried to take its place as one of the great powers, a key player in international peace and security.

Three things have historically prevented India from realizing these grand strategic goals. First, the partition of the South Asian subcontinent along religious lines (first into India and Pakistan, in 1947, then into India, Pakistan, and Bangladesh, in 1971) left India with a persistent conflict with Pakistan and an internal Hindu-Muslim divide. It also physically separated India from historically linked states such as Afghanistan, Iran, and the nations of Southeast Asia. The creation of an avowedly Islamic state in Pakistan caused especially profound problems for India's engagement with the Middle East. Such tensions intertwined with regional and global great-power rivalries to severely constrict India's room for maneuver in all three concentric circles.

The second obstacle was the Indian socialist system, which caused a steady relative economic decline and a consequent loss of influence in the years after independence. The state-socialist model led India to shun commercial engagement with the outside world. As a result, India was disconnected from its natural markets and culturally akin areas in the extended neighborhood.

Finally, the Cold War, the onset of which quickly followed India's independence, pushed India into the arms of the Soviet Union in response to Washington's support for Pakistan and China — and thus put the country on the losing side of the great political contest of the second half of the twentieth century. Despite being the largest democracy in the world, India ended up siding with the opposite camp on most global issues.

The last decade of the twentieth century liberated India from at least two of these constraints; state socialism gave way to economic liberalization and openness to globalization, and the Cold War ended. Suddenly, New Delhi was free to reinvent its foreign policy — positioning itself to face the rise of China, shifting its strategic approach to its other neighbors, and beginning to work closely with the world's existing great powers.

VARIETIES OF INFLUENCE

India's recent embrace of openness and globalization has had an especially dramatic effect on the country's role in the region. As the nations of the subcontinent jettison their old socialist agendas, India is well positioned to promote economic integration. Although the pace has been relatively slow, the process has begun to gain traction. The planned implementation of the South Asian Free Trade Agreement this summer signals the coming reintegration of the subcontinent's markets, which constituted a single economic space until 1947.

At the same time, optimism on the economic front must be tempered by an awareness of the problematic political developments in India's smaller neighbors. The struggle for democracy and social justice in Nepal, interminable political violence and the rise of Islamic extremism in Bangladesh, and the simmering civil war in Sri Lanka underscore the potential dangers of failing states on the subcontinent. There are also the uncertain futures of Pakistan and Afghanistan: defeating religious extremism and creating modern and moderate states in both countries is of paramount importance to India. A successful Indian strategy for promoting peace and prosperity within the region would require preventing internal conflicts from undermining regional security, as well as resolving India's own conflicts with its neighbors.

In the past, great-power rivalries, as well as India's own tensions with Pakistan and China, have complicated New Delhi's effort to maintain order in the region. Today, all of the great powers, including the United States and China, support the Indian objective of promoting regional economic integration. The Bush administration has also started to defer to Indian leadership on regional security issues. Given the new convergence of U.S. and Indian interests in promoting democracy and countering extremism and terrorism, New Delhi no longer suspects Washington of trying to undercut its influence in the region. As a result, it is more prepared than ever to work with the United States and other Western powers to pursue regional goals.

Meanwhile, the external environment has never been as conducive as it is today to the resolution of the Indo-Pakistani conflict over Kashmir. The conflict has become less and less relevant to India's relations with the great powers, which has meant a corresponding willingness on New Delhi's part to work toward a solution. Of particular importance has been the steady evolution of the U.S. position on Kashmir since the late 1990s. The support extended by President Bill Clinton to India in its limited war with Pakistan in 1999 removed the perception that Washington would inevitably align with Islamabad in regional conflicts. But India remained distrustful of the Clinton administration's hyperactive, prescriptive approach to Kashmir. It has been more comfortable with the low-key methods of the Bush administration, which has avoided injecting itself directly into the conflict. The Bush administration has also publicly held Pakistan responsible for cross-border terrorism and has extracted the first-ever assurances from Pakistan to put an end to the attacks. New Delhi does not entirely believe these promises, but it has nonetheless come to trust Washington as a source of positive of influence on Islamabad.

These developments have opened the way for a peace process between the two governments. With the growing awareness that the normalization of relations with Pakistan would end a debilitating conflict and help India's regional and global standing, New Delhi has begun to negotiate seriously for the first time in decades. Although the pace of talks has not satisfied Pakistan, the two sides have agreed on a range of confidence-building measures. Indian Prime Minister Manmohan Singh has rejected the idea of giving up territory, but he has often called for innovative solutions that would improve living conditions and for common institutions that would connect Kashmiris across the Line of Control. Singh has made clear that the Indian leadership is ready to risk political capital on finding a diplomatic solution to Kashmir.

India's recent effort to resolve its long-standing border dispute with China has been just as bold. New Delhi decided in 2003 to seek a settlement with Beijing on a political basis, rather than on the basis of legal or historical claims. As a result, during Chinese Premier Wen Jiabao's visit to New Delhi in April 2005, India and China agreed on a set of principles to guide the final settlement. The two governments are now exploring the contours of mutually satisfactory territorial compromises.

India's search for practical solutions to the disputes over Kashmir and its border with China suggests that the country has finally begun to overcome the obsession with territoriality that has consumed it since its formation. Ironically, the nuclearization of India and Pakistan in 1998 may have helped in this regard: although nuclearization initially sharpened New Delhi's conflicts with both Islamabad and Beijing, it also allowed India to approach its territorial problems with greater self-assurance and pragmatism.

INDIA UNBOUND

Progress on the resolution of either of these conflicts, especially the one over Kashmir, would liberate India's political and diplomatic energies so that the country could play a larger role in the world. It would also finally release India's armed forces from the constraining mission of territorial defense, allowing them to get more involved in peace and stability operations around the Indian Ocean. Even with all the tensions on the subcontinent, the armies of India, Pakistan, and Bangladesh have been among the biggest contributors to UN peacekeeping operations. The normalization of Indo-Pakistani relations would further free up some of the best armed forces in the world for the promotion of the collective good in the greater Middle East, Africa, and Asia.

Even as the Kashmir and China questions have remained unsettled, India's profile in its extended neighborhood has grown considerably since the early 1990s. India's outward economic orientation has allowed it to reestablish trade and investment linkages with much of its near abroad. New Delhi is negotiating a slew of free- and preferential-trade agreements with individual countries as well as multilateral bodies including the Association of Southeast Asian Nations (ASEAN), the Gulf Cooperation Council (GCC), and the Southern African Development Community. Just as China has become the motor of economic growth in East Asia, a rising India could become the engine of economic integration in the Indian Ocean region.

After decades of being marginalized from regional institutions in different parts of Asia, India is also now a preferred political partner for ASEAN, the East Asian Summit, the GCC, the Shanghai Cooperation Organization, and the African Union. Moreover, it has emerged as a major aid donor; having been an aid recipient for so long, India is now actively leveraging its own external assistance to promote trade as well as political objectives. For example, India has given $650 million in aid to Afghanistan since the fall of the Taliban.

Meanwhile, the search for oil has encouraged Indian energy companies to tail their Western and Chinese counterparts throughout the world, from Central Asia and Siberia and to western Africa and Venezuela.

On the security side, India has been actively engaged in defense diplomacy. Thanks to the strength of its armed forces, India is well positioned to assist in stabilizing the Indian Ocean region. It helps that there has been a convergence of U.S. and Indian political interests: countering terrorism, pacifying Islamic radicalism, promoting democracy, and ensuring the security of sea-lanes, to name a few. The Indian navy in particular has been at the cutting edge of India's engagement with the region — as was evident from its ability to deploy quickly to areas hit by the tsunami at the end of 2004. The Indian navy today is also ready to participate in multinational military operations.

AXES AND ALLIES

The end of the Cold War freed India to pursue engagement with all the great powers — but especially the United States. At the start of the 1990s, finding that its relations with the United States, China, Japan, and Europe were all underdeveloped, India moved quickly to repair the situation. Discarding old socialist shibboleths, it began to search for markets for its products and capital to fuel its long-constrained domestic growth. Economic partnerships were easy to construct, and increasing trade flows provided a new basis for stability in India's relations with other major powers. India's emergence as an outsourcing destination and its new prowess in information technology also give it a niche in the world economy — along with the confidence that it can benefit from economic globalization.

Barely 15 years after the collapse of the Soviet Union, India's omnidirectional engagement with the great powers has paid off handsomely. Never before has India had such expansive relations with all the major powers at the same time — a result not only of India's increasing weight in the global economy and its growing power potential, but also of New Delhi's savvy and persistent diplomacy.

The evolution of Sino-Indian ties since the 1990s has been especially important and intriguing. Many see violent conflict between the two rising Asian powers as inevitable. But thanks to New Delhi's policy of actively engaging China since the late 1980s, the tensions that characterized relations between them from the late 1950s through the 1970s have become receding memories. Bilateral trade has boomed, growing from less than $200 million in the early 1990s to nearly $20 billion in 2005. In fact, China is set to overtake the European Union and the United States as India's largest trading partner within a few years. The 3,500-kilometer Sino-Indian border, over which the two countries fought a war in 1962, is now tranquil. And during Wen's visit to India in April 2005, India and China announced a "strategic partnership" — even though just seven years earlier New Delhi had cited concerns over China as a reason for performing nuclear tests, prompting a vicious reaction from Beijing.

India has also cooperated with China in order to neutralize it in conflicts with Pakistan and other smaller neighbors. In the past, China tended to be a free rider on regional security issues, proclaiming noninterference in the internal affairs of other nations while opportunistically befriending regimes in pursuit of its long-term strategic interests. This allowed India's subcontinental neighbors to play the China card against New Delhi when they wanted to resist India's attempts to nudge them toward conflict resolution. But now, Beijing has increasingly avoided taking sides in India's disputes, even as its economic and security profile in the region has grown.

China is not the only Asian power that India is aiming to engage and befriend. Japan has also emerged as an important partner for India, especially since Japanese Prime Minister Junichiro Koizumi has transformed Japanese politics in the last few years. During a visit to New Delhi just a couple of weeks after Wen's in April 2005, Koizumi announced Japan's own "strategic partnership" with India. (This came despite Japan's harsh reaction to India's nuclear test in 1998, which prompted Japanese sanctions and an effort by Tokyo to censure India in the United Nations and other multilateral forums.) Amid growing fears of a rising China and the incipient U.S.-Indian alliance, Japan has elevated India to a key player in its long-term plans for Asian security.

Recognizing the need to diversify its Asian economic portfolio, Tokyo has also, for political reasons, begun to direct some of its foreign investment to India (which has overtaken China as the largest recipient of Japanese development assistance). Since the start of the Bush administration, Japan has also shown increasing interest in expanding military cooperation with India, especially in the maritime domain. India, too, has recognized that it shares with Japan an interest in energy security and in maintaining a stable balance of power in Asia. Japan actively supported India's participation in the inaugural East Asian Summit, in December 2005, despite China's reluctance to include New Delhi. Neither India nor Japan wants to base their political relationship exclusively on a potential threat from China, but both know that deepening their own security cooperation will open up new strategic options and that greater coordination between Asian democracies could limit China's impact.

India's relations with Europe have been limited by the fact that New Delhi is fairly unimpressed with Europe's role in global politics. It senses that Europe and India have traded places in terms of their attitudes toward the United States: while Europe seethes with resentment of U.S. policies, India is giving up on habitually being the first, and most trenchant, critic of Washington. As pessimism overtakes Europe, growing Indian optimism allows New Delhi to support unpopular U.S. policies. Indians consistently give both the United States and the Bush administration very favorable marks; according to a recent Pew Global Attitudes poll, for example, the percentage of Indians with a positive view of the United States rose from 54 percent in 2002 to 71 percent in 2005. And whereas a declining Europe has tended to be skeptical of India's rise, the Bush administration has been fully sympathetic to India's great-power aspirations.

Still, India does have growing economic and political ties with some European powers. Although many smaller European countries have been critical of the U.S.-Indian nuclear deal, the continent's two nuclear powers, France and the United Kingdom, have been supportive. Paris, in particular, bet long ago (well before Washington did, in fact) that a rising India would provide a good market for high-tech goods; with this in mind, it shielded New Delhi from the ire of the G-8 (the group of eight highly industrialized nations) after India tested nuclear weapons in May 1998. In the last several years, the United Kingdom has also started to seize economic opportunities in India and has been generally accommodating of New Delhi's regional and global aspirations.

In the wake of the Soviet Union's collapse, India also worked to maintain a relationship with Russia. The two states resolved residual issues relating to their old semi-barter rupee-ruble trading arrangements, recast their 1971 peace and friendship treaty, and maintained military cooperation. When President Vladimir Putin succeeded Boris Yeltsin, in 2000, India's waiting game paid off. A newly assertive Moscow was determined to revive and expand its strategic cooperation with India. New Delhi's only problems with Moscow today are the weakening bilateral trade relationship and the risk of Russia's doing too much to strengthen China's military capabilities.

CHARM OFFENSIVE

At the end of the Cold War, the prospect of India's building a new political relationship with the United States seemed remote. Washington had long favored Pakistan and China in the region, India had in turn aligned itself with the Soviet Union, and a number of global issues seemed to pit the two countries against each other. Yet after the Cold War, India set about wooing the United States. For most of the Clinton administration, this sweet-talking fell on deaf ears, in part because Clinton officials were so focused on the Kashmir dispute and nonproliferation. Clinton, driven by the unshakable assumption that Kashmir was one of the world's most dangerous "nuclear flashpoints" and so needed to be defused, emphasized "preventive diplomacy" and was determined to "cap, roll back, and eventually eliminate" India's nuclear capabilities. Of course, Clinton's approach ran headlong into India's core national security concerns — territorial integrity and preserving its nuclear option. Pressed by Washington to circumscribe its strategic capabilities, New Delhi reacted by testing nuclear weapons.

But even as it faced U.S. sanctions, New Delhi also began to proclaim that India was a natural ally of the United States. Although the Clinton administration was not interested in an alliance, the nuclear tests forced the United States to engage India seriously for the first time in five decades. That engagement did not resolve the nuclear differences, but it did bring Clinton to India in March 2000 — the first American presidential visit to India in 22 years. Clinton's personal charm, his genuine empathy for India, and his unexpected support of India in the 1999 war with Pakistan succeeded in improving the atmospherics of the relations and in putting New Delhi on Washington's radar screen in a new way.

It took Bush, however, to transform the strategic context of U.S.-Indian relations. Convinced that India's influence will stretch far beyond its immediate neighborhood, Bush has reconceived the framework of U.S. engagement with New Delhi. He has removed many of the sanctions, opened the door for high-tech cooperation, lent political support to India's own war on terrorism, ended the historical U.S. tilt toward Pakistan on Kashmir, and repositioned the United States in the Sino-Indian equation by drawing closer to New Delhi.

India has responded to these sweeping changes by backing the Bush administration on missile defense, the International Criminal Court, and finding alternative approaches to confronting global warming. It lent active support to Operation Enduring Freedom in Afghanistan by protecting U.S. assets in transit through the Strait of Malacca in 2002, agreed to work with the United States on multinational military operations outside of the UN framework, and, in 2005 and 2006, voted twice with Washington against Iran — an erstwhile Indian ally — at the International Atomic Energy Agency. India also came close to sending a division of troops to Iraq in the summer of 2003 before pulling back at the last moment. Every one of these actions marked a big departure in Indian foreign policy. And although disappointed by India's decision to stay out of Iraq, the Bush administration recognized that India was in the midst of a historic transformation of its foreign policy — and kept faith that India's own strategic interests would continue to lead it toward deeper political cooperation with Washington. New Delhi's persistence in reaching out to Washington since 1991 has been driven by the belief that only by fundamentally changing its relationship with the world's sole superpower could it achieve its larger strategic objectives: improving its global position and gaining leverage in its relations with other great powers.

But India's ability to engage everyone at the same time might soon come to an end. As U.S.-Chinese tensions grow and Washington looks for ways to manage China's influence, questions about India's attitude toward the new power politics will arise: Can India choose to remain "nonaligned" between the United States and China, or does India's current grand strategy show a clear bias toward the United States?

The nuclear pact unveiled by Bush and Singh in July 2005 — and consolidated when Bush went to New Delhi in March 2006 — was an effort by Washington to influence the ultimate answer to that question. Bush offered to modify U.S. nonproliferation laws (subject to approval by Congress, of course) and revise the global nuclear order to facilitate full cooperation with India on civilian nuclear energy. New Delhi, in return, has promised to separate its civilian and military nuclear programs, place its civilian nuclear plants under international safeguards, and abide by a range of nonproliferation obligations. India's interest in such a deal has been apparent for a long time. Having failed to test weapons before the Nuclear Nonproliferation Treaty was drafted, in 1968, India was trapped in an uncomfortable position vis-à-vis the nuclear order: it was not willing to give up the nuclear option, but it could not be formally accommodated by the nonproliferation regime as a nuclear weapons state.

India's motives for wanting a change in the nuclear regime are thus obvious. But for the Bush administration, the deal is less about nuclear issues than it is about creating the basis for a true alliance between the United States and India — about encouraging India to work in the United States' favor as the global balance of power shifts. Ironically, it was the lack of a history of mutual trust and cooperation — stemming in part from past nuclear disputes — that convinced the Bush administration that a nuclear deal was necessary.

AN IMPOSSIBLE ALLY?

Many critics argue that the Bush administration's hopes for an alliance are misplaced. They insist that the traditionally nonaligned India will never be a true ally of the United States. But such critics misunderstand India's nonalignment, as well as the nature of its realpolitik over the past 60 years. Contrary to a belief that is especially pervasive in India itself, New Delhi has not had difficulty entering into alliances when its interests so demanded. Its relationship with the Soviet Union, built around a 1971 peace and friendship treaty, had many features of an alliance (notwithstanding India's claim that such ties were consistent with nonalignment); the compact was in many ways a classic response to the alignment of Washington, Beijing, and Islamabad. India has also had treaty-based security relationships with two of its smaller neighbors, Bhutan and Nepal, that date back to 1949-50 — protectorate arrangements that were a reaction to China's entry into Tibet.

In fact, there is no contradiction between India's alleged preference for "moralpolitik" (in opposition to pure power politics, or Machtpolitik) and the Bush administration's expectation of an alliance with India. New Delhi is increasingly replacing the idea of "autonomy," so dear to Indian traditionalists, with the notion of India's becoming a "responsible power." (Autonomy is thought appropriate for weak states trying to protect themselves from great-power competition but not for a rising force such as India.) As India starts to recognize that its political choices have global consequences, it will become less averse to choosing sides on specific issues. Alliance formation and balancing are tools in the kits of all great powers — and so they are likely to be in India's as well.

That India is capable of forming alliances does not, however, mean that it will necessarily form a long-term one with the United States. Whether it does will depend on the extent of the countries' shared interests and their political capacity to act on them together. The Bush administration expects that such shared interests — for example, in balancing China and countering radical Islam in the Middle East — will provide the basis for long-term strategic cooperation. This outcome is broadly credible, but it is by no means inevitable, especially given the United States' seeming inability to build partnerships based on equality.

When it comes to facing a rising China, India's tendency to engage in regional balancing with Beijing has not come to an end with the proclamation of a strategic partnership between the two nations. Indeed, preventing China from gaining excessive influence in India's immediate neighborhood and competing with Beijing in Southeast Asia are still among the more enduring elements of India's foreign policy. Despite Western concerns about the military regime in Myanmar, New Delhi has vigorously worked to prevent Yangon from falling completely under Beijing's influence, and India's military ties with the Southeast Asian nations are expanding rapidly. In 2005, when Pakistan pushed for giving China observer status in the South Asian Association for Regional Cooperation, India acted quickly to bring Japan, South Korea, and the United States in as well. Given India's deep-seated reluctance to play second fiddle to China in Asia and the Indian Ocean region — and the relative comfort of working with a distant superpower — there is a structural reason for New Delhi to favor greater security cooperation with Washington.

In the Middle East, too, India has a common interest with the United States in preventing the rise of radical Islam, which poses an existential threat to India. Given its large Muslim population — at nearly 150 million, the third largest in the world — and the ongoing tensions stemming from the subcontinent's partition, India has in the past acted on its own to avert the spread of radical Islam. When Washington aligned with conservative Islamic forces in the Middle East during the Cold War, India's preference was for secular nationalist forces in the region. When the United States acted ambivalently toward the Taliban in the mid-1990s, India worked with Russia, Iran, and the Central Asian states to counter the Taliban by supporting the Northern Alliance. Now, although some in India are concerned that alignment with the United States might make India a prime target for Islamist extremists, there is no way India can compromise with radical Islam, which threatens its very unity.

But shared interests do not automatically produce alliances. The inequality of power between the two countries, the absence of a habit of political cooperation between them, and the remaining bureaucratic resistance to deeper engagement in both capitals will continue to limit the pace and the scope of strategic cooperation between India and the United States. Still, there is no denying that India will have more in common with the United States than with the other great powers for the foreseeable future.

While New Delhi has acknowledged that U.S. support is necessary for India's rise to be successful, Washington has recognized India's potentially critical role in managing emerging challenges to global order and security. As a major beneficiary of accelerating globalization, India could play a crucial role in ensuring that other developing countries manage their transitions as successfully as it has, that is, by taking advantage of opportunities while working to reduce the pain of disruption. Given the pace of its expansion and the scale of its economy, India will also become an important force in ensuring that the unfolding global redistribution of economic power occurs in an orderly fashion. Meanwhile, India could become a key player in the effort to modernize the politics of the Middle East. If nothing else, India's success in ensuring the rights and the integration of its own Muslim minority and in reaching peace with Pakistan would have a powerful demonstration effect.

To secure a long-term partnership with India, Washington must build on the argument of "Indian exceptionalism" that it has advanced in defense of the recent nuclear pact, devising a range of India-specific policies to deepen cooperation. India is unlikely, however, to become a mere subsidiary partner of the United States, ready to sign on to every U.S. adventure and misadventure around the world. It will never become another U.S. ally in the mold of the United Kingdom or Japan. But nor will it be an Asian France, seeking tactical independence within the framework of a formal alliance.

Given the magnitude of the global security challenges today, the United States needs more than meek allies. It should instead be looking to win capable and compatible partners. A rising India may be difficult at times, but it will act broadly to defend and promote the many interests it shares with Washington. Assisting India's rise, then, is in the United States' own long-term interest.

C. RAJA MOHAN is Strategic Affairs Editor at The Indian Express and a member of India's National Security Advisory Board. His most recent book is Impossible Allies: Nuclear India, United States, and the Global Order.

© Foreign Affairs

The India Model

Gurcharan Das

Indian Prime Minister Manmohan Singh at the National Development Council meeting in New Delhi, June 27, 2005.

AN ECONOMY UNSHACKLED

Although the world has just discovered it, India's economic success is far from new. After three postindependence decades of meager progress, the country's economy grew at 6 percent a year from 1980 to 2002 and at 7.5 percent a year from 2002 to 2006 — making it one of the world's best-performing economies for a quarter century. In the past two decades, the size of the middle class has quadrupled (to almost 250 million people), and 1 percent of the country's poor have crossed the poverty line every year. At the same time, population growth has slowed from the historic rate of 2.2 percent a year to 1.7 percent today — meaning that growth has brought large per capita income gains, from $1,178 to $3,051 (in terms of purchasing-power parity) since 1980. India is now the world's fourth-largest economy. Soon it will surpass Japan to become the third-largest.

The notable thing about India's rise is not that it is new, but that its path has been unique. Rather than adopting the classic Asian strategy — exporting labor-intensive, low-priced manufactured goods to the West — India has relied on its domestic market more than exports, consumption more than investment, services more than industry, and high-tech more than low-skilled manufacturing. This approach has meant that the Indian economy has been mostly insulated from global downturns, showing a degree of stability that is as impressive as the rate of its expansion. The consumption-driven model is also more people-friendly than other development strategies. As a result, inequality has increased much less in India than in other developing nations. (Its Gini index, a measure of income inequality on a scale of zero to 100, is 33, compared to 41 for the United States, 45 for China, and 59 for Brazil.) Moreover, 30 to 40 percent of GDP growth is due to rising productivity — a true sign of an economy's health and progress — rather than to increases in the amount of capital or labor.

But what is most remarkable is that rather than rising with the help of the state, India is in many ways rising despite the state. The entrepreneur is clearly at the center of India's success story. India now boasts highly competitive private companies, a booming stock market, and a modern, well-disciplined financial sector. And since 1991 especially, the Indian state has been gradually moving out of the way — not graciously, but kicked and dragged into implementing economic reforms. It has lowered trade barriers and tax rates, broken state monopolies, unshackled industry, encouraged competition, and opened up to the rest of the world. The pace has been slow, but the reforms are starting to add up.

India is poised at a key moment in its history. Rapid growth will likely continue — and even accelerate. But India cannot take this for granted. Public debt is high, which discourages investment in needed infrastructure. Overly strict labor laws, though they cover only 10 percent of the work force, have the perverse effect of discouraging employers from hiring new workers. The public sector, although much smaller than China's, is still too large and inefficient — a major drag on growth and employment and a burden for consumers. And although India is successfully generating high-end, capital-and knowledge-intensive manufacturing, it has failed to create a broad-based, labor-intensive industrial revolution — meaning that gains in employment have not been commensurate with overall growth. Its rural population, meanwhile, suffers from the consequences of state-induced production and distribution distortions in agriculture that result in farmers' getting only 20 to 30 percent of the retail price of fruits and vegetables (versus the 40 to 50 percent farmers in the United States get).

India can take advantage of this moment to remove the remaining obstacles that have prevented it from realizing its full potential. Or it can continue smugly along, confident that it will get there eventually — but 20 years late. The most difficult reforms are not yet done, and already there are signs of complacency.

A 100-YEAR TALE

For half a century before independence, the Indian economy was stagnant. Between 1900 and 1950, economic growth averaged 0.8 percent a year — exactly the same rate as population growth, resulting in no increase in per capita income. In the first decades after independence, economic growth picked up, averaging 3.5 percent from 1950 to 1980. But population growth accelerated as well. The net effect on per capita income was an average annual increase of just 1.3 percent.

Indians mournfully called this "the Hindu rate of growth." Of course, it had nothing to do with Hinduism and everything to do with the Fabian socialist policies of Prime Minister Jawaharlal Nehru and his imperious daughter, Prime Minister Indira Gandhi, who oversaw India's darkest economic decades. Father and daughter shackled the energies of the Indian people under a mixed economy that combined the worst features of capitalism and socialism. Their model was inward-looking and import-substituting rather than outward-looking and export-promoting, and it denied India a share in the prosperity that a massive expansion in global trade brought in the post-World War II era. (Average per capita growth for the developing world as a whole was almost 3 percent from 1950 to 1980, more than double India's rate.) Nehru set up an inefficient and monopolistic public sector, overregulated private enterprise with the most stringent price and production controls in the world, and discouraged foreign investment — thereby causing India to lose out on the benefits of both foreign technology and foreign competition. His approach also pampered organized labor to the point of significantly lowering productivity and ignored the education of India's children.

But even this system could have delivered more had it been better implemented. It did not have to degenerate into a "license-permit-quota raj," as Chakravarthi Rajagopalachari first put it in the late 1950s. Although Indians blame ideology (and sometimes democracy) for their failings, the truth is that a mundane inability to implement policy — reflecting a bias for thought and against action — may have been even more damaging.

In the 1980s, the government's attitude toward the private sector began to change, thanks in part to the underappreciated efforts of Prime Minister Rajiv Gandhi. Modest liberal reforms — especially lowering marginal tax rates and tariffs and giving some leeway to manufacturers — spurred an increase in growth to 5.6 percent. But the policies of the 1980s were also profligate and brought India to the point of fiscal crisis by the start of the 1990s. Fortunately, that crisis triggered the critical reforms of 1991, which finally allowed India's integration into the global economy — and laid the groundwork for the high growth of today. The chief architect of those reforms was the finance minister, Manmohan Singh, who is now prime minister. He lowered tariffs and other trade barriers, scrapped industrial licensing, reduced tax rates, devalued the rupee, opened India to foreign investment, and rolled back currency controls. Many of these measures were gradual, but they signaled a decisive break with India's dirigiste past. The economy returned the favor immediately: growth rose, inflation plummeted, and exports and currency reserves shot up.

To appreciate the magnitude of the change after 1980, recall that the West's Industrial Revolution took place in the context of 3 percent GDP growth and 1.1 percent per capita income growth. If India's economy were still growing at the pre-1980 level, then its per capita income would reach present U.S. levels only by 2250; but if it continues to grow at the post-1980 average, it will reach that level by 2066 — a gain of 184 years.

PECULIAR REVOLUTION

India has improved its competitiveness considerably since 1991: there has been a telecommunications revolution, interest rates have come down, capital is plentiful (although risk-averse managers of state-owned banks still refuse to lend to small entrepreneurs), highways and ports have improved, and real estate markets are becoming transparent. More than 100 Indian companies now have a market capitalization of over a billion dollars, and some of these — including Bharat Forge, Jet Airways, Infosys Technologies, Reliance Infocomm, Tata Motors, and Wipro Technologies — are likely to become competitive global brands soon. Foreigners have invested in over 1,000 Indian companies via the stock market. Of the Fortune 500 companies, 125 now have research and development bases in India — a testament to its human capital. And high-tech manufacturing has taken off. All these changes have disciplined the banking sector. Bad loans now account for less than 2 percent of all loans (compared to 20 percent in China), even though none of India's shoddy state-owned banks has so far been privatized.

For now, growth is being driven by services and domestic consumption. Consumption accounts for 64 percent of India's GDP, compared to 58 percent for Europe, 55 percent for Japan, and 42 percent for China. That consumption might be a virtue embarrasses many Indians, with their ascetic streak, but, as the economist Stephen Roach of Morgan Stanley puts it, "India's consumption-led approach to growth may be better balanced than the resource-mobilization model of China."

The contrast between India's entrepreneur-driven growth and China's state-centered model is stark. China's success is largely based on exports by state enterprises or foreign companies. Beijing remains highly suspicious of entrepreneurs. Only 10 percent of credit goes to the private sector in China, even though the private sector employs 40 percent of the Chinese work force. In India, entrepreneurs get more than

80 percent of all loans. Whereas Jet Airways, in operation since 1993, has become the undisputed leader of India's skies, China's first private airline, Okay Airways, started flying only in February 2005.

What has been peculiar about India's development so far is that high growth has not been accompanied by a labor-intensive industrial revolution that could transform the lives of the tens of millions of Indians still trapped in rural poverty. Many Indians watch mesmerized as China seems to create an endless flow of low-end manufacturing jobs by exporting goods such as toys and clothes and as their better-educated compatriots export knowledge services to the rest of the world. They wonder fearfully if India is going to skip an industrial revolution altogether, jumping straight from an agricultural economy to a service economy. Economies in the rest of the world evolved from agriculture to industry to services. India appears to have a weak middle step. Services now account for more than 50 percent of India's GDP, whereas agriculture's share is 22 percent, and industry's share is only 27 percent (versus 46 percent in China). And within industry, India's strength is high-tech, high-skilled manufacturing.

Even the most fervent advocates of service-based growth do not question the desirability of creating more manufacturing jobs. The failure of India to achieve a broad industrial transformation stems in part from bad policies. After India's independence, Nehru attempted a state-directed industrial revolution. Since he did not trust the private sector, he tried to replace the entrepreneur with the government — and predictably failed. He shackled private enterprise with byzantine controls and denied autonomy to the public sector. Perhaps the most egregious policy was reserving around 800 industries, designated "small-scale industries" (SSI), for tiny companies that were unable to compete against the large firms of competitor nations. Large firms were barred from making products such as pencils, boot polish, candles, shoes, garments, and toys — all the products that helped East Asia create millions of jobs. Even since 1991, Indian governments have been afraid to touch this "SSI holy cow" for fear of a backlash from the SSI lobby. Fortunately, that lobby has turned out to be mostly a phantom — little more than the bureaucrats who kept scaring politicians by warning of a backlash. Over the past five years, the government has been pruning the list of protected industries incrementally with no adverse reaction.

In the short term, the best way for India to improve the lot of the rural poor might be to promote a second green revolution. Unlike in manufacturing, India has a competitive advantage in agriculture, with plenty of arable land, sunshine, and water. To achieve such a change, however, India would need to shift its focus from peasant farming to agribusiness and encourage private capital to move from urban to rural areas. It would need to lift onerous distribution controls, allow large retailers to contract directly with farmers, invest in irrigation, and permit the consolidation of fragmented holdings.

Indian entrepreneurs also still face a range of obstacles, many of them the result of lingering bad policies. Electric power is less reliable and more expensive in India than in competitor nations. Checkpoints keep trucks waiting for hours. Taxes and import duties have come down, but the cascading effect of indirect taxes will continue to burden Indian manufacturers until a uniform goods-and-services tax is implemented. Stringent labor laws continue to deter entrepreneurs from hiring workers. The "license raj" may be gone, but an "inspector raj" is alive and well; the "midnight knock" from an excise, customs, labor, or factory inspector still haunts the smaller entrepreneur. Some of these problems will hopefully diminish with the planned designation of new "economic zones," which promise a reduced regulatory burden.

Economic history teaches that the Industrial Revolution as it was experienced by the West was usually led by one industry. It was textile exports in the United Kingdom, railways in the United States. India, too, may have found the engine that could fuel its takeoff and transform its economy: providing white-collar services that are outsourced by companies in the rest of the world. Software and business-process outsourcing exports have grown from practically nothing to $20 billion and are expected to reach $35 billion by 2008. The constraining factor is likely to be not demand but the ability of India's educational system to produce enough quality English-speaking graduates.

Meanwhile, high-tech manufacturing, a sector where India is already demonstrating considerable strength, will also begin to expand. Perhaps in a decade, the distinction between China as "the world's workshop" and India as "the world's back office" will slowly fade as India's manufacturing and China's services catch up.

RISING DESPITE THE STATE

It is an amazing spectacle to see prosperity beginning to spread in today's India even in the presence of appalling governance. In the midst of a booming private economy, Indians despair over the lack of the simplest public goods. It used to be the opposite: during India's socialist days, Indians worried about economic growth but were proud of their world-class judiciary, bureaucracy, and police force. But now, the old centralized bureaucratic Indian state is in steady decline. Where it is desperately needed — in providing basic education, health care, and drinking water — it has performed appallingly. Where it is not needed, it has only started to give up its habit of stifling private enterprise.

Labor laws, for example, still make it almost impossible to lay off a worker — as the infamous case of Uttam Nakate illustrates. In early 1984, Nakate was found at 11:40 AM sleeping soundly on the floor of the factory in Pune where he worked. His employer let him off with a warning. But he was caught napping again and again. On the fourth occasion, the factory began disciplinary proceedings against him, and after five months of hearings, he was found guilty and sacked. But Nakate went to a labor court and pleaded that he was a victim of an unfair trade practice. The court agreed and forced the factory to take him back and pay him 50 percent of his lost wages. Only 17 years later, after appeals to the Bombay High Court and the national Supreme Court, did the factory finally win the right to fire an employee who had repeatedly been caught sleeping on the job.

Aside from highlighting the problem of India's lethargic legal system, Nakate's case dramatizes how the country's labor laws actually reduce employment, by making employers afraid to hire workers in the first place. The rules protect existing unionized workers — sometimes referred to as the "labor aristocracy" — at the expense of everyone else. At this point, the labor aristocracy comprises only 10 percent of the Indian work force.

No single institution has come to disappoint Indians more than their bureaucracy. In the 1950s, Indians bought into the cruel myth, promulgated by Nehru, that India's bureaucracy was its "steel frame," supposedly a means of guaranteeing stability and continuity after the British raj. Indians also accepted that a powerful civil service was needed to keep a diverse country together and administer the vast regulatory framework of Nehru's "mixed economy." But in the holy name of socialism, the Indian bureaucracy created thousands of controls and stifled enterprise for 40 years. India may have had some excellent civil servants, but none really understood business — even though they had the power to ruin it.

Today, Indians believe that their bureaucracy has become a prime obstacle to development, blocking instead of shepherding economic reforms. They think of bureaucrats as self-serving, obstructive, and corrupt, protected by labor laws and lifetime contracts that render them completely unaccountable. To be sure, there are examples of good performance — the building of the Delhi Metro or the expansion of the national highway system — but these only underscore how often most of the bureaucracy fails. To make matters worse, the term of any one civil servant in a particular job is getting shorter, thanks to an increase in capricious transfers. Prime Minister Singh has instituted a new appraisal system for the top bureaucracy, but it has not done much.

The Indian bureaucracy is a haven of mental power. It still attracts many of the brightest students in the country, who are admitted on the basis of a difficult exam. But despite their very high IQs, most bureaucrats fail as managers. One of the reasons is the bureaucracy's perverse incentive system; another is poor training in implementation. Indians tend to blame ideology or democracy for their failures, but the real problem is that they value ideas over accomplishment. Great strides are being made on the Delhi Metro not because the project was brilliantly conceived but because its leader sets clear, measurable goals, monitors day-to-day progress, and persistently removes obstacles. Most Indian politicians and civil servants, in contrast, fail to plan their projects well, monitor them, or follow through on them: their performance failures mostly have to do with poor execution.

The government's most damaging failure is in public education. Consider one particularly telling statistic: according to a recent study by Harvard University's Michael Kremer, one out of four teachers in India's government elementary schools is absent and one out of two present is not teaching at any given time. Even as the famed Indian Institutes of Technology have acquired a global reputation, less than half of the children in fourth-level classes in Mumbai can do first-level math. It has gotten so bad that even poor Indians have begun to pull their kids out of government schools and enroll them in private schools, which charge $1 to $3 a month in fees and which are spreading rapidly in slums and villages across India. (Private schools in India range from expensive boarding schools for the elite to low-end teaching shops in markets.) Although teachers' salaries are on average considerably lower in private schools, their students perform much better. A recent national study led by Pratham, an Indian nongovernmental organization, found that even in small villages, 16 percent of children are now in private primary schools. These kids scored 10 percent higher on verbal and math exams than their peers in public schools.

India's educational establishment, horrified by the exodus out of the public educational system, lambastes private schools and wants to close them down. NIIT Technologies, a private company with 4,000 "learning centers," has trained four million students and helped fuel India's information technology revolution in the 1990s, but it has not been accredited by the government. Ironically, legislators finally acknowledged the state's failure to deliver education a few months ago when they pushed through Parliament a law making it mandatory for private schools to reserve spots for students from low castes. As with so many aspects of India's success story, Indians are finding solutions to their problems without waiting for the government.

The same dismal story is being repeated in health and water services, which are also de facto privatized. The share of private spending on health care in India is double that in the United States. Private wells account for nearly all new irrigation capacity in the country. In a city like New Delhi, private citizens cope with an irregular water supply by privately contributing more than half the total cost of the city's water supply. At government health centers, meanwhile, 40 percent of doctors and a third of nurses are absent at any given time. According to a study by Jishnu Das and Jeffrey Hammer, of the World Bank, there is a 50 percent chance that a doctor at such a center will recommend a positively harmful therapy.

How does one explain the discrepancy between the government's supposed commitment to universal elementary education, health care, and sanitation and the fact that more and more people are embracing private solutions? One answer is that the Indian bureaucratic and political establishments are caught in a time warp, clinging to the belief that the state and the civil service must be relied on to meet people's needs. What they did not anticipate is that politicians in India's democracy would "capture" the bureaucracy and use the system to create jobs and revenue for friends and supporters. The Indian state no longer generates public goods. Instead, it creates private benefits for those who control it. Consequently, the Indian state has become so "riddled with perverse incentives ... that accountability is almost impossible," as the political scientist Pratap Bhanu Mehta reported. In a recent study of India's public services, the activist and author Samuel Paul concluded that "the quality of governance is appalling."

There are many sensible steps that can be taken to improve governance. Focusing on outcomes rather than internal procedures would help, as would delegating responsibility to service providers. But what is more important is for the Indian establishment to jettison its faith in, as the political scientist James Scott puts it, "bureaucratic high modernism" and recognize that the government's job is to govern rather than to run everything. Government may have to finance primary services such as health care and education, but the providers of those services must be accountable to the citizen as though to a customer (instead of to bosses in the bureaucratic hierarchy).

None of the solutions being debated in India will bring accountability without this change in mindset. Fortunately, the people of India have already made the mental leap. The middle class withdrew from the state system long ago. Now, even the poor are depending more and more on private services. The government merely needs to catch up.

REFORM SCHOOL

India's current government is led by a dream team of reformers — most notably Prime Minister Singh, a chief architect of the liberalization of 1991. Singh's left-wing-associated National Congress Party was swept into power two years ago even though the incumbent BJP (Bharatiya Janata Party) had presided over an era of unprecedented growth. The left boasted that the election was a revolt of the poor against the rich. In reality, however, it was an anti-incumbent backlash — specifically, a vote against the previous government's poor record in providing basic services. What matters to the rickshaw driver is that the police officer does not extort a sixth of his daily earnings. The farmer wants a clear title to his land without having to bribe the village headman, and his wife wants the doctor to be there when she takes her sick child to the health center. These are the areas where government touches most people's lives, and the sobering lesson from India's 2004 elections is that high growth and smart macroeconomic reforms are not enough in a democracy.

Still, the left saw the Congress victory as an opportunity. Unfortunately, it stands rigidly against reform and for the status quo, supporting labor laws that benefit 10 percent of workers at the expense of the other 90 percent and endorsing the same protectionist policies that the extreme right also backs — policies that harm consumers and favor producers. Thus, Singh and his reformist allies often seem to be sitting, frustrated, on the sidelines. For example, the new government has pushed through Parliament the National Rural Employment Guarantee Act, which many fear will simply become the biggest "loot for work" program in India's history. Although some of the original backers of the bill may have had good intentions, most legislators saw it as an opportunity for corruption. India's experience with job-creation schemes is that their benefits usually do not reach the poor; and they rarely create permanent assets even when they are supposed to: the shoddy new road inevitably gets washed away in the next monsoon. There is also the worry that the additional 1 percent of GDP borrowed from the banks to finance this program will crowd out private investment, push up interest rates, lower the economy's growth rate, and, saddest of all, actually reduce genuine employment.

Singh knows that India's economic success has not been equally shared. Cities have done better than villages. Some states have done better than others. The economy has not created jobs commensurate with its rate of growth. Only a small fraction of Indians are employed in the modern, unionized sector. Thirty-six million are reportedly unemployed. But Singh also knows that one of the primary reasons for these failures is rigid labor laws — which he wants to reform, if only the left would let him.

Singh's challenge is to get the majority of Indians united behind reform. One of the reasons that the pace of reform has been so slow is that none of India's leaders has ever bothered to explain to voters why reform is good and just how it will help the poor. (Chinese leaders do not face this problem, which is peculiar to democracies.) Not educating their constituents is the great failure of India's reformers. But it is not too late for Singh and the reformers in his administration — most notably finance Minister Palaniappan Chidambaram and the head of the Planning Commission, Montek Singh Ahluwalia — to start appearing on television to conduct lessons in basic economics. If the reformers could convert the media and some members of Parliament, the bureaucracy, and the judiciary to their cause, Indians would be less likely to fall hostage to the seductive rhetoric of the left. If they were to admit honestly that the ideas India followed from 1950 to 1990 were wrong, people would respect them. If they were to explain that India's past regulations suppressed the people and were among the causes of poverty, people would understand.

PEOPLE POWER

Shashi Kumar is 29 years old and comes from a tiny village in Bihar, India's most backward and feudal state. His grandfather was a low-caste sharecropper in good times and a day laborer in bad ones. His family was so poor that they did not eat some nights. But Kumar's father somehow managed to get a job in a transport company in Darbhanga, and his mother began to teach in a private school, where Kumar was educated at no cost under her watchful eye. Determined that her son should escape the indignities of Bihar, she tutored him at night, got him into a college, and, when he finished, gave him a railway ticket for New Delhi.

Kumar is now a junior executive in a call center in Gurgaon that serves customers in the United States. He lives in a nice flat, which he bought last year with a mortgage, drives an Indica car, and sends his daughter to a good private school. He is an average, affable young Indian, and like so many of his kind he has a sense of life's possibilities. Prior to 1991, the realization of these possibilities was open only to those with a government job. If you got an education and did not get into the government, you faced a nightmare that was called "educated unemployment." But now, Kumar says, anyone with an education, computer skills, and some English can make it.

India's greatness lies in its self-reliant and resilient people. They are able to pull themselves up and survive, even flourish, when the state fails to deliver. When teachers and doctors do not show up at government primary schools and health centers, Indians just open up cheap private schools and clinics in the slums and get on with it. Indian entrepreneurs claim that they are hardier because they have had to fight not only their competitors but also state inspectors. In short, India's society has triumphed over the state.

But in the long run, the state cannot merely withdraw. Markets do not work in a vacuum. They need a network of regulations and institutions; they need umpires to settle disputes. These institutions do not just spring up; they take time to develop. The Indian state's greatest achievements lie in the noneconomic sphere. The state has held the world's most diverse country together in relative peace for 57 years. It has started to put a modern institutional framework in place. It has held free and fair elections without interruption. Of its 3.5 million village legislators, 1.2 million are women. These are proud achievements for an often bungling state with disastrous implementation skills and a terrible record at day-to-day governance.

Moreover, some of the most important post-1991 reforms have been successful because of the regulatory institutions established by the state. Even though the reforms have been slow, imperfect, and incomplete, they have been consistent and in one direction. And it takes courage, frankly, to give up power, as the Indian state has done for the past 15 years. The stubborn persistence of democracy is itself one of the Indian state's proudest achievements. Time and again, Indian democracy has shown itself to be resilient and enduring — giving a lie to the old prejudice that the poor are incapable of the kind of self-discipline and sobriety that make for effective self-government. To be sure, it is an infuriating democracy, plagued by poor governance and fragile institutions that have failed to deliver basic public goods. But India's economic success has been all the more remarkable for its issuing from such a democracy.

Still, the poor state of governance reminds Indians of how far they are from being a truly great nation. They will reach such greatness only when every Indian has access to a good school, a working health clinic, and clean drinking water. Fortunately, half of India's population is under 25 years old. Based on current growth trends, India should be able to absorb an increasing number of people into its labor force. And it will not have to worry about the problems of an aging population. This will translate into what economists call a "demographic dividend," which will help India reach a level of prosperity at which, for the first time in its history, a majority of its citizens will not have to worry about basic needs. Yet India cannot take its golden age of growth for granted. If it does not continue down its path of reform — and start to work on bringing governance up to par with the private economy — then a critical opportunity will have been lost.

GURCHARAN DAS is former CEO of Procter & Gamble India and the author of India Unbound: The Social and Economic Revolution From Independence to the Global Information Age.

America's New Strategic Partner?

Ashton B. Carter

President George W. Bush and India's Prime Minister Manmohan Singh in New Delhi, March 2, 2006.

SEEING THE BIG PICTURE

Last summer, Indian Prime Minister Manmohan Singh announced that India and the United States had struck a deal for a far-reaching "strategic partnership." As part of the agreement, President George W. Bush broke with long-standing U.S. policy and openly acknowledged India as a legitimate nuclear power, ending New Delhi's 30-year quest for such recognition.

Much of the debate surrounding "the India deal," as the agreement has come to be known since it was finalized last March, has focused on nuclear issues. Opponents charge that Bush's historic concession to India could deal a serious blow to the international nonproliferation regime and could set a dangerous precedent for Iran, North Korea, and other aspiring nuclear powers. They also note that the Bush administration obtained no meaningful commitments from New Delhi — no promises that India would limit its growing nuclear arsenal or take new steps to help combat nuclear proliferation and international terrorism. Why, the critics ask, did Washington give India so much for so little?

These detractors are both right and wrong. They are right to say that the deal is unbalanced and seems to have been struck with little regard for some of its implications. But they overstate the damage it will do to nonproliferation — an important cause, without doubt — and their understanding of the deal's objectives is too narrow. When the nuclear arrangements of the agreement are understood — as they should be — as just one part of a sweeping strategic realignment that could prove critical to U.S. security interests down the road, the India deal looks much more favorable. Washington gave something away on the nuclear front in order to gain much more on other fronts; it hoped to win the support and cooperation of India — a strategically located democratic country of growing economic importance — to help the United States confront the challenges that a threatening Iran, a turbulent Pakistan, and an unpredictable China may pose in the future. Washington's decision to trade a nuclear-recognition quid for a strategic-partnership quo was a reasonable move.

Critics rightly note, however, a serious asymmetry in the arrangement: whereas the deal is clear about what the United States conceded, it is vague about what India will give in return. India obtained nuclear recognition up front; the gains for the United States are contingent and lie far ahead in the uncertain future. This imbalance leaves Washington at the mercy of India's future behavior: there is still a chance that India will not deliver on the strategic partnership, especially if cooperating with the United States means abandoning positions it once endorsed as a leader of the Nonaligned Movement (NAM) and siding decisively with Washington on a range of security issues. It remains to be seen, for example, if India, once a staunch detractor of the nonproliferation regime, will now become one of its supporters.

The truth is that it is too soon to tell whether the promise of the India deal will be realized. It is too soon to tell even whether the deal will be consummated at all. To take effect, the White House's nuclear concessions to India must be written into U.S. law. Only Congress can do that, and many of its members are seeking to rebalance the deal in the United States' favor. Some legislators are eager to do so by taking back some of Washington's nuclear concessions, including on nuclear recognition — a recanting that would cast a lasting cloud over U.S.-Indian relations. Recognizing the danger of this approach, other legislators, backed by reputable nonproliferation experts, are advocating imposing new technical conditions on India. They hope to limit what they perceive to be the danger posed by the India deal to the nonproliferation regime. But the damage will likely be manageable, and haggling over technical details is unlikely to restore whatever loss to its reputation as a proponent of nonproliferation Washington has already suffered. New Delhi might view such conditions as punitive or as only a begrudging acceptance of the deal, a result that would undermine the goodwill Washington sought to build by launching a broad strategic partnership.

The deal, no matter how problematic its nuclear provisions, should not be recast or curtailed. Rather, Congress must support it in its entirety and approve it with implementation language that clearly states the concrete geopolitical advantages the United States expects to gain from a strategic partnership with India.

RECOGNITION AT LAST

Previous U.S. administrations adopted the stance that India's nuclear arsenal, which was first tested in 1974, was illegitimate and should be eliminated or at least seriously constrained. They did so for two reasons. First, they feared that legitimating the Indian arsenal might spur an arms race in Asia because Pakistan, India's archrival, and China might be tempted to keep pace with India's activities. Second, Washington wanted to stick strictly to the principles underlying the Nuclear Nonproliferation Treaty (NPT): parties to the treaty could engage in peaceful nuclear commerce; states that stood outside the NPT regime, such as India, could not. U.S. policymakers feared that compromising these principles might both give states with nuclear aspirations reason to think they could get around the NPT if they waited long enough and dishearten those other states that loyally supported the treaty against proliferators.

A stance, however, is not a policy. And eliminating India's arsenal became an increasingly unrealistic stance when Pakistan went nuclear in the 1980s — and then became a fantasy in 1998, when India tested five bombs underground and openly declared itself a nuclear power. After India's tests, the Clinton administration sought to nudge New Delhi in directions that would limit counteractions by China and Pakistan and above all prevent an Indo-Pakistani nuclear war. All the while Washington firmly maintained that U.S. recognition of India's nuclear status was a long way off. After the attacks of September 11, 2001, which prompted Washington to take a fresh look at U.S. policies in South Asia, the Bush administration first reached out to Pakistan to secure its help against Islamist terrorists.

But then it also turned toward New Delhi, and in the summer of 2005 finally granted India de facto nuclear recognition. In a stroke, Washington thereby invited India to join the ranks of China, France, Russia, the United States, and the United Kingdom — the victors of World War II — as a legitimate wielder of the influence that nuclear weapons confer. When, earlier this year, the Bush administration negotiated the specific terms of its nuclear arrangement with New Delhi, Washington abandoned, against the advice of nonproliferation specialists, any efforts to condition the deal on constraints that would keep India from further increasing its nuclear arsenal.

Under the terms of the deal, the United States commits to behave, and urge other states to behave, as if India were a nuclear weapons state under the NPT, even though India has not signed the treaty and will not be required to do so. (Even if the Bush administration had wished to make India a de jure nuclear weapons state under the

NPT, such a change probably would not have been possible, as it would have required unanimously approval by all 188 parties to the treaty.) Washington has also undertaken to stop denying civil nuclear technology to India and has determined to require India to apply the safeguards of the International Atomic Energy Agency (IAEA) only to nuclear facilities it designates as being for purely civil purposes. India is now also authorized to import uranium, the lack of which had long stalled the progress of its nuclear program.

Nuclear recognition will bring enormous political benefits to the Indian government. Naturally, the deal is popular with domestic constituencies, which were already well disposed toward the United States. (In 2005, a poll by the Pew Research Center found that 71 percent of Indian respondents had a favorable view of the United States — the highest percentage among the 15 leading nations polled.) Singh supporters in the National Congress Party have downplayed the importance of the few obligations that India has undertaken, such as the commitment to voluntarily subject some of its nuclear facilities to inspections, a routine practice in all the other recognized nuclear states, including the United States. Criticism from the opposition BJP (Bharatiya Janata Party) has been narrow and technical — and it probably reflects the BJP's chagrin that the agreement was secured while the National Congress Party was in power. Although some members of the marginal Left Front parties have criticized the terms of the deal, their complaints have smacked of antiquated NAM politics, and the detractors are unlikely to be able to block the deal's approval by the Indian Parliament. Barring the imposition of new conditions by the U.S. Congress, the deal is thus likely to sail through the legislature in India.

American critics of the deal contend that India's past behavior does not warrant this free pass. They argue that Washington should at least ask India to stop making fissile material for bombs, as the NPT's acknowledged nuclear powers have already done, rather than wait for the proposed fissile Material Cutoff Treaty to come into existence. Others contend that India should be required to place more nuclear facilities under IAEA safeguards, to prevent any diversion of fissile materials from its nuclear power program to its nuclear weapons program. Still others want India to sign the Comprehensive Test Ban Treaty rather than be allowed merely to abide by a unilateral moratorium on further underground testing, as it has done since 1998.

The Indian government, backed by Indian public opinion, has resisted all attempts to impose such technical constraints on its nuclear arsenal. So far, the U.S. government has effectively supported New Delhi's position by insisting that the India deal is not an arms control treaty but a broader strategic agreement. The Bush administration has described the nuclear issue as the "basic irritant" in U.S.-Indian relations and has argued that once the issue is out of the way, India will become a responsible stakeholder in the nonproliferation regime, jettison its vestigial NAM posturing, take a more normal place in the diplomatic world — and become a strategic partner of the United States.

COLLATERAL DAMAGE

The most serious charge against the deal is that Washington, by recognizing India's de facto nuclear status and effectively rewarding noncompliance, hurt the integrity of the nonproliferation regime. There is no question that such an abrupt reversal of U.S. policy was a blow to nonproliferation efforts, but the damage is manageable and will not affect the most worrisome near-term cases.

To begin with, the impact of the Bush-Singh deal on so-called rogue states is likely to be minimal. It is safe to assume that as North Korea's Kim Jong Il calculates how far he can go with his nuclear breakout, he hardly worries about the internal consistency of the NPT regime (much like Saddam Hussein, who eventually stopped paying it any heed). Pyongyang's governing ideology is not communism so much as a fanatical embrace of autarky and self-reliance, which seems to include open defiance of international norms such as nonproliferation. North Korea's tolerance for ostracism by the international community is legendary. Stopping its nuclear program — by measures short of war — would require tough and focused diplomacy, with incentives and sanctions, in which the NPT would play little part.

The India deal's impact on Iran, another country driving for nuclear power status, will also be modest. Tehran's ongoing cat-and-mouse game with the IAEA, the United States, the United Kingdom, France, and Germany suggests that Iranian leaders have at least a smidgen of sensitivity to international opinion. India's nuclear recognition may give Tehran a new talking point — if India gets a free pass, why not Iran? — but that is about it. Iran's nuclear program, like that of North Korea, has deep roots in the country's sense of insecurity and its national pride, and these factors matter far more than the NPT. Besides, because Tehran continues to claim that it seeks only nuclear power, not nuclear weapons, it would be hard-pressed to point to India as a relevant precedent.

The deal's impact will mostly be felt among two other groups of countries: states that are not rogues but have flirted or continue to flirt with nuclear status ("the in-betweens") and states that faithfully uphold the rules, whether or not they have nuclear weapons ("the stalwarts"). South Africa, Argentina, Brazil, Ukraine, Kazakhstan, Belarus, South Korea, Taiwan, and, more recently, Libya have all been in-betweens at some point. Although they eventually forwent nuclear weapons for reasons specific to their own circumstances, all of them were in some way swayed by the fear that they would suffer lasting international ostracism if they flouted the NPT regime. With India's sweet deal now suggesting that forgiveness comes to proliferators who wait long enough, some states might be tempted to stray. (Brazil, which is now trying to enrich uranium, comes to mind.)

Curiously, the India deal might have the greatest effect on the stalwarts of nonproliferation, including the five states that are formally entitled to hold nuclear weapons under the NPT. Not only do these countries play an important role in confronting rogue states and keeping in-betweens in bounds; they also provide direct technical support to the nonproliferation regime by denying critical exports to governments that infringe the NPT's rules. The Nuclear Suppliers Group, in particular, coordinates controls on exports by nations with advanced nuclear power technology. The nsg was the result of a U.S. initiative, and the United States has long helped prevent the group's members from giving in to pressure from their nuclear industries to sell technology more liberally abroad. Now that Washington has suddenly changed its policy, the nsg states might consider themselves free to pick and choose when they will and will not apply nonproliferation rules. The Chinese could be tempted to make deals with Pakistan, the Russians with Iran, and the Europeans with everyone else.

Limiting the damage caused by the Bush-Singh deal must therefore center on managing the in-between and stalwart states. (Developing a plan for doing so would have been a logical part of the U.S. diplomatic initiative toward India in 2005-6, yet the Bush administration failed to devise one.) Such an effort should be possible, and the U.S. government's belated consultations with the leaders of such states have had promising results. In fact, most of the countries whose adherence to the NPT regime remains critical will wind up supporting the deal or at least acquiescing in it, for three reasons. First, they tend to accept Washington's arguments that New Delhi's possession of nuclear weapons is an irreversible fact and that India has controlled the transfer of sensitive technology responsibly — there has apparently been no Indian Abdul Qadeer Khan (known as A. Q. Khan, he ran a black-market nuclear supply ring from Pakistan). Second, India is not a rogue state but a stable democracy that is likely to play a large and constructive role in the global order in the years to come. Third, India's 30 years in the penalty box, which long exacted a heavy price from New Delhi in terms of both prestige and technology, should be sufficient to establish that adherents to the nonproliferation regime are serious about punishing those who infringe its norms. Such arguments have won over many members of the nonproliferation community, notably Mohamed ElBaradei, the IAEA director general and a Nobel Peace Prize laureate. Although the Bush-Singh deal has caused some grumbling within the NPT regime, a revolt of its members or the regime's collapse is not likely. The damage to nonproliferation will ultimately be limited.

THE REAL DEAL

Just as the deal's critics have exaggerated its costs to the nonproliferation regime, its proponents have exaggerated — or misstated — its benefits. The Bush administration claims, for example, that the India deal will require New Delhi to improve its laws and procedures for controlling exports or diversions of sensitive nuclear technology. But India already is bound to exert such controls under the U.S.-sponsored un Security Council Resolution 1540. Moreover, Washington is touting better compliance as a plus of the deal, even as it lauds India's apparently solid record of controlling nuclear exports — effectively trying to argue the point both ways.

Bush administration spokespeople have also defended the deal as critical to preventing India's economic rise from posing a threat to the world's oil security and to the environment. Both New Delhi and Washington want India to be able to satisfy its huge population's spiking energy needs — which are projected to grow fourfold within 25 years (faster than the country's gdp is expected to increase) — without aggravating its dependence on oil from the Middle East or excessively contributing to pollution and global warming. Nuclear power can play a part in helping India address these problems, but it will not make a critical difference. It can do little to slake the thirst of the principal oil-consuming sector in India — transportation — because cars and trucks do not run off the electrical grid and will not for a long time. Electricity in India will be mostly produced by coal-burning power plants for the foreseeable future; even under the most extravagant projections, nuclear plants will provide less than ten percent of India's electricity. (Today, they produce only three percent.) Burning coal more cheaply and more cleanly would do more for India's economy and the environment than would expanding the country's nuclear power capacity.

The real benefits of the India deal for Washington lie in the significant gains, especially in terms of security, that the broader strategic relationship could deliver down the road. For one thing, with New Delhi as an informal ally, Washington should expect to have India's help in curbing Iran's nuclear ambitions, even if India's assistance would risk compromising its friendly relations with Iran. There have been some promising signs. At meetings of the IAEA Board of Governors over the past year, India joined the United States and its European partners in finding that Iran had violated its NPT obligations and then in referring the matter to the un Security Council — two welcome signs that India supports the international campaign to curb Iran's nuclear ambitions. Whether India actively cooperates with the United States against Iran or persists in offering rhetorical support for the spread of nuclear-fuel-cycle activities (uranium enrichment and plutonium reprocessing) will be the clearest test of whether nuclear recognition "brings India into the mainstream" of nonproliferation policy, as the Bush administration predicts will happen.

The United States will also want India's assistance in dealing with a range of dangerous contingencies involving Pakistan. Pakistan's stock of nuclear weapons, along with Russia's, is the focus of urgent concern about nuclear terrorism. Whatever version of the A. Q. Khan story one believes — that the Pakistani government and military were unaware of Khan's activities or that they permitted them — its moral is worrisome. It suggests that terrorists could buy or steal the materials (namely, plutonium or enriched uranium) necessary to building nuclear bombs from Pakistan thanks to diversion by radical elements in the Pakistani elite or if the Musharraf regime crumbles. And if an incident were to originate in Pakistan, the United States would want to respond in concert with as many regional players as possible, including India.

Such risks are still difficult for Washington and New Delhi to acknowledge publicly, however, as both governments try to maintain a delicately balanced relationship with Islamabad. The United States needs Pervez Musharraf's support to search for Osama bin Laden and other terrorists on Pakistani territory, prevent the radicalization of Pakistan's population, and stabilize Afghanistan; it can ill afford to be perceived as tilting too far toward India. The Indian government, for its part, also seems intent on improving its relations with Islamabad. But it is still reeling from the fallout of the bombings on the Indian Parliament last year, which have been attributed to Pakistani terrorists. And India, too, could be a victim of loose nukes in the event of disorder in Pakistan.

Down the road, the United States might also want India to serve as a counterweight to China. No one wishes to see China and the United States fall into a strategic contest, but no one can rule out the possibility of such a competition. The evolution of U.S.-Chinese relations will depend on the attitudes of China's younger generation and new leaders, on Chinese and U.S. policies, and on unpredictable events such as a possible crisis over Taiwan. For now, the United States and India are largely eager to improve trade with China and are careful not to antagonize it. But it is reasonable for them to want to hedge against any downturn in relations with China by improving their relations with each other. Neither government wishes to talk publicly, let alone take actions now, to advance this shared interest, but they very well might in the future.

The India deal could also bring the United States more direct benefits, militarily and economically. Washington expects the intensification of military-to-military contacts and hopes eventually to gain the cooperation of India in disaster-relief efforts, humanitarian interventions, peacekeeping missions, and postconflict reconstruction efforts, including even operations not mandated by or commanded by the United Nations, operations in which India has historically refused to participate. Judging from the evolution of the United States' security partnerships with states in Europe and Asia, the anticipation of such joint action could lead over time to joint military planning and exercises, the sharing of intelligence, and even joint military capabilities. U.S. military forces may also seek access to strategic locations through Indian territory and perhaps basing rights there. Ultimately, India could even provide U.S. forces with "over-the-horizon" bases for contingencies in the Middle East.

On the economic front, as India expands its civilian nuclear capacity and modernizes its military, the United States stands to gain preferential treatment for U.S. industries. The India deal theoretically creates economic opportunities in the construction of nuclear reactors and other power infrastructure in India. These should not be exaggerated, however. The United States would have to secure preferences at the expense of Russian and European competitors and would need to persuade India's scientific community to focus its nuclear power expansion on conventional reactors rather than on the type of exotic and expensive technologies (for example, fast-breeder reactors) it currently favors. India is also expected to increase the scale and sophistication of its military, in part by purchasing weapons systems from abroad. The United States can reasonably anticipate some preferential treatment for U.S. vendors. Early discussions have concerned the sale of f-16 and f-18 tactical aircraft and p-3c maritime surveillance aircraft.

THE ONLY WAY TO GO

Of course, there can be no guarantees that the United States will benefit from India's partnership in these matters. As befits a great nation on its way to global prominence, India will have its own opinions about how best to live up to the deal — or not, as the case may be — while pursuing its own interests.

Proponents of the India deal have compared it to President Richard Nixon's opening to China in 1971. It is true that both overtures were bold moves based on a firm foundation of mutual interest and that both were leaps of trust rather than shrewd bargains. But there are sobering differences between the two fledgling partnerships. Nixon and Mao Zedong shared a clear and present enemy — the Soviet Union — not an uncertain set of possible future dangers, as do Bush and Singh now. More important, India today, unlike Mao's China, is a democracy. No government in New Delhi can turn on a dime in regard to a policy followed for decades or suddenly commit India to a broad set of actions that support U.S. interests; only a profound and probably slow evolution in the views of India's elites could produce such changes. India's diplomats and civil servants are notorious for adhering to independent positions regarding the world order, economic development, and nuclear security. The architects of the India deal have suggested that such habits will quickly yield in the face of the United States' recent accommodations on the nuclear issue. But their expectation is naive. Americans may see Washington's turnabout on long-standing U.S. nonproliferation policy as a serious concession, but Indians view it as a belated and much deserved acknowledgment. The United States could come to regret having played its trump card so early.

Although the deal's critics are understandably worried, they risk expressing their concern in counterproductive ways, most notably by seeking to rebalance the U.S.-India deal by imposing additional constraints on India's nuclear program. Preventing an arms race between India, China, and Pakistan is an important goal, but it is best pursued in nontechnical ways. New Delhi has stated its intention to pursue a "minimum deterrent" — not an all-out arms race — and the Bush administration should hold it to this pledge.

Rather than pull back, the Bush administration and Congress should move forward. A better approach than subtracting benefits from India's side of the ledger would be to add benefits to the United States' side so as to ensure that Washington will obtain what it rightly expects of New Delhi: not just nuclear restraint and a new level of support in handling potential proliferators such as Iran, but a broad strategic realignment. It is too soon to tell whether the United States' goals are shared by India and whether they will be reached. But the United States can do no better to serve its interests than to state its high expectations of this strategic partnership and then give it a real chance of being fully realized.

ASHTON B. CARTER is Professor of Science and International Affairs at Harvard's Kennedy School of Government and was Assistant Secretary of Defense in the first Clinton administration.

India's Democratic Challenge

Ashutosh Varshney

Indian traders protest against a tax reform in Amritsar, March 30, 2005.

CHARTING A NEW PATH

India is attempting a transformation few nations in modern history have successfully managed: liberalizing the economy within an established democratic order. It is hard to escape the impression that market interests and democratic principles are uneasily aligned in India today. The two are not inherently contradictory, but there are tensions between them that India's leaders will have to manage carefully.

Students of political economy know that market-based policies meant to increase the efficiency of the aggregate economy frequently generate short-term dislocations and resentment. In a democratic polity, this resentment often translates at the ballot box into a halt or a reversal of pro-market reforms. In the West, such tensions have remained moderate for at least three reasons: universal suffrage came to most Western democracies only after the Industrial Revolution, which meant that the poor got the right to vote only after those societies had become relatively rich; a welfare state has attended to the needs of low-income segments of the population; and the educated and the wealthy have tended to vote more than the poor.

The Indian experience is different on all three counts. India adopted universal suffrage at the time of independence, long before the transition to a modern industrialized economy began. The country does not have an extensive welfare system, although it has made a greater effort to create one of late. And, defying democratic theory, a great participatory upsurge has marked Indian politics, a phenomenon that is only beginning to be understood by scholars and observers: since the early 1990s, India's plebeian orders have participated noticeably more in elections than its upper and middle classes. In fact, the recent wisdom about Indian elections turns standard democratic theory on its head: the lower the caste, income, and education of an Indian, the greater the odds that he will vote. The ruling United Progressive Alliance (UPA), a coalition with the Indian National Congress at its core, counts on the lower social orders as its most important voting bloc.

India's development experience is also likely to be distinct from East Asia's. South Korea and Taiwan embraced universal-franchise democracy only in the late 1980s and the mid-1990s, two decades after their economic upturn began. Other economically successful countries in the region, such as China and Singapore, have yet to become liberal democracies. Periodic renewals of mass mandates through the ballot box are not necessary in authoritarian countries, but they are in India. Democratic politics partly explains why, for example, privatization has gone so slowly in India compared to in China. In India, workers have unions and political parties to protect their interests. In China, labor leaders who resist job losses due to privatization are tried and jailed for treason and subversion, something entirely inconceivable in India's democracy.

So far, the reform process of the last 15 years has had positive results: by most conventional standards, India's economy is booming. After registering a 6 percent average annual growth rate for nearly a quarter century, the Indian economy has picked up even greater speed. Over the last three years, it has grown at over 8 percent annually, and forecasts for the next few years promise more of the same. Investment as a proportion of GDP has been steadily climbing, exceeding 30 percent lately and raising hopes of an investment boom like that which propelled East Asia's economies. Total foreign direct investment for the current financial year is likely to exceed $10 billion (compared with $100 million in 1990-91) and is rising. Exports are growing at a fast clip, with India's trade-to-GDP ratio more than doubling in 2006 from its 1991 level of 15 percent. The manufacturing sector, like the services sector, is becoming a key engine of the economy, and India's world-class information technology sector continues to grow exponentially, employing less than 0.5 percent of India's labor force but producing about 5 percent of the nation's GDP. Corporate dynamism, rarely associated with India in the past, is fast changing the business map of the country, and India, in turn, is rapidly becoming an important factor in the global strategies of the world's leading international firms.

But how long will the boom last? That depends on India's democratic politics, where economic growth has fed pressures for the redistribution of wealth. Mainstream economic theory about markets and human welfare holds that markets will benefit all in the long run. But long-term perspectives do not come naturally to democratic politicians, who must focus on winning elections in the short term. Accordingly, a low-income democracy such as India must nurture the energies of its entrepreneurs while, in the short run, responding to the reservations and resentments of the masses. How well India's politicians walk this tightrope will determine the outcome of the country's economic transformation.

HOW IT ALL BEGAN

In keeping with the prevailing theories in development planning after World War II, in the 1950s India opted for a centrally planned economy with a closed trade regime, heavy state intervention, and an industrial policy that emphasized import substitution. This pro-state and trade-pessimistic development model was characterized by three sets of controls: internal, external, and those relating to the special role of the public sector. The internal regulatory regime heavily employed investment and production controls through an infamous industrial licensing system that regulated aspects of economic activity as varied as plant capacity, output prices, the quantity of capital, the quantity and type of inputs, technology, and the sectors or industries that were required to be reserved for small-scale investors. A host of tariff and quantitative controls were created to protect "infant" domestic producers from external competition. And the public sector was allowed extraordinary authority over the commanding heights of the economy, including the steel, power, telecommunications, and heavy machinery industries.

It was within this thicket of protectionist policies that, in July 1991, reformers in the Congress-led government began to push hard for economic transformation under the looming prospect of a balance-of-payments crisis. Some reforms had already been put in place by Prime Minister Rajiv Gandhi in the mid-1980s, but the big thrust came in 1991-92 as a result of that looming crisis. The finance minister at the time, Manmohan Singh (currently India's prime minister), argued that the macroeconomic stabilization necessary to stave off a crisis was not enough; it had to be reinforced by reforms to make the decision-making and operational environment of firms more market-based. Thus began a series of incremental reforms, which the BJP (Bharatiya Janata Party) continued after it came to power at the head of the National Democratic Alliance (NDA) coalition in 1998.

In some areas of economic policy, progress has been dramatic; in others, little or no progress has been made. India's investment regime has undergone the most extensive reform. The industrial licensing system has been almost completely abolished. Firms are free to make decisions about investment, pricing, and technology. Only three industries — rail transport, military aircraft and ships, and atomic energy generation

— are now reserved for the public sector (instead of 18 in the past), and these, too, are beginning to welcome collaboration with private industry on some activities. The rules governing foreign investment have been substantially liberalized. Complete foreign private ownership in a large number of industries, and majority private ownership in most industries, is allowed, excluding airlines, insurance companies, and the major retail trade. And since 1992, foreign institutions have been allowed to buy and sell stocks in Indian firms. Indian companies, in turn, are now free to issue equity in foreign markets.

A great deal of progress has also been made in reforming India's trade and exchange-rate regimes. India now has a flexible exchange-rate system. The average tariff on imports has come down from over 100 percent to just under 25 percent today, and all quota restrictions on trade have been lifted.

Progress has been limited, however, in five areas: fiscal policy, privatization, small-scale industry, agriculture, and labor law. India's fiscal deficits continue to be high. Large agricultural subsidies for inputs, grain, and power are some of the main contributors to these deficits, and almost every attempt at lowering the subsidies has been met by political protests on behalf of farmers. A start toward privatization was made in 2001, but unions and some political parties have vigorously resisted it. To help millions of small producers, many manufactured products continue to be reserved for "small-scale investors" (a status that caps investment at $250,000 per industrial unit), although in 2001, garments, toys, shoes, and auto components were finally removed from the reserved list. No proposal for a complete dereservation of all industries has yet been seriously entertained, hampering the ability of many Indian companies to compete with their counterparts in other developing countries, notably China. And labor laws have not been reformed, meaning that no company operating in India employing more than 100 workers can fire any without government permission — and permission is almost never granted.

WHAT'S IN IT FOR ME?

Who has really reaped the benefits of the reforms? India has always had a small number of affluent individuals, symbolized by its maharajahs and business tycoons. Now the proportion of the population that is rich has undoubtedly increased, and a substantial middle class has emerged, numbering anywhere between 200 million and 250 million, depending on the measure used. In what is fast becoming an emblem of the rising Indian middle class, six million cell phones are bought every month, making India the fastest-growing market for cell phones in the world. Businesses in the cities are booming, five-star hotels are fully booked, airports are clogged, and flights are regularly oversold.

At the same time, the begging bowls and emaciated faces of malnourished children, historically the most visible signs of mass deprivation on the streets of Indian cities, have not appreciably receded. Poverty has clearly decreased since the reforms began, when roughly a third of the country was below the poverty line, but close to a fourth of the population still lives on less than $1 a day, much to the disappointment of many reformers who had expected a faster decline. The nation's growth on the whole has not been employment-intensive.

Where inequality is concerned, two issues are hotly debated: urban-rural imbalances and the interpersonal income distribution. Over the last ten years, India's economy as a whole may have grown at more than 6 percent per annum, but agriculture, which still supports, fully or in part, around 60 percent of the country's population, has grown at a mere 2.2 percent annually. To be sure, growth rates in agriculture are rarely as high as those in manufacturing and services, but the gap in India has become noticeably large. It is now widely accepted throughout India that urban-rural inequalities have grown since the reforms began.

The statistics on interpersonal income distribution are less conclusive, partly because such data tend to be highly unreliable for developing countries. But opinion polls make it quite clear that a very large proportion of the population believes the reforms have mostly benefited "the rich," which in the public's eye includes the middle class in India. The largest-ever sample drawn for election analysis in India, by the National Election Study (NES) in 2004, showed that those who believed the reforms had benefited only the affluent outnumbered those who thought the reforms had benefited the whole nation; the more one climbs down the social ladder, the greater the former belief. Upper-caste respondents were nearly split on the question, but a wide margin of respondents lower on the socioeconomic scale — especially ex-untouchables, Muslims, and other underprivileged groups — believed the reforms had mainly benefited the rich. The survey results also showed that those who believed the reforms had benefited the whole country voted in large numbers for the BJP-led NDA, whereas those who thought the rich were the only beneficiaries voted disproportionately for Congress and its allies.

These perceptions may not necessarily match reality. It is particularly unclear how the masses interpret the term "reforms." The NES polls focused on only one side of the economic reforms by asking questions such as whether the number of employees in government service should be reduced, whether public-sector businesses should be privatized, and whether foreign companies should be allowed to freely enter the Indian economy. But other questions, reflecting a fuller view, were not asked: Should import tariffs be dropped further so as to allow for the greater availability of cheap consumer goods? Should the rules regulating how banks and post offices function be made easier and more transparent? Should big companies continue to be protected by the government, or should new and smaller companies be allowed to emerge and compete with them? Should the government interfere less in regard to where and at what price to sell grain? Should loss-making government firms be privatized if a substantial proportion of their proceeds could be reserved for public health and education? It is unclear how the masses would respond to a complete picture of reforms and, accordingly, whether the underprivileged segments of society would support deeper reforms.

Whatever better statistics may finally prove, mass perceptions matter in politics. And the overall picture that emerges from current perceptions of the reform process is one of two Indias: an India of booming businesses, growing cities, and a vibrant middle class and an India of struggling agriculture, poor villages, and a large lower class. The rising tide produced by economic liberalization appears to have lifted many boats, but not all. Too large a segment of the population feels ignored by the new economic policies. The current Indian government has thus unsurprisingly made two objectives clear regarding the economy: keep growth strong, but make it more inclusive through public policy. Leaving markets entirely to themselves is not politically feasible in a low-income democracy such as India.

THE DEMOCRATIC CONSTRAINT

There are two aspects to the challenge reformers face within India's democratic context: perceptions of the reforms to date and the short-term pain likely to accompany the deeper reforms to come. The economic reforms undertaken thus far have not been those that would directly affect the lives of India's poor masses, and this has fed their resentment against the reforms, which they believe have only benefited the upper and middle classes. The employment effect of the reforms — while significant in skill-and capital-intensive sectors — has not been substantial enough throughout the economy to ameliorate this resentment. Further pro-market reforms — the large-scale privatization of public-sector firms, the implementation of a hire-and-fire employment policy, changes in agricultural policy, radical changes in small-industry sectors, and the drastic reduction of fiscal deficits — will undoubtedly have a direct effect on the lives of the masses, but the long-term benefits of these reforms for India's lower classes are likely to be accompanied by considerable short-term pain. The electoral consequence of this likelihood has meant that Indian politicians have proceeded gingerly on these deep reforms, embracing instead those that directly affect the elite.

It is therefore helpful to think of India's reform politics as following two tracks: what may be termed elite politics and mass politics. This distinction is absolutely crucial in understanding India's reform dynamics. In India, the elite consists mainly of English-speaking upper-caste and urban citizens. Elite politics in India typically takes place in the upper realms of the public sphere: in the interactions between business and government and in the dealings between New Delhi and foreign governments and international financial institutions. Outside government, the upper end of the public sphere includes English-language newspapers and television and the Internet. To the elite, India's economic future has never looked brighter.

But India's mass politics is dancing to a different tune. It is the plebeian social orders that make up this political constituency. Streets and the ballot box are the primary sites of the mass politics, and voting, demonstrations, and riots its major manifestations. Economic reforms are viewed by the poor masses as a revolution primarily for everyone but them. Economists may recommend a more passionate embrace of neoliberalism as a solution to India's poverty, but the poor appear to have plenty of reservations about economic reforms — and they have voting clout in India's democracy.

One can therefore see why elite-oriented reforms (making investment in real estate easier, deregulating the stock market, liberalizing civil aviation) have continued under the current government in India, whereas more radical reforms (changing labor laws, privatizing public enterprises, eliminating agricultural subsidies) have stalled. The latter have run into what might be called a mass-politics constraint. As a result, it is now customary to argue that India has a "strong consensus on weak reforms."

Three factors are typically critical in determining whether any particular policy enters the arena of mass politics: the number of people affected by the policy, how organized those people are, and whether the effect is direct and immediate or indirect and over a long time horizon. The more people affected by a policy choice, the more organized they are, and the more direct the policy's effects, the more likely it is that a policy will generate mass concern.

By this logic, some economic issues are more likely to arouse mass opposition than others. Inflation, for example, quickly becomes a contentious matter in mass politics because it affects most segments of the population. A financial meltdown has a similar effect, because a large number of banks and firms collapse and millions of people lose their jobs. In comparison, stock markets directly concern mainly shareholders, whose numbers are not likely to be large or very organized in a poor country such as India. As a result, short of a financial collapse, stock-market issues rarely, if ever, enter the fray of mass politics in less developed countries. Ethnocommunal conflicts, not economic issues, have until now driven mass politics in India. The consequences of ethnic cleavages and ethnically based policies tend to be obvious to most people, and ethnic groups are either already organized or can organize quickly.

Unlike the economic reforms already implemented, the deeper changes that many economists argue India needs for long-term growth are, by directly affecting the masses — and affecting them negatively to begin with — likely to arouse the passions of the lower class. In India's highly adversarial democracy, political leaders will continue to find it extremely difficult to stake their political fortunes on economic reforms that are expected to cause substantial short-term dislocations and are likely to produce rewards only in the long term. Meanwhile, identity politics — especially caste-based affirmative action and Hindu-Muslim relations — continue to occupy the center of the political stage, consuming substantial political attention and determining electoral fortunes. As a result, what is of great consequence to mainstream economists is of secondary importance to politicians, who prefer predictability in and control over their political universe.

THE SOURCES OF CONGRESS' CONDUCT

Nonetheless, economic reform has been growing in importance in India's electoral politics over the last decade. In a survey of mass political attitudes in India conducted in 1996, only 19 percent of the electorate reported any knowledge of the economic reforms that had been implemented, even though the reforms had been in existence since 1991. In the countryside, where more than 70 percent of Indians then lived, only about 14 percent had heard of the reforms (compared with 32 percent of voters in cities). Nearly 66 percent of college graduates were aware of the dramatic changes in economic policy, compared with only 7 percent of the illiterate poor. (In contrast, close to 75 percent of the electorate — urban and rural, literate and illiterate, rich and poor — reported knowing of the demolition of the mosque in Ayodhya in 1992, and 87 percent took a stand on caste-ased affirmative action.) Economic reforms were a nonissue in the 1996 and 1998 parliamentary elections. In the 1999 elections, the biggest reformers either lost or did not campaign on pro-market platforms.

The 2004 parliamentary elections that returned Congress to power, however, hinted at the rising importance of economic reforms to India's mass politics. In dramatic contrast to 1996, when a mere 19 percent of voters even knew of the reforms implemented up to that point, in 2004, according to the NES election survey, over 85 percent expressed clear judgments of them — and the main verdict was that the reforms were primarily elite-serving.

To be sure, economic issues were still not the main reason for the NDA's election defeat in 2004. Its loss had more to do with regional politics and party alliances. Coalition partners in India tend to be regional parties that are strong only in one or two states (India is made up of 28 states), and national parliamentary elections consequently depend heavily on how regional parties in the large states perform. In two significant states, Andhra Pradesh and Tamil Nadu, the regional allies of the BJP did disastrously. The key issues in these and other states were more regional in nature, rather than related to national or economic issues. The way coalition arithmetic translates to parliamentary seats further undermined the NDA. In a first-past-the-post parliamentary system such as India's, parliamentary seats are not allocated in strict proportionality to ballots won. In the 2004 election, although the BJP-led NDA trailed the Congress-centered UPA by a mere 0.6 percent of the overall popular vote, the latter won a 33-seat advantage (222 seats as opposed to 189 for the NDA).

Nevertheless, the 2004 electoral results suggest that the pressure on politicians to make reforms relevant to the masses is rising, even if it has not yet reached a critical threshold. Resentment of reforms may well prove decisive in the next election, due by 2009. The increasing mass disaffection with the economic reforms helps explain the economic policies of the current government. The 2004 election led Congress' strategists to the conclusion that the party needed to focus its program on the lower and middle echelons of society, which have become the party's main constituency. The Indian government today has some of the ace reformers of post-1991 India, including Prime Minister Singh, Finance Minister Palaniappan Chidambaram, and the economic planning czar, Montek Singh Ahluwalia. But two of its biggest initiatives have been distinctly antimarket: the National Rural Employment Guarantee Act and the extension of affirmative action in higher education. The first measure, passed by Parliament in August 2005, guarantees every unemployed rural household that each year at least one of its members will get 100 days of work. (The scheme, currently in operation in 200 districts, is slated to be extended to the entire country over the next two years.) The second reform reserves 27 percent of the spaces in government-aided institutions of higher education, including the Indian Institutes of Technology and the Indian Institutes of Management, for the "other backward castes."

The UPA is dependent on the left for its parliamentary majority, but this is only part of the story that explains these antimarket measures. More germane is the character of the constituency that now forms the main pillar of Congress' support. Until the mid-1980s, Congress was an umbrella party drawing substantial support from all segments of society, but the BJP and its coalition have since come to represent the socially privileged, the educated, and high-income groups. The upper segments of society constitute no more than 25-30 percent of India's population. Given the kind of support they have given the BJP and its allies over the last ten years, getting them back under the Congress umbrella is not as electorally promising as consolidating gains in the much larger middle and lower segments — especially given the latter's higher rates of voter turnout. It is therefore no surprise that targeted antimarket interventions on behalf of the lower social orders form the centerpiece of Congress' new political strategy.

The BJP, although less constrained than Congress, cannot entirely escape these pressures either. If the BJP is to regain and hold on to power, it will have to resolutely move down the socioeconomic ladder for support, something it has already begun doing. Even a BJP-led government would therefore be expected to push a program of targeted state interventions. Unless the upper segments of Indian society regroup and begin to participate in elections more, they will dwindle as a power in electoral politics, in spite of their control of the press. And until the middle class becomes a majority of the population and starts to participate more vigorously in elections, the plebeian pressures will remain in politics and India's economic reforms will continue to have an ostrich-like character: moving ahead on policies directly affecting the elite but lagging behind on policies that directly, and negatively, hit the masses.

A TORTOISE TO CHINA'S HARE?

Although the mass-politics constraint on India's economic reforms is now beginning to emerge, it need not be a reason for alarm. India's democracy is a short-term constraint but a long-term asset for pro-market reformers. The stability of Indian democracy is not in question. Whichever coalition of parties comes to power, reforms on the whole will continue. Since 1991, four coalitions have ruled India, and none has departed from the path of reforms. The differences have been those of degree and pace, not direction. There is no going back to the old statist economic regime. A middle class with rising incomes that boasts 200 million to 250 million people will continue to attract investor attention. The nation's remarkable human capital at the middle-class level will also draw investors. Moreover, there will continue to be economic reforms largely impervious to the constraints of mass politics: changes to the financial sector, greater rationalization of tax structures, further simplification of investment rules, the liberalization of real estate development, and the modernization of airports.

The mass-politics constraint does mean, however, that reformers in India will have to juggle two separate tasks in the short to medium term: continuing reforms in the elite-oriented sectors and responding to mass needs through further antimarket state interventions. And if market-oriented economic reforms are to be embraced in areas directly relevant to the masses, politicians will have to answer the following questions: How will the privatization of public enterprises, the reform of labor laws, and the lifting of agricultural subsidies benefit the masses? And how long will the benefits take to trickle down? All of these reforms are likely to enhance mass welfare in the long run. Therefore, for democratic politicians, this problem will effectively mean taking measures such as reserving a substantial proportion of the proceeds from privatization for public health and primary education, constructing safety nets for workers as labor laws are reformed, and coming up with a plan for a second green revolution in agriculture in return for drawing down the current huge agricultural subsidies. The last one, in particular, will require both opening up agriculture to market forces and greater public investment in irrigation, agricultural research, and rural infrastructure and education.

But although democratic politics makes life challenging for reformers, it could also turn out to be a huge benefit in the long run. Consider the counterexample of China. It is hard to believe that the single-party state in China will not eventually be challenged from within the existing party structure, by the burgeoning middle class, or by rising peasant and labor unrest. The attendant economic consequences of a political transition or upheaval in China are uncertain. In contrast, democratic India has a viable solution to the problem of political transition: the party, or coalition of parties, that wins elections will run the government. Transition rules are now deeply institutionalized in India, and long-term political stability is a virtual certainty.

The long-term benefits of India's democracy are enhanced by its rule of law and advanced capital markets. Firm-level innovation is normally facilitated by copyright laws and the rewards that capital markets bring to innovative firms. The rule of law continues to evade China, and its capital markets are heavily government-dominated. Who knows what will happen to China's economic progress when, faced with competitive pressure from lower-cost producers, it loses its comparative advantage in labor-intensive mass production. India's innovative firms and skilled labor, on the other hand, are already beginning to make a mark on the international scene — a trend that is likely to continue in the coming years.

Ashutosh Varshney is Professor of Political Science at the University of Michigan and the author of "Ethnic Conflict and Civic Life: Hindus and Muslims in India" and "Democracy, Development, and the Countryside: Urban-Rural Struggles in India."

The Promise of Modinomics

How the New Prime Minister Can Bring Back Growth

Arvind Panagariya

A construction site in New Delhi, November 20, 2013.

For the first time in India's modern history, a non–Congress Party outsider with no prior involvement in running the central government has won an absolute majority in the parliament. But as the euphoria associated with Narendra Modi's extraordinary election gives way to the duties of the office, the new prime minister must turn to the hard work of delivering the economic promises he made during the campaign. For Modi, that will raise three key questions: Is sustained rapid growth, which is essential for his development and employment plans, even feasible? If it is, what reforms should the government undertake now and in the longer run to achieve it? And what obstacles will he face in carrying out these reforms?

WHAT AILS INDIA?

Until the 2012 fiscal year, the Indian economy had grown at eight percent per year for nearly a decade. That track record busted apart the myth that democracy hinders economic growth — a common conclusion among many looking at the economic growth of authoritarian China, Singapore, Taiwan, and (in an earlier age) South Korea. Although policy mistakes have resulted in a sharp decline in India's growth rate to below five percent in the last two fiscal years, sustained policy reform could bring the country near-double-digit growth over the next two decades.

There are three reasons for this. First, throughout the last decade, India's national savings rate has been consistently at 30 percent of GDP or higher. Those savings guarantee that India has plenty of investible resources to grow the stock of capital, an important ingredient in growth. Second, demographically, India is young, and it is predicted to become even younger, with a healthy growth in population. It will not, therefore, face the labor shortages that have already hit many other economies, including China. In fact, the working population will rise as a proportion of the total population, which, in turn, could lead to a further increase in the savings rate. Finally, with a per-capita income of around only $1,500 per year, India still has vast room to catch up. It remains very far from the global productivity frontier and can grow rapidly as it races toward it.

So renewed Indian growth is possible. But how can the government promote it? That depends on what caused the recent downturn. The outgoing government's favorite explanation was that the global economy was weak. But closer examination points to domestic factors. In 2007–08, the economy grew 9.3 percent. In September 2008, the Lehman crisis hit. But it only mildly dented the Indian economy, forcing the growth rate down to 6.7 percent during 2008–09. In the following two years, the growth rate quickly returned to a higher level, averaging 8.75 percent. It is only in subsequent years, a period during which little has changed in the global economy, that growth rate has averaged just 4.6 percent.

The key to this sharp decline in growth is paralysis in the central government, which resulted from three factors. First, corruption scandals led to the jailing of several of top-level politicians and bureaucrats. That created gridlock; worried about the risk of being called out for corruption, officials prudentially put off making decisions. Second, the environment ministry inordinately delayed decisions on environmental clearances on projects worth more than a hundred billion dollars, adding to investors' woes. Finally, an ineffective prime minister's office slowed things down even more by failing to coordinate across ministries. (Most decisions in India require agreement among two or more ministries.)

BUDGET BREAKDOWN

The new government will need to overcome all three sources of paralysis. It must convince senior officers that they can make legitimate decisions without fear of future prosecution. It should appoint a pragmatic environment minister. (The current minister, although he fulfills that need, is in charge of the ministry only temporarily.) And it will have to build a strong prime minister's office to ensure that disagreements across ministries do not get in the way of policymaking.

Overcoming the deadlock in New Delhi must be complemented by the creation of healthier partnerships with India's state government. New Delhi must be readier to sign off on state initiatives to attract investors. And it must also get more serious about evaluating states' progress in meeting those goals in a timely fashion.

The final budget for 2014–15, which is due for presentation in early July and will replace the interim budget of the previous government, provides the Modi government with several opportunities. The first concerns the fiscal deficit. The interim budget pegs the deficit at 4.1 percent of GDP. But most commentators have argued that the figure was calculated based on overly optimistic assumptions about revenues and expenditures. On the revenue front, the calculation assumes a nominal GDP growth of 13.4 percent, which would translate into net tax revenue growth of 18 percent and proceeds from sales of equity in government-owned enterprises yielding more than $6 billion. On the expenditure side, the calculation assumes that subsidies to the poor will stay at the same level in nominal terms as last year. It also makes inadequate provision for recapitalization of banks. Because of these issues, one of India's leading banks, Kotak Mahindra, has noted that a "more realistic" deficit would be 4.5 percent of the GDP. The new government must thus ensure that the fiscal deficit does not exceed at 4.1 percent if the calculation in the interim budget is right and 4.5 percent if it is wrong.

The budget must also clearly signal the government's intention to restart reforms that stalled under the outgoing government, particularly liberalizing trade and lowering the top tariff rate on nonagricultural goods from ten percent to seven — and possibly even five — percent. It must also commit to completing the Goods and Services Tax (GST) reform within two years. That will entail replacing all indirect national-and state-level taxes with a uniform value-added tax on all goods and services except for essential items such as food and medicines, which will be exempted, and so-called demerit goods, such as alcohol and tobacco, which will be taxed at higher rates. It should also commit to completing the direct-tax simplification and codification within one year. That would involve clarifying tax rules and eliminating some exemptions, leaving less room for bureaucrats to use their own discretion on tax day. Finally, it must end retrospective taxation, which was introduced in 2012 to force a multinational into paying a tax that, according to a later supreme court ruling, it did not owe under the then-existing laws.

Next, it is important to improve the quality of expenditures. Two steps in particular are necessary. First, the government must cut subsidies to the middle class more aggressively than what the interim budget proposes. Petrol and diesel subsidies must be eliminated entirely within the current calendar year. Cooking gas subsidies should be reduced from 12 cylinders per year to six. The budget must also rebalance the composition of expenditures. In particular, it should shift toward capital expenditures — spending on highways, rural roads, ports, and electrical transmission and distribution lines. Overall, capital expenditures must rise from 1.76 percent of the GDP in the interim budget to two percent.

Beyond getting the deficit right, the Modi government must immediately address the health of public-sector banks, which suffer from exceedingly high levels of restructured and nonperforming loans. The government has three options: recapitalizing the banks using public funds, diluting government equity in the banks by pushing the banks to raise equity from the market, or closing some of the weakest banks or merging them with stronger banks. Given the fiscal constraints, it is unlikely that sufficient public funds will be available to rely on recapitalization alone. Nor would that be desirable, since the other two steps offer the opportunity to introduce additional banking sector reforms. The second option would create pressure for banking efficiency. And the third would promote consolidation of an industry that currently consists of one gigantic public sector bank and numerous much smaller banks.

Finally, the government must also use the budget to show its seriousness about giving the states greater legislative and fiscal power. To this end, it should commit to giving states timely permission to amend the laws within the purview of the Concurrent List of the Constitution, which consists of areas in which both the center and state can legislate. Normally, central laws in these areas take precedence over state laws, but the constitution allows the center to permit states to override its laws. The commitment would open the door for speedy labor and land-acquisition reform.

ON TRACK

Once the budget is complete, Modi must turn his attention to longer-term reforms. In our recent book, Why Growth Matters, CFR Senior Fellow Jagdish Bhagwati and I classified reforms into two categories: Track I and Track II. Track I reforms are those aimed at accelerating and sustaining employment-friendly growth, and Track II reforms are aimed at expanding social spending and making it more effective at combating poverty, illiteracy, and poor health.

Track I reforms require, first and foremost, the reform of India's labor laws. Highly rigid labor laws have made entrepreneurs terrified of hiring workers. Large corporations in India have systematically avoided entering low-skilled and labor-intensive sectors such as apparel, footwear, and electronics assembly — in all of which

China excels. Rather, they have chosen to invest in capital-intensive or skills-intensive industries, such as auto and auto parts, heavy machinery, chemicals, pharmaceuticals, telecommunications, and software. Even when operating in these sectors, they choose the most capital-and skilled-labor-intensive technologies and prefer hiring contract workers when they need low-skilled labor.

As a result, in the most labor-intensive economic sector, clothing and accessories, India's exports have been less in absolute terms than those of Bangladesh, a smaller country, for many years. They have now fallen below even tiny Vietnam. When compared to a country of its own size, China, India comes nowhere close: China exports more than ten times as much clothing and accessories. With nearly 500 million workers who are overwhelmingly unskilled or low skilled, this poor performance has meant that millions of workers are left without decent jobs. Instead, they have ended up in informal jobs in small shops or the domestic service and local transportation industries, receiving low pay.

Labor laws relating to industrial disputes, trade unions, apprenticeship, pensions, provident fund, and insurance have been the major obstacles to the entry of large formal-sector firms into low-skilled labor-intensive industries. Their effect has been reinforced by the absence of proper bankruptcy laws that would allow firms to close rapidly in case of failure. For example, in some case, firms with 100 or more workers are not permitted to make layoffs. There are plenty of horror stories about formal-sector firms existing for two years and then taking 20 years to wind down their operations.

With such onerous bankruptcy laws, firms hesitate to enter the formal sector in the first place. The result is a stagnant formal sector and a large and ever-growing informal sector. In the next five years, then, the Modi administration will need to think seriously about reforming India's labor laws and introducing mechanisms that permit the smooth exit of failing firms.

The government also needs to accelerate the development of highways, railways, and electricity. The previous government slowed down investment in these areas even as the economy grew at eight percent. The result is a huge deficit in infrastructure. Apart from building more and better infrastructure, the new government will need update its policies toward those sectors. Railways, currently state-run, should be broken up into four or five independent corporations. Those corporations could then compete for passengers and freight contracts. In the electricity sector, it is time to free up distribution companies and regulatory commissions in the states from political interference. In addition, modernization and economic transformation will also require the movement of workers from rural areas into urban industries and services. Cities, then, will also need cheap rental housing. Otherwise, the slums will only grow larger. India will also need to build many, many new cities.

In addition, the government must restart efforts to privatize public-sector enterprises, especially those engaged in such activities as manufacturing fertilizers, chemicals, and electronic and engineering goods. It makes particularly little sense to hold on to the enterprises that have been absorbing massive public revenues with little to show for it. But there is also a case to privatize profitable enterprises; research sponsored by the Program on Indian Economic Policies at Columbia University has shown that enterprises such as Bharat Aluminum Co., Ltd., and Hindustan Zinc, Ltd., which were privatized during the last BJP-led coalition government, have performed much better than those that were chosen for privatization but were not fully privatized.

Finally, successive governments have neglected to introduce any reforms whatsoever in higher education. As a result, higher education in India is governed by the same education policies that it created in the 1950s. The United Kingdom, whose framework India borrowed, reformed its system more than 20 years ago. The government's first step, then, should be to end its own bureaucratic stranglehold on the university system. It should abolish such government bodies as the University Grants Commission, which set and enforce standards for all Indian universities, and replace them with lighter regulatory bodies. These could set some basic norms. Any institution that can meet them should be allowed university status. Institutions must also be free to set their own tuition and teacher salaries.

HEALTH IS WEALTH

Alongside Track I, the government should also reform Track II policies, aimed at addressing the food security, employment, education, health, and wellness of the Indian public.

In previous years, rapid growth, which brought extra revenue, allowed the government to expand social spending. Unfortunately, that money has not been put to good use, mostly due to the poor design of social programs. Both the National Rural Employment Guarantee Act (NREGA) program and the food security program lose massive amounts of money to waste and corruption each year. Ideally, those programs should be replaced with cash transfers, which are shown to be more efficient. But since politics may not favor an outright switch to cash transfers, the government could give the bottom half of households that receive aid the option to choose between 10,000 rupees (almost $170) per year (to be given to the senior-most woman of the household) and access to NREGA and subsidized food. In all likelihood, most households will opt for cash. This will empower the households and help the government wind down the massive state-run distribution chains for subsidized goods and jobs.

There are Track II reforms for elementary education as well. The Right to Education Act of 2009 set norms for funding, teachers, and buildings and other physical infrastructure for each school. But the act set no expectations for learning. It also outlawed board examinations for students and mandated automatic promotions of pupils all the way up to the eighth grade. Because of that, the performance of teachers cannot be measured. In addition, teacher absenteeism is rampant. As a result, systematic surveys by Pratham, an Indian nongovernmental organization, show a sharp decline in the language and mathematical skills of children in public schools.

The problems in Indian public schools might be fixable, or they might not be. Either way, it is worth giving poor parents the same option that the richer parents have: access to private schools. It is sensible to start with education vouchers, which the parent can use for the school of his or her choice. If public schools can provide a decent education, the voucher money will flow right back to the government. If not, children will flee public schools and the government and teachers there might be forced to reconsider their lackadaisical attitudes.

As growth is restored and money begins to flow, the government will also need to address health policy in a major way, namely through its sanitation and vaccination programs. It will need to increase provision of modern toilet facilities. And Indian cities will need to do better job of waste management, drainage, and cleaning of sewage. These are activities that require state intervention since their benefits become automatically available to all without consumers, regardless of whether those consumers pay, and are therefore not profitable for private firms to undertake.

Perhaps not surprisingly, the government has performed very poorly in providing medical services to the public. Despite decades of efforts and investments to build up sub-centers, primary health centers, and community health centers in rural areas, 80 percent of patients who need outpatient care and 55 percent who need inpatient care go to private providers. And here, too, then the private sector needs to be given a greater role: the government should give poor households the money for day-to-day outpatient health care and insurance for episodic illnesses involving large expenditures, mainly surgeries requiring hospitalization.

MODI'S MANDATE

Modi wants to be transformational and intends to be in office for multiple terms. With him, India has an unusual opportunity to transform itself. If it can grow at ten percent per year over the next two decades — an entirely feasible ambition — by 2030 it will be the world's third-largest economy. By then, it would have also brought prosperity and modern amenities to a very large section of its population.

But the road to reform is not without obstacles. At least three roadblocks are worth noting. First, many within the BJP who now hold ministerial posts shared the previous government's general economic philosophy. They voted for nearly all legislation that the government passed. In other words, the new prime minister will need to bring them on board.

Second, Modi's coalition lacks a majority in the Rajya Sabha, the Indian Parliament's upper house. Therefore, it will have to skillfully negotiate with the Congress Party and other parties to pass major legislations. It also has two other options for pressing forward legislation. First, in areas covered by the Concurrent List of the Constitution, such as labor and land, it can transfer powers to reform laws to the states. Second, it can bring legislation to a joint meeting of both houses of the parliament. According to the Indian constitution, in such joint sessions, parliamentarians can pass laws with a simple majority.

Finally, India's judiciary has lately become very active. It, too, could throw barriers in the way of reforms. In part, that activism has resulted from the failures of the past executive to do his minimal duties. With a renewed focus on efficiency in the executive branch, judicial activism may decline on its own. But that is by no means certain, and the government may have to negotiate its way with the judges as it proceeds with reforms.

Either way, the new government's forthcoming budget will be the first sign of whether the world's largest democracy intends to take advantage of this historic opportunity or squander it yet one more time.

ARVIND PANAGARIYA is the Jagdish Bhagwati Professor of Indian Political Economy in the Department of International and Public Affairs and of Economics. He is author, with Jagdish Bhagwati, of *Why Growth Matters*.

Modi's Money Madness

Will the BJP Learn the Wrong Lessons From Demonetization?

James Crabtree

Indian Prime Minister Narendra Modi in Mumbai, December 2016.

No one quite knows which Narendra Modi will turn up to fight for reelection in 2019: the reformist technocrat pledging to create jobs or the tub-thumping populist armed with giveaways. For most of his first term, the Indian prime minister has struck a fair balance between the two, and last month he passed his third anniversary in power with a good growth record and strong poll numbers. But his calculations appeared to change last November, when he tilted toward populism by launching demonetization, a surprise move to scrap two high-denomination banknotes. This has proved to be one of the most disruptive experiments in recent economic history, and one from which Modi's administration now risks learning all the wrong lessons.

The fact that demonetization has been bad for short-term growth is no longer in doubt. Last week, India released GDP figures for the first quarter of 2017, the period when Modi's demonetization had its largest impact. Over those three months, hundreds of millions of Indians were forced to line up at cash machines and bank counters to replace their old 500-rupee (about $7) and 1000-rupee (about $15) notes, which made up about nine-tenths of the value of all currency in circulation. The crunch hit the poor particularly hard, and brought swaths of commercial activity in India's cash-dependent economy — and especially in its large semi-legal gray market — to a standstill.

Sure enough, the new data bear this out. From January to March of this year, Indian growth sank to six percent, down from seven percent in the previous quarter. Although high by Western standards, these figures lost India its title as the world's fastest-growing major economy, pushing China back into first place. They also brought growth over the last twelve months down to its lowest point for three years. Modi's Bharatiya Janata Party (BJP) government, eager to defend demonetization, blamed other factors, such as weaker global trade performance, for the slowdown. It also pointed to the policy's potential longer-term benefits, such as higher rates of tax collection. But demonetization's impact was especially clear in the collapse of spending on construction, which is heavily dependent on informal cash transactions.

Demonetization has proved to be one of the most disruptive experiments in recent economic history.

The problem is that although a drop of a percentage point or so in growth is large, it is not that large. Many economists feared a drop many magnitudes bigger. Now that the worst has worn off, demonetization remains popular. At least at first, Modi justified the measure on anticorruption grounds — by scrapping notes, so the argument went, the government was taking a swipe at black money, or the illicit cash piles thought to be held by everyone from criminals and terrorists to corrupt bureaucrats — and the public appears to have believed him. Yet there is little evidence that any of the criminals suffered more than temporary inconvenience. As their eyes turn toward reelection, the risk is that BJP leaders will have learned to dismiss expert warnings about the cost of populism and press ahead with more of it.

Understanding why demonetization has been less harmful than feared is therefore important. The World Bank's most recent India Development Update, published in late May, provides some clues. It shows that the impact of the cash crunch was cushioned by other factors, including a third year of good monsoon rains, which are crucial to agriculture. A recent uptick in global growth helped too, as did higher public spending unrelated to demonetization. And when the demonetization crunch did hit, India's economy proved more resilient than expected: the remaining cash in the economy circulated more quickly, informal credit was provided to consumers and farmers, and some wealthier people switched to digital payments.

Put another way, Modi got lucky. But now there is a real risk that he will take more populist measures in the same vein. When his party won a resounding post-demonetization victory in crucial elections in the bellwether state of Uttar Pradesh this spring, Modi went on to install the firebrand Hindu cleric Yogi Adityanath as chief minister. Adityanath responded by canceling nearly six billion dollars' worth of bank loans to farmers. This cancellation started off a chain of events in other states, which some estimate is likely to result in tens of billions of further debt forgiveness, raising pressure on public finances.

Meanwhile, for the long-term benefits of demonetization to be felt, Modi needs to push what the World Bank report calls "complementary reforms," including improvements to tax administration and the reduction of complex business barriers, to encourage more of India's vast informal economy to move into the formal sector. There is a good chance that no such reforms will emerge. So far Modi's economic achievements are real, but his record on delivering growth-enhancing reforms, especially those that risk upsetting the public, is mixed. Although his grand gesture of demonetization made little sense economically, it has proved enduringly popular, and it appears to have made only a minor dent in the GDP. As he approaches 2019, it is not hard to see the lesson that he might learn.

An earlier version of this article referred to India's "surprise move to scrap two low-denomination banknotes." The notes in question were high-denomination.

JAMES CRABTREE is Senior Visiting Research Fellow at the Lee Kuan Yew School of Public Policy NUS in Singapore, on sabbatical from his previous position at the *Financial Times*, where he was Mumbai Bureau Chief.

India at 70

The World's Biggest Democracy Celebrates Its Birthday

Madhav Khosla and Milan Vaishnav

People celebrated India's Independence Day in Delhi, August 2017.

Seventy years ago, independent India was born. Having shaken off the yoke of the British Empire, the country embarked on what was — and remains — the world's most radical democratic experiment. Never before had a nation with such a low per capita level of income extended universal voting rights to its citizens; throw in varied topography, unparalleled ethnic and religious diversity, the inheritance of a socially rigid and unequal caste system, and the fact that India resides in a fractious geopolitical neighborhood, and its flourishing democracy looks even more remarkable. Today, the country features more than 1,000 political parties. Women participate in the electoral process in larger numbers than their male counterparts. Historically disadvantaged groups, such as Dalits (formerly "untouchables"), are reshaping politics and gaining social mobility.

But the Indian democratic experiment is marred by a central flaw. Indian democracy has worked well during elections. But — as the historian Ramachandra Guha has noted — democracy between elections is much less robust. It is commonplace to observe that democracy is not just about voting, and it is in this respect that modern India is coming up short. The Indian democratic project is held back, in short, by ineffectual governance and a patchy record on civil liberties.

In part, the reason is that India's democratic journey is an inversion of the standard Western process of democratization. In most examples of the latter, such as the United Kingdom, or even the United States, a reasonably strong and centralized state was in place before democratic norms and institutions were codified. This state had powers one associates with modern sovereign regimes: a monopoly on the use of force, an ability to extract tax revenue, and a system to deliver (basic) public services. In most historical Western examples, democracy was laid atop these foundations, even then, only brick by gradual brick. In the United States, for instance, women waited over a century for even the de jure right to the vote.

India's democratic journey is an inversion of the standard Western process of democratization.

India experienced no such gradual sequencing. After the British departed in 1947, India's leaders were pressed to fulfill dual objectives: preserve the new nation's unity and satisfy citizens' longing for political freedom. These weighty decisions took place against a backdrop of the bloody partition of the subcontinent. For the key protagonists in India's independence movement, therefore, immediate universal suffrage and continuity with British institutions was a short-term solution for survival, as well as a long-term statement of national principle.

This legacy defines India to this day and is the basis of the first vital threat to its democracy: a bureaucratic state that is heavy on paperwork and light on essential services. This is a direct inheritance of empire: to manage their far-flung colony, the British employed relatively few people and extraordinary volumes of paperwork. These twin realities — minimal staffing and excessive red tape — still characterize Indian governance. About 31 million cases are pending in India's judicial system, winding their way through a creaky and poorly resourced process. More than a quarter of police posts sit vacant.

And, like the British Empire before it, the Indian state compounds the shortage of human capital with a Kafkaesque regulatory maze of bureaucratic procedure. According to the World Bank's 2017 ease of doing business indicators, India ranks 130 out of 190 countries, sandwiched between Cabo Verde and Cambodia. The state's regulatory heavy-handedness, in turn, creates a readymade avenue for politicians and bureaucrats to trade favors in exchange for bribes or campaign cash.

The second vital threat to Indian democracy comes from the state's own mixed record on civil liberties. Though this is partly the consequence of weak state capacity and an ineffectual system of law enforcement and administration, the deeper cause is ideological. In twenty-first-century India, sedition remains a jailable offense, defamation attracts both civil and criminal penalties and homosexuality is a crime. To be sure, the existence and enforcement of these laws predate the current government of Prime Minister Narendra Modi.

But here is also where state-led backslide may be greatest. The rising Hindu majoritarianism of Modi's Bharatiya Janata Party — evident in anti-Muslim mob violence, a rise in lynchings in the name of protecting cows (held holy by some Hindus), and nationalist rhetoric — has gathered speed as the BJP's footprint has rapidly expanded under Modi's leadership. The problem is not simply that these divisive and sometimes violent transgressions undermine individual freedom and rule of law — it is that the state has granted such attacks moral legitimacy. Quite frequently, opposition parties have acquiesced in these violations of fundamental civil liberties.

With India three decades away from its centennial birthday, the time to address these shortcomings is overdue. A familiar lament is that India — pluralistic and fractious — is not more like China, where an autocratic central state "gets things done." But this critique gets it backwards; it flows from a misreading of India's history and present infirmities. India's problem is not too much democracy — it is that democracy is too often conflated with voting. But democratic norms and practices must extend to clean governance and individual rights between elections as well. To borrow a phrase from independent India's first prime minister, Jawaharlal Nehru: India's tryst with destiny has been successful because of its democratic nature, not in spite of it. Instead, its current leadership must grapple with the nation's most pressing dilemma: reforming a state that is active in places where it should not be, yet too often absent in places it should.

MADHAV KHOSLA is a junior fellow at the Harvard Society of Fellows. MILAN VAISHNAV is Senior Fellow and Director of the South Asia Program at the Carnegie Endowment for International Peace.

Will India Start Acting Like a Global Power?

New Delhi's New Role

Alyssa Ayres

Indian Prime Minister Narendra Modi and the leaders of the other BRICS countries in Goa, India, October 2016.

The country with the world's third-largest military by personnel strength, fifth-largest defense budget, and seventh-largest economy isn't a member of the UN Security Council. It isn't even a member of the G-7, the exclusive club of major industrialized economies. It is India, a country long regarded as an emerging power rather than a major global player.

In fairness, for years, this assessment was not off the mark, and India's reality did not match up to its vaunted potential. And indeed, India still faces daunting developmental challenges. It is home to around 270 million people living in extreme poverty. Its infrastructure is in need of major investment — to the tune of $1.5 trillion over a decade, according to India's finance minister. Discrimination among India's famously diverse population persists, whether on the basis of gender, caste, religion, or region.

Because of these challenges, and because the country has been kept on the margins of the global institutions central to U.S. diplomacy, India's impressive economic power and defense capabilities have often gone unnoticed. But that is changing. A more confident India has already begun to shape the global agenda on climate change, clean energy, and worker mobility. And spurred by China's increasingly assertive regional posture, India has ramped up its own military capacity.

India has long chafed at the fact that despite its size and its democracy, the world does not see it as a major power. Unlike China, it does not have a coveted permanent seat on the UN Security Council. Considering India's growing economy and enhanced military capabilities, Indian leaders are pushing for their country's "due place in global councils," as former Prime Minister Manmohan Singh put it. Under the current prime minister, Narendra Modi, India has begun to see itself as a "leading power," laying overt claim to a new, more central place in the world.

As India leaves behind some of its old defensiveness on the world stage, a vestige of its nonaligned worldview, it is time for U.S. policy to evolve, as well. Relations between the United States and India have come a long way from the days in which the diplomat and historian Dennis Kux could write of the two as "estranged democracies," and both countries now talk of being "strategic partners"—a relationship of cooperation, but not a formal alliance. U.S. President Donald Trump has not yet fully articulated his plans for relations with India, although he did remark in June that they have "never looked brighter," and in a departure from the Washington playbook, he has explicitly asked India to do more on economic development in Afghanistan.

As the president and his team grapple with India's rise, they should reconceptualize the U.S.-Indian relationship to better manage differences with a power that prizes policy independence above all. And they must address the inequity of India's exclusion from major institutions of global governance by championing Indian membership and giving New Delhi a long-overdue place at the table.

Working with a rising India will not always be easy. The country remains fiercely protective of its policy independence, shuns formal alliances, and remains ever willing to break global consensus, as it has done most famously on trade negotiations. It can be a close defense partner, but not in the familiar template of most U.S. alliances. India wants an improved trade and economic relationship, but it will not be easily persuaded by U.S. entreaties for increased market access. Still, Democratic and Republican administrations alike have prioritized forging closer ties with New Delhi, rightly regarding a tighter relationship as a vote for the importance of democracy and a bet on shared prosperity and stability in Asia.

Indian Air Force soldiers during a rehearsal for Indian Air Force Day at the Hindon air force station on the outskirts of New Delhi, October 2016.

PROSPERITY AND POWER

As with China, the economy has been at the center of India's global transformation. While many outside India are aware of the country's great potential, few realize that the Indian economy, with a GDP of over $2 trillion at current exchange rates, has now surpassed the economies of Canada and Italy (both members of the G-7). U.S. government projections anticipate that India will be the world's third-largest economy by 2029, lagging behind only China and the United States. A slowdown in China and contractions in Brazil and Russia have increased India's share of global GDP as measured by purchasing power parity, which the International Monetary Fund (IMF) projects will exceed eight percent by 2020—above that of Japan in 1995 and that of China in 2000. If the world at large doesn't yet see India as akin to those economic powerhouses, CEOs around the world do: a 2016 survey conducted by the firm KPMG found that India had moved up four notches to become their top pick for growth opportunities in the next three years.

India's sheer size and its youthful demographics offer the prospect of enormous economic growth. According to UN estimates, India will overtake China as the world's most populous country sometime around 2024, and it will do so with a significantly younger population. India's large working-age population will continue to grow until 2050, while Japan, China, and western Europe age. By then, Japan's median age is expected to stand at 53 years, China's at nearly 50, and western Europe's at 47. The median-age Indian will be just 37 years old.

Although India remains home to the world's largest number of poor, its middle class is growing and now consists of anywhere from 30 million (as the Pew Research Center estimates) to 270 million people (as the National Council of Applied Economic Research estimates), depending on how "middle class" is measured. A 2007 McKinsey report estimated that the Indian middle class, if defined as those with an annual disposable household income of $4,000 to $22,000, could balloon to nearly 600 million people by 2025. A growing middle class wields market power, which explains why giant multinational companies, from Apple and Xiaomi to Bosch and Whirlpool, have India in their sights: all those four are now manufacturing goods in India for the growing Indian market. India surpassed China as the world's largest market for motorcycles and scooters in 2016, but it has also become a global hub for automobile manufacturing, producing nearly one in three small cars sold worldwide. India does not yet come to mind as an automotive powerhouse, but Ford, Hyundai, Maruti Suzuki, and Tata are all making cars there. Collectively, the Indian automotive industry built only slightly fewer automobiles in 2016 than South Korea and more than Mexico, both major car-producing nations. Although India needs to do much more to develop its manufacturing base, its advances in the auto industry represent an about-face from just 15 years ago.

India has begun to see itself as a "leading power," laying overt claim to a new, more central place in the world.

Increasingly, India is translating its economic might into military power. It already counts itself as part of a select club of countries with advanced defense technology, including a nuclear weapons program. India is also a space power: it sent a probe to the moon in 2008 and has another in the works, and in 2014, it placed a vehicle in orbit around Mars (at a fraction of the cost of NASA's latest Mars orbiter).

With its sights set on primacy in the Indian Ocean, New Delhi is strengthening its defense ties with countries across the region and building a blue-water navy. According to the International Institute for Strategic Studies, India now has a force strength of nearly 1.4 million troops on active duty and nearly 1.2 million reservists. The Stockholm International Peace Research Institute estimates that India became the world's fifth-largest military spender in 2016, ahead of France and the United Kingdom. Now the world's top importer of military equipment for the last five years, India has accelerated its procurements from U.S. companies from essentially zero to more than $15 billion worth over the past decade. But even as defense ties with the United States grow, India is not going to end its long-standing relationship with Russia, and recognizing that is part of working with New Delhi. Indeed, Russia remains a major defense supplier for India, as are France and Israel; India is simply diversifying its strategic bets by doing business with multiple partners.

India is also increasingly producing its own advanced defense technologies, instead of importing them. Although it recently replaced its aging aircraft carrier in a much-delayed deal with Russia in 2013, it now has a second carrier under construction, developed and built at home, although it may not be ready for as long as a decade. India has a third carrier scheduled for construction, also to be made domestically, and it has plans to add at least three nuclear-powered submarines to its fleet. In fact, in a major departure from the past, the country has begun to export military equipment to other countries in the region. India began transferring a series of naval patrol vessels to Mauritius in 2015, and it has been in discussions with Vietnam to sell it cruise missiles.

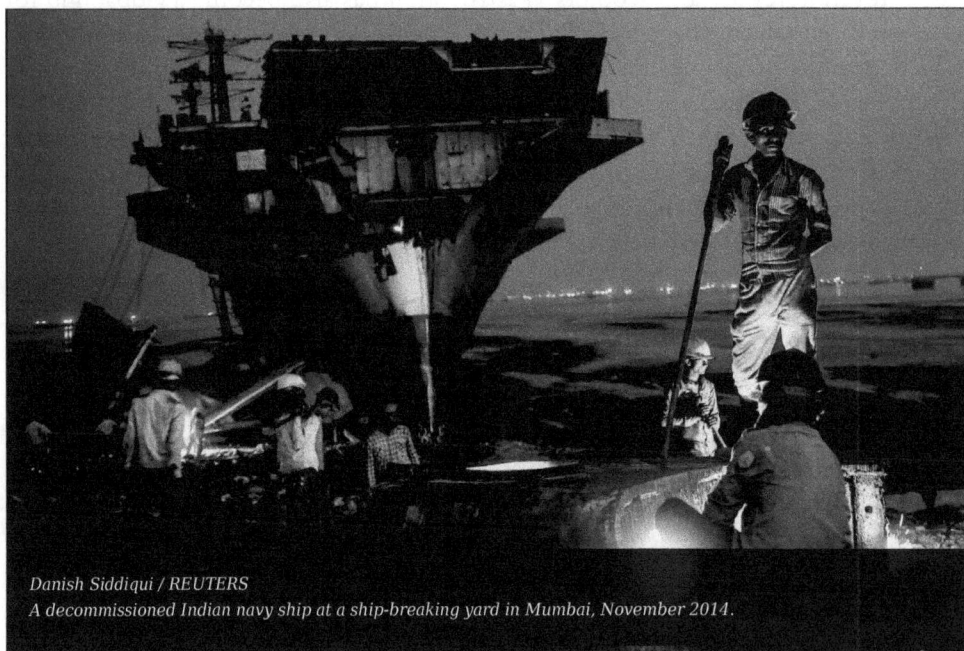

Danish Siddiqui / REUTERS
A decommissioned Indian navy ship at a ship-breaking yard in Mumbai, November 2014.

A NEW SWAGGER

A more confident India, eager to shape, rather than simply react to, global events, has already made its presence felt diplomatically. Take climate change. In the long-running multilateral climate negotiations, India moved, in less than a decade, from playing defense to taking the lead in setting the global climate agenda. For years, India had refused to acquiesce to proposals to cap carbon emissions. Indians considered it deeply unfair that the developed West was looking for cuts from developing India, a country with a historically small contribution to climate change, low per capita emissions, and large future development needs. But at the 2015 Paris climate conference, a new Indian stance emerged. Along with François Hollande, then France's president, Modi announced a new international solar power alliance to be headquartered in India, with a focus on promoting the rapid deployment of solar energy and cutting the costs of financing and development. Given India's ambitious and expensive goal of ramping up domestic solar energy production to 100 gigawatts by 2022, the alliance has allowed India to take on an international leadership role that complements its preexisting domestic energy plans. The Paris agreement showcased a different style of Indian diplomacy — this was not the India that helped scuttle the World Trade Organization's Doha negotiations in 2008 but a new, problem-solving India.

On defense and security, India has strengthened its capacity over the past decade to such an extent that U.S. secretaries of defense now routinely refer to India as a net provider of regional security. India's maritime ambitions, especially its goal of primacy in the Indian Ocean, are a response to China's more assertive presence across South Asia. Beijing's intensified infrastructure development assistance to Bangladesh, the Maldives, Sri Lanka, and, especially, Pakistan — as well as a new military base in Djibouti — have expanded China's Indian Ocean reach. A 2012 decision upped India's naval ship requirement to 198 from its earlier level of 138. In 2015, New Delhi quietly reached an agreement with the Seychelles to host its first overseas military base. That same year, India took the lead in rescuing nearly 1,000 foreign citizens from 41 countries stranded in Yemen, including Americans. And when Japan joined India and the United States that year as a permanent participant in the annual Malabar naval exercises, India was able to showcase its warships, planes, and submarines beside the two most powerful democracies in the Asia-Pacific region.

While deepening its ties with the West, New Delhi has also shown a determination to invest in alternative international organizations over the course of the past decade. India does not seek to overturn the global order; rather, it merely wants such institutions as the UN Security Council, the Asia-Pacific Economic Cooperation (APEC), the World Bank, the IMF, the Nuclear Suppliers Group, and others to expand to accommodate it. But as reform of these organizations drags on, New Delhi has put some of its eggs in other baskets.

Take the BRICS, comprising Brazil, Russia, India, China, and South Africa. In less than a decade, the group has become an important diplomatic forum and has accomplished more than most observers expected. At their 2012 summit, the BRICS began discussions on the New Development Bank — which announced its first loans in 2016—an institution in which these five countries could have an equal voice, unlike their disproportionately low representation in the World Bank and the IMF. And in 2014, they agreed to form the BRICS Contingent Reserve Arrangement, an alternative to IMF support in times of economic crisis. India also supported the Chinese-led creation of the Asian Infrastructure Investment Bank, and it is now the bank's second-biggest contributor of capital.

In 2017, India also joined the Shanghai Cooperation Organization, and it maintains an active presence in other institutions far outside the United States' orbit, such as the Conference on Interaction and Confidence Building Measures in Asia. Although New Delhi's top priority remains a seat commensurate with its size and heft within the traditional global organizations still dominated by the West, India has shown that it is also willing to help build other arenas in order to have a greater voice. India will likely continue to maintain this diverse array of relationships even as it strengthens its ties with the United States; regardless, granting New Delhi the place it deserves in major Western international forums would help, rather than hinder, U.S. interests. At a time when international coordination has become far more complex, the increase in new organizations creates "forum-shopping" opportunities, as the political scientist Daniel Drezner and others have argued. More forums and more options make it harder to get things done internationally — and also decrease Washington's influence.

Eduardo Munoz / REUTERS
Indian Prime Minister Narendra Modi at the United Nations headquarters in New York, September 2014.

A SEAT AT THE TABLE

Successive U.S. administrations have viewed the relationship with India as one of the United States' great strategic opportunities, offering a chance to overcome historical differences and strengthen ties with a fast-growing market, a stable pillar in a region of turmoil, and a large country that can provide a balance of power across Asia and a bulwark against Chinese dominance. The George W. Bush administration sought to reframe the U.S.-Indian relationship by striking a 2005 deal concerning civilian nuclear cooperation, bridging what had been a 30-year divide on nonproliferation. The Obama administration continued the momentum, with various efforts to expand defense, economic, and diplomatic cooperation.

But shared goals do not always translate into shared approaches. Such was the case with Russia's annexation of Crimea: Indian officials walked a tightrope, saying little publicly about it beyond an anodyne tweet from a Ministry of External Affairs spokesperson ("We are closely watching fast evolving situation and hope for a peaceful resolution") rather than clearly condemning Russia's violation of Ukrainian sovereignty.

On questions of grand strategy, India's desire to be recognized as a major global power includes an indelible commitment to its own ideas of autonomy. Although New Delhi has shifted over the years from reflexive nonalignment to a recent philosophy of "strategic autonomy" to the present Indian government's vision of "the world is one family" (from the Sanskrit phrase vasudhaiva kutumbakam), the connecting thread remains policy independence. But that sense of independence can sometimes clash with the United States' tendency to believe that its partners and allies should support it across the board.

Part of the problem is that Washington has no template for a close defense relationship outside of the obligations inherent in a formal alliance. The U.S. government's designation of India last year as a "major defense partner"—a status created and accorded only to India, as a means to facilitate advanced defense cooperation — illustrates the unique situation and marks the beginning of a new way to think through this relationship. Even though New Delhi seeks deeper ties, including obtaining U.S. technology, Indians do not want to sign themselves up for every U.S.-led initiative around the world. There is a difference between being "natural allies," in the words of former Indian Prime Minister Atal Bihari Vajpayee, and the extensive commitments of a formal alliance. New Delhi seeks the rhetorical flourish of the former without the restrictive expectations of the latter.

Given that U.S. and Indian interests are converging across Asia, military ties between the two countries will no doubt deepen. But as they do, U.S. policymakers will have to manage their expectations and not be disappointed when India, say, improves ties with Iran. In order to ward off frustrations with India's inevitable departures from U.S. preferences, the United States should frame its relationship with India differently, conceiving of it more as a joint venture in business than a traditional alliance. That would mean insulating shared initiatives from areas of disagreement, such as policy toward Iran or ties with Russia.

Given the size of India's economy, it is past time for the country to be brought into agenda-setting institutions.

On economics, too, Washington at times differs sharply with New Delhi, despite a commitment on both sides to expanding bilateral trade. Indeed, India has never hesitated to break global consensus to protect its perceived economic interests. A decade ago, New Delhi and Beijing made common cause to protect their agricultural sectors, leading to the July 2008 stalemate that ended the Doha round of international trade negotiations. Then, in 2014, India backed out of the Trade Facilitation Agreement, which sought to cut red tape, despite having previously agreed to it. It took extensive talks to revive the deal. More recently, India's powerful information technology sector has raised trade in services to the very top of India's economic negotiating agenda, since one way to provide information technology services is to perform work on location — including in another country. New Delhi is pushing other countries to accept greater numbers of Indian temporary workers while remaining resistant to opening its own market further to goods and services. In 2016, India filed a formal dispute against the United States in the World Trade Organization over increases in visa fees that India claimed would hit its information technology workers especially hard; the outcome will set a precedent for managing worker mobility across the globe.

Despite these disagreements, there is ample room for progress on the economic relationship. India's global ambitions rest on sustained economic growth, and for that, India needs to maintain ongoing reforms. While only India's own political process will determine the trajectory of those efforts, the United States can and should do a better job of including India in the international networks conducive to economic growth and job creation. Historically, decades of self-sufficiency and a relatively small economy locked India out of productive economic institutions such as APEC, the Organization for Economic Cooperation and Development (OECD), and the International Energy Agency (IEA)—all bodies that set standards and provide a meaningful place for cooperation on trade, development, and economic policy.

Given the size of India's economy, it is past time for the country to be brought into such agenda-setting institutions. An APEC missing Asia's third-largest economy lacks legitimacy and makes little economic sense. Washington should support Indian membership, something it has so far refrained from doing. The same argument holds for the OECD, especially because India has emerged as a major donor of development aid across South Asia and Africa. In recent years, the OECD has created a category of states called "key partners"—a group that includes India, along with Brazil, China, and Indonesia — which it consults but does not count as members. Locking India out of the OECD also keeps it out of the IEA, for arcane historical reasons, thus excluding one of the world's largest energy consumers. If the G-7 is to remain a central economic-agenda-setting institution for the world's leading democracies, at some point, it, too, will have a hard time rationalizing its exclusion of India given the rapidly growing size of the Indian economy. Concerns that bringing India into the fold will disrupt consensus in these economic institutions are overblown, since these are not binding negotiating forums. If anything, giving India a place at the table will help pull it into a cohort of countries already committed to economic openness and transparency.

Finally, on the security front, India is right to see its continued exclusion from permanent UN Security Council membership as unfair, given its population and contributions to UN peacekeeping (India is among the top troop contributors annually). Washington should seek to make good on its promise of working toward permanent membership for India "in a reformed and expanded" Security Council, as President Barack Obama pledged before the Indian Parliament in 2010. Promoting India's membership could present challenges to many U.S. positions, but the perspective Indian diplomats bring on some of the world's most intractable problems deserves to be heard in the same room as the perspectives from China, France, Russia, and the United Kingdom. Unfortunately, the UN Security Council has not budged on the issue of expansion since Obama first voiced support for Indian inclusion. Reform has been held hostage to competing demands from other deserving countries — such as Brazil, Germany, and Japan — not to mention a lack of consensus on the size of expansion and whether new permanent members should have veto powers.

Even if the UN remains plagued by inertia, there are many other forums where India could make a contribution, with a little help from Washington. The United States must do a better job of normalizing the reality of India's rise and overtly emphasizing the country's importance to U.S. national interests and to the world, just as Washington assumes the importance of so many of its close European partners. Despite their political differences, both Modi and his predecessor, Singh, shared a conviction: that for India on the world stage, "our time has come." Washington should embrace — rather than merely await — its arrival.

ALYSSA AYRES is Senior Fellow for India, Pakistan, and South Asia at the Council on Foreign Relations and the author of the forthcoming book *Our Time Has Come: How India Is Making Its Place in the World* (Oxford University Press, 2018), from which this essay is adapted. Copyright © 2018 Oxford University Press. All rights reserved.

www.ingramcontent.com/pod-product-compliance
Lightning Source LLC
Chambersburg PA
CBHW081150270326
41930CB00014B/3106